Irma Jepson
Memorial
Fund

The Reflective Parent

THE REFLECTIVE PARENT

---

*How to Do Less and Relate More
with Your Kids*

REGINA PALLY

W. W. NORTON & COMPANY
Independent Publishers Since 1923
New York • London

For information about permission to reproduce selections from this book, write to Permissions, W. W. Norton & Company, Inc., 500 Fifth Avenue, New York, NY 10110

For information about special discounts for bulk purchases, please contact W. W. Norton Special Sales at specialsales@wwnorton.com or 800-233-4830

Manufacturing by LSC Harrisonburg
Production manager: Christine Critelli

Library of Congress Cataloging-in-Publication Data

Names: Pally, Regina, author.
Title: The reflective parent : how to do less and relate more with your kids / Regina Pally.
Description: First edition. | New York : W.W Norton & Company, [2017] | Includes bibliographical references and index.
Identifiers: LCCN 2016029057 | ISBN 9780393711332 (hardcover)
Subjects: LCSH: Parent and child. | Parenting.
Classification: LCC HQ755.85 .P3426 2017 | DDC 649/.1—dc23 LC record available at https://lccn.loc.gov/2016029057

W. W. Norton & Company, Inc., 500 Fifth Avenue, New York, N.Y. 10110
www.wwnorton.com

W. W. Norton & Company Ltd., 15 Carlisle Street, London W1D 3BS

1 2 3 4 5 6 7 8 9 0

I dedicate this book to my three children who taught me everything important I needed to know about parenting, and to my husband who supports me and boosts up my confidence whenever I start to doubt myself.

Contents

EIGHT

Parenting from Infancy through Childhood   178

NINE

Parenting from Adolescence through Adulthood   206

Acknowledgments

There are so many people whose ideas, encouragement, and advice went into the writing of this book. I am eternally grateful to all my friends, family, and colleagues who supported me, listened to all my ideas, and helped in the early drafts of this book. I want to especially acknowledge, Nancy Rosser, Dorli Burge, Kathy Reuter, Joan Gurfield, Sharon Polkinghorn, Martha Slagerman, Julie Tepper and Jonathan Salk. I am indebted to the whole team at Center for Reflective Communities, especially Diane Reynolds, John Grienenberger, Bronwyn Talbot, Wendy Denham, Natalie Levine, Melissa Jacobs and Kevin Gruenberg who so generously give of their time to promote healthy development in children through reflection and relationship building, and who so graciously share with me all their knowledge about child development and parenting. I want to thank Paulene Popek who first introduced me to the concept of Reflective Parenting and helped me to launch Center for Reflective Communities. I am grateful to Dan Siegel, who first got me involved in learning about the brain, and for his support of the reflective work I do, and to Hans Miller and John Schummann, who guided my neuroscience learning for many years. I am so grateful to my mentor Beatrice Beebe, who lovingly nurtures all my writing efforts. I want to thank the scientific researchers Pat Levitt, Marco Iacoboni, and Peter Whybrow for their advice. Finally I want to deeply thank my editors at Norton for all their excellent suggestions and assistance.

Introduction

WHY I WROTE THIS BOOK

This book is the one I needed when I was a young parent raising my three children. At that time, I read all the parenting books. They all had great advice. But, unfortunately, the answers often left me feeling less confident than before. It was as if there were a "right" way to parent and, if I did not fit the mold, I might be harming my child. I felt as if I had a precious package to transport, but I was walking along a narrow path on a high cliff without guardrails. Every move had to be perfect or something terrible might happen.

What I eventually learned is that there is a lot more leeway in parenting than I realized and that I could be trusted to figure out for myself what my child needed from me. I learned that the path is much wider than most people think and that there are strong guardrails to protect you and your child from falling off the cliff. In fact, figuring out what I needed to know as a parent became part of my life's work, professionally and personally. This book is my effort to share what I have learned. It seems to me from the parents I talk with these days that they need it now as much as I did back then.

This book draws on what I learned from my pediatric, psychiatric, and psychoanalytic training; my clinical work with patients; my studies in neuroscience; my personal experiences; and most recently my involvement with the nonprofit organization Center for Reflective Communities (CRC),[1] whose mission is to promote healthy child development by

---

1 CRC began in 2008 as the Center for Reflective Parenting. The name was changed in 2015. CRC is a training, service, and research organization that works primarily with

strengthening the relationship bonds that children have with all the people who care for them. Through them, I learned that a parent's reflective capacity is the factor most closely associated with healthy child development and can be protective against the negative impact of stress and adversity. CRC's guiding principle is that *what matters most in life is relationships and that being* reflective *strengthens the relationships we have with all the people in our life.*

Reflective parenting means understanding that everything your child does and says is motivated or triggered by something going on inside their mind, such as a feeling, an intention, or a belief, and that the same is true for you. Everything you do or say is motivated or triggered by something going on inside your mind. Reflective parenting involves two-way perspective-taking, in which you see the world from your child's perspective as well as your own. Being reflective enables you to do all the things that research shows are associated with children doing better throughout their *whole life*:

- Understanding your child's perspective as well as your own
- Having an open, flexible, and positive attitude toward your child
- Tolerating ambiguity and uncertainty
- Maintaining balance in how you parent
- Regulating your child's distress and negative emotions
- Finding solutions that best fit who your child is and who you are as a person
- Fostering closeness while also promoting age-appropriate independence

---

agencies and organizations serving low-income, disadvantaged, and at-risk children and their families. Because all children, the poor as well as the affluent ones, need a reflective adult in their life, CRC makes its reflective programs available to parents, teachers, and others throughout the community.

What I have to say may be a little harder to take in than much of what is presented in other parenting books or offered by well-intentioned parenting experts, because I encourage parents to trust their own instincts and think on their own. I am hoping to counteract a tendency I see in much of what parents are reading and hearing about. All too often, ideas are presented in an overly simplified and formulaic way, which conveys the message that this is *the* right way to do it. The focus is frequently on what parents are doing wrong, while hardly any attention is given to what they are doing right. Many parents complain that they end up doubting themselves and feeling bad or guilty if they don't follow the steps advised. I hear similar feedback from teachers and clinicians working with parents: that so many parents believe there is some specific script or set of behaviors they should use, and that if they don't say or do things exactly right, they have messed up.

Much of what the books and the experts have to say is good, even terrific. But as good as it is, critical points are being missed. What is missing is a sense of nuance, flexibility, and openness to the fact that everyone is different. There tends to be an absence of humility, a lack of recognition that life is messy and so is parenting—a failure to acknowledge that no matter how reflective we are or how well we do as parents, we will never be able to become perfect parents or to create children who have no problems. There is a lack of acceptance of the reality that so many situations are simply uncertain and ambiguous and that we can't always know what to do. There is also a tendency to ignore the biological perspective that even good things can go too far.

Although many parents believe that all they need is the right answer, I believe there are no right answers and that the best answer is one that the parent figures out is best for who their child is and who they are as a parent. I have chosen for the most part not to offer specific answers or advice for specific problems. There are plenty of these to be had from other sources, and I encourage you to find them if you need or want them. My contribution is a bit different. Instead of telling you what to do as a parent, I intend to help you *think about how* you parent and how you want to parent. It's a way of honing your thinking skills *about* yourself and your child. It's a way, I believe, that is more likely to bring you a sense of optimism and confidence about your relationship and about how your child will grow up into the adult he or she is to become. The angle I present is more focused on possibilities, seeing situations from multiple perspectives, and realizing that there are many equally good ways to parent.

The following section comprises three exercises to warm up your reflective mind and get you thinking about the ideas I present in this book. The first captures a bit of what it's like to be a child, the second what it's like to be a parent, and the third what it's like to think reflectively.

GETTING STARTED: REFLECTIVE THOUGHT EXPERIMENTS

Imagine yourself being dropped off on Mars. You know nothing about how to survive on Mars. Hopefully, a kindly Martian takes you under their wing, keeps you safe, and teaches you the ropes. You need to be taught the Martian language, how to get along with other Martians, what is acceptable Martian behavior and what is not, what foods Martians eat and which to avoid, and so on. If you're lucky, your Martian guide understands and accepts that *you know almost nothing* and *need to learn everything* and recognizes that you need empathy and support in the difficult process of becoming a well-functioning Martian.

Imagine yourself as a gardener. You've purchased a new type of plant to grow in your garden, though no one told you exactly what the plant is. All you know is that it needs soil, sunlight, water, and fertilizer, but you don't know the right amount or type. You are an observant gardener, however. You see whether you are doing it right by how the leaves and flowers look. Are they bright and vibrant, or wilted and yellowing? The plant grows and sends out branches every which way. You have to prune it so that it fits well in the garden. Your goal is to discover exactly what plant you have on your hands and what environment you need to provide in order to maximize its optimal development. You wonder, are you dealing with a rose bush, a cherry tree, an onion, or an orchid? What mixture of soil, sun, water, and food is best suited to the plant? What type of pruning is required? There are books, classes, and other gardeners to help, but as any gardener knows, each plant and each garden is a bit unique.

Imagine yourself as an archeologist. You are digging in the desert among ancient ruins and pick up a curved object. You look at it carefully before you decide what it is. You conclude it is a broken piece of pottery. After you have figured out *what* the object is, you must figure out how it was used. You can see the object perfectly clearly and are quite certain it is part of a bowl. The purpose of the object, however, is more opaque because it's so ancient. All you can do is guess at or infer all the various possibilities. Perhaps the bowl was used for washing, cooking, or for some ritual practice. As good as your guess may be, you remain humble, realizing you don't know for certain.

BEING REFLECTIVE IS THE NATURAL WAY

Being reflective may sound like a special or unusual ability. However, it is actually the most ordinary and natural way human beings understand each other and understand themselves. The ability to be reflective is essential for relating well to others, because it enables us to try to see the world from the other person's perspective as well as our own and to accept that there is always more than one way to view a situation. This concept is captured by two common sayings: "One man's meat is another man's poison" and "There is more than one way to skin a cat."

REFLECTIVE PARENTING BENEFITS PARENTS AND CHILDREN

Using a reflective approach to parenting is good for your child and good for you as a parent. This approach is designed to lessen the tensions and anxieties of parenting by counteracting many of the pressures our modern culture puts on parents. Today's parents have come to believe in a narrow view of what it means to be successful—that there is a correct way to get there and that it is their job to provide their child with all the right opportunities for success. Unfortunately, this leads to children being overscheduled, oversupervised, and overhelped. All this pressure to do it right is literally choking the self-reliance and resiliency out of our children. Additionally, it contributes to an atmosphere among parents that is anxious, insecure, and competitive as they try to create the perfect child.

A reflective approach offers several antidotes to today's parents' excessive stress and anxiety about child-rearing. It recommends that parents embrace two fundamental truths: that there are no right answers and that there is no one right way to parent. Doing so will increase the confidence of parents and children and boost their capacity to manage stressful times. Another recommendation is to do less and relate more. Parents tend to assume that their child's future success requires them to focus on academic achievement and extracurricular activities. However, the relationship between parent and child provides the richest source for the life lessons children need to learn in order to do well in life—emotionally, socially, and even academically. And, as a side benefit, it doesn't cost money or require any driving.

REFLECTIVE PARENTING PUTS SCIENCE TO GOOD USE

Scientific knowledge about how children develop and how they experience the world is often used these days for the wrong purposes. The current climate encourages us to use it to promote more achievement in our children at the expense of the relationship. When parents focus so much on how to get kids to learn more, achieve more, do better in school, have more activities, have more accomplishments, have more play dates, and be better prepared for getting into a good college, they are inadvertently doing a disservice to their children. While it is true that achievement and accomplishment are important, they end up being empty unless the child feels nurtured and grounded in a secure relationship with a parent. Even efforts to help economically disadvantaged children or children living with other types of adversity often put the cart before the horse. It is good to provide all children with good schools and teachers, but unless we also put enough effort into making sure every child grows up with a nurturing and secure relationship with an adult who takes care of them, those efforts will not be as effective.

This book places parenting and child development within a framework of neuroscience. The science supports the use of a reflective approach to parenting and emphasizes the central role of relationships in all healthy child development. Science also demonstrates that the capacity to be reflective is crucial to social competence, learning, achievement, and overall well-being. In fact, the capacity to be reflective is so important that the human brain has several regions dedicated to it.

The science explains why, even though being reflective is an ordinary and natural human skill and even though the brain is built to be reflective, we don't always understand other people accurately. We still have plenty of misunderstanding and conflict. This is where a reflective approach becomes essential. The reflective approach keeps parents on the lookout for the possibility of misunderstanding their child and guides them in managing conflict when it occurs. A reflective approach enables a parent's brain and mind to work together to raise a child who has the best chance of reaching their full potential.

HOW I LEARNED TO BE A REFLECTIVE PARENT

My three children are now all grown up. It has taken me a long time to gather my thoughts together into the overall philosophy and approach I describe in this book. Along the way I had so much to learn. Although I had gone to medical school, was a practicing psychiatrist, and had supported myself for years, I was shocked at just how challenging parenting really was. Life with young children while balancing work and career is chaotic, and there is always so much not getting done. My husband and I had very different perspectives and had to work out our differences while having less sleep and three little ones to care for. Most of all, I had no idea I had so many "buttons" a child could push to rile me up emotionally, leaving me feeling confused and upset.

I also found that other parents were not too open about sharing their difficulties in an honest way. This made it appear to me as if I were the only one with so many problems and that everyone else was getting it *right*. But maybe because I was a psychiatrist, or maybe because of who I am as a person, I made it my mission to find a different way to think about things, one that would make me feel more competent and help me enjoy being a parent more. I feel fortunate that out of all the confusion and emotional upheaval, I found an approach to parenting that not only was helpful to me, but also proved helpful to many other parents as well.

Everything I learned about parenting and being reflective, I learned on the job. The learning did not come all at once. Nor did it come without times of doubt and conflict. It was years before I had a clear vision for what approach to use, and it wasn't until much later in my professional career that I even discovered the term *reflective parenting*. It was my colleagues at the nonprofit organization Center for Reflective Communities who inspired me to write this book and helped me to better articulate my ideas.

I want to emphasize that it is not just the experiences themselves that helped to change me. I had to learn that it is *how you interpret events*, not the events themselves, that matters most. I had to work hard to interpret experiences in a more positive way in order to parent differently. I tried to think about difficult incidents not as roadblocks, impediments, failures, or evidence of trouble, but as opportunities to develop a more open and health-promoting attitude and especially as experiences to learn from.

Following are some personal stories of experiences I had with my children and my husband that stand out in my mind as key moments of learning and developing the approach presented in this book. First and foremost, I had to learn to be humble—to acknowledge that even I, a competent and organized professional, could end up feeling totally at loose ends, not knowing what to do and leaving tasks uncompleted for weeks. It was really hard and I certainly made plenty of mistakes. I went through a lot of trial-and-error learning. But, as you will discover in this book, I have come to understand that that is "what nature had in mind."

Learning to Be Kinder to Myself

My older son lost some of his vision when he was about 20 months old. The doctors said it would be only partially reversible, but they also told us it might not have been as bad if it had been picked up earlier. I felt it was my fault for not noticing it earlier. I felt like a terrible mother, cried a lot, and became really irritable. My husband finally got annoyed at me and said, "Stop blaming yourself. You're putting so much energy into self-blame that it's depleting you. Your son needs you to put all your energy into helping him." That started me on the *no-blame path*.

Learning to Be More Flexible

My younger son was easygoing. The other two children were more difficult, needing lots of attention and extra help. It was a rule in our family that no toy guns were allowed. My older son, despite his more difficult temperament, never argued about it, so I felt certain about my "no guns" policy. The younger boy, however, wouldn't let it go. He pushed, argued and complained that he wanted a toy gun. Finally, I decided I was going to have to do it another way with him. As much as I didn't believe in guns, and as much as it went against my values, this kid seemed to need a toy gun. I wasn't sure why, especially since he was so easygoing. But his constant asking for it was so unusual for him that I decided to get him one. On a trip to Disneyland, I bought him a Daniel Boone gun and coonskin cap. I was immediately happy I had shifted my approach. He played with the gun in his room for hours on end, making up all kinds of creative stories that he acted out. That reinforced for me the reality that *there is no one right way to parent.*

Learning It's OK for My Child to Be Upset

At age seven, my older son really started giving me a hard time. He was angry all the time, he would refuse to do what I asked, and his attitude when he did things was very negative. I was at my wits' end. I sat down to talk with him, saying how much I loved him and tried to help him and how I was upset because he was angry with me so often. He ran out of the room as he shouted, "You know what your problem is, Mom? You think you can always fix things!"

Wow. That was a shock to hear. I started to follow him down the hall and was just about to knock on his door when I realized he was absolutely right. I was proving it there and then. I was just about to go into his room and "fix things"—to help him be less upset. I realized that I was always trying to swoop in and make everyone happy, but now my son was telling me that, *from his perspective,* it was backfiring. I had to look hard at myself and acknowledge that I had a problem with tolerating conflict or my kids' being in distress. Now I was learning that sometimes it is better to *allow room for your child to be upset.*

Learning to Adjust My Parenting to Who My Child Is

My daughter was a very good student, but starting in about fourth grade she stopped reading for pleasure. She read what was required of her for school, nothing more. Reading was important to me and to my husband, and the rest of the family read a lot. We believed it was something everyone should do. My daughter's lack of interest was a big disappointment to me, and I even felt rejected that she wasn't reading. I tried everything I could think of, including bribing her to read more. Nothing worked. It was only causing more tension. The truth was, no matter how much I wanted my daughter to read, it was just not something she was going to do. End of story! If I didn't accept that, we were both going to be unhappy. I realized it was best for me to raise the child I had and not keep wishing for her to be a different child. When I did that, the tension disappeared. It was still hard to let go of the disappointment, but I realized it was my problem, not hers. That incident convinced me that *adjusting my parenting to the needs of my child* was essential for my daughter but also good for me as well.

Learning to Trust Myself More

In high school, my daughter begged me to let her go to a sleepover party. I was unsure about it because I didn't know the parents, but all her friends were going to the party. So, against my instincts, I reluctantly said yes. Oddly, she kept bothering me about it. She kept bringing up that she knew I really didn't want her to go, followed by arguments as to why she should go to the party. Finally it dawned on me that maybe she didn't really want to go. So I went with my gut and said, "Sorry, I've changed my mind. It's not a good weekend for you to go to this party. There's just too much else going on." She said in a grumpy voice, "OK, if that's how you feel." But the arguing stopped. I had been trying to *feel more confident and listen to myself more*, and this incident was the extra boost I needed.

Learning There Is Always Another Way to Look at It

A particular incident with my husband really crystallized my thinking about being reflective. He had been quite ill for a long while. In addition to the medical care he received, I took it upon myself to try to nurse him back to health—fluffing his pillows, preparing him chicken soup, bringing cold compresses for his forehead. When he was well, I told him how hurt and disappointed I was that he hadn't been more appreciative of all I'd done for him. He told me, "Regina, not everyone is like you. You like TLC when you're sick, but I like to be left alone!" If that isn't a booster shot for being reflective, I don't know what is.

THE STRUCTURE OF THIS BOOK

Throughout this book, the ideas and skills of reflective parenting are interwoven with what we know about child development, the parent–child relationship, and the neuroscience of human social relationships. **Brain Basics** at the beginning of each chapter highlight the aspect of brain function being discussed. Scattered throughout each chapter, **"Science Says"** boxes present scientific experiments that support the concepts being discussed, in more scientific detail. At the end of each chapter, **Stories of Parents and Children** provide short examples of parent–child interactions that illustrate the points being made; a **Putting It into Words** section gives a few examples of the reflective language a parent might use in talking with their child; and **Take-Home Lessons** give tips and suggestions that parents can try at home to strengthen their own reflective parenting and their relationship with their child.

THIS BOOK IS FOR YOU

The role of parenting is to raise a child to become a well-functioning adult. Therefore, this book discusses reflective parenting from infancy through adolescence. Reflective parenting is extremely flexible. It can be used anywhere, for any situation, with any type of child, no matter what their age. Whether you are having difficulties or simply want to learn more in order to enhance your experience of being a parent, this book will be useful to you. Be prepared for a no-right-answers approach. This may make some parents more anxious because they believe that they need the right answer, that right answers exist, and that someone has them. By the end of the book, it is my hope that you will be relieved to discover that there is never any one right answer, that there are always many possible answers, and that the answers you come up with yourself are the best ones to have.

The Reflective Parent

ONE

10 Principles of Reflective Parenting

BRAIN BASICS

The human brain is designed to develop properly only in the context of human relationships.

HOW YOU RELATE IS MORE IMPORTANT THAN ANYTHING YOU DO

The *relationship you have with your child is the most valuable tool in your parenting toolbox.* When that relationship is strong, your child is more likely to reach their full potential in all the areas you care about as a parent: social-emotional development, academic achievement, competence, and resilience. Reflective parenting uses a strong parent–child relationship as the vehicle for raising a well-functioning child who develops into a well-functioning adult (Figure 1.1). It is similar to how a parent buys a safe car to drive their child around in, or the way a parent buys healthy food to deliver the proper proteins and vitamins to their child. The reason it is called a *reflective* approach to parenting is that the best predictor of a strong parent–child relationship is the parent's capacity to be reflective (Grienenberger, Kelly, & Slade, 2005; Slade, Grienenberger, Bernbach, Levy, & Locker, 2005).

A strong parent–child relationship is a balance of many different kinds of qualities: flexible yet firm, containing yet freeing, guiding with-

Figure 1.1. The relationship is the vehicle.

out being dogmatic, and comforting without being overprotective. It is like a rubber band that can expand without breaking; like a bread pan that holds the sides of the dough in shape while the top is rising; like a pressure cooker lid that holds in the steam but also releases pressure to avoid an explosion; like a map with a number of possible good routes to take to your destination; like a thermostat that can be adjusted to keep the room temperature comfortable. To achieve these relationships qualities, a parent must interact with their child in a reflective way.

Here is an example of what is meant by a strong parent–child relationship and being reflective. A child comes home crying because they didn't do well on a test. The parent offers a soothing touch and comforting words. The parent inquires more about what happened, but the child doesn't answer the question and keeps complaining about the test. The parent allows the child to express their distress and tell what they think happened. The child says, "I hate that teacher. She made the test too hard." The parent feels upset and disappointed with the child for not taking responsibility and for blaming the teacher but doesn't share it. This is because the parent senses that the child is too distraught to learn anything from the situation right now. Later, when things are calmer, the parent has a discussion with the child. Here the parent explores whether there was some way the child could have been better prepared for the test. The parent guides the child in learning the importance of taking responsibility for one's actions rather than blaming others.

When parents are not reflective, they tend to be more reactive. For example, it can weaken a relationship if a parent is consistently too quick to give a consequence or to lecture on the need to study hard for a test. Neither is it good for the relationship if a parent is consistently too quick to jump in to take the child's side or complain to the teacher about the tests.

Even if your relationship is already strong, a reflective approach will help you to be more relaxed, worry less, feel better about your child, and feel better about your parenting. This chapter presents guidelines for how a parent can be as reflective as possible and explains in more depth what being reflective entails.

Parenting Is Not a Job; It's a Relationship

Even though parenting takes work, parenting is not a job. Parenting is a *relationship* between you and your child. Every aspect of reflective parenting is directed at building a *strong* relationship with your child. According to neuroscientists, this is because children learn and function best only in the context of a strong relationship with the primary person or persons who care for them. The brain is designed to build strong relationships out of a messy combination of understanding and misunderstanding, getting along and having conflict, being close and being separate. What keeps the mess and the misunderstanding from getting out of hand and harming the child is the parent's reflective capacity. Your brain's reflective capacity operates as a type of GPS system to navigate you through the messiness of relationships in general, and in this case the parent–child relationship.

3

Reflective Parenting 101

Reflective parenting is an all-purpose relationship tool for raising a child of any age. It is especially good for dealing with the stressful and difficult parts of parenting. Because the essence of reflective parenting is to be flexible, understanding, and accepting of who your child is and who you are as a parent, it is an approach that will apply no matter what type of parent you are, what type of child you have, or what type of family circumstances you are experiencing.

This approach is called reflective parenting because it involves a parent's use of their reflective capacity in all aspects of their relationship with their child. *Reflective capacity* is technically defined as a mental skill in which the mind is able to recognize (a) that all human behavior has meaning in terms of what is going on inside a person's mind, such as their feelings, desires, intentions, motivations, and beliefs, and that this applies to one's own behavior as well as the behavior of others; (b) that all people have a mind that is subjective, separate, and private; and (c) that what is in one person's mind may be the same or may be different from what is going on inside someone else's mind.

In everyday language, *reflective capacity* means understanding that what your child is doing is caused by something going on internally, inside your child's mind, and that what you do in response to your child's action is caused by something in your own mind. Additionally, since your child's mind is hidden from view, what you assume to be the reason for your child's behavior may or may not be correct. Therefore, try as you might to be as reflective as possible, misunderstandings are bound to happen from time to time.

Reflective parenting is always relationship focused. It encourages parents to (a) maintain a primary focus on the parent–child relationship, (b) have an understanding of the role that the minds of the child and of the parent play in that relationship, and (c) see the relationship from multiple perspectives. This is captured a bit in one of the mottos of reflective parenting: "It is not *what* you do. It is *how you do* what you do." The point to be emphasized is that whether you are playing a game, helping with homework, teaching an important life lesson, comforting your child's distress, setting limits, or disciplining your child, the quality of how you relate to your child will have more impact than any of your words or actions.

THE 10 GUIDING PRINCIPLES OF REFLECTIVE PARENTING

Reflective parenting brings together a parent's capacity for reflective thinking with a set of guiding principles to follow when interacting with a child. The principles of reflective parenting are derived from what science has shown helps parents to be as reflective as possible and to give their children what they most need for all aspects of healthy development. The 10 principles of reflective parenting are as follows:

1. **The parent–child relationship is paramount.** Make sure to slow down and be in the moment, because relationships cannot be hurried or rushed. When in doubt, focus on the relationship. No matter what else you do, the relationship should come first. The relationship matters more than anything else, including academics, after-school enrichment, limits, and even discipline. The relationship is the fertile soil in which your child's roots are planted so that your child can flourish and bloom.

2. **There is no perfect parent, and there are no "right" or "best" answers or ways of parenting.** There are a broad range of parenting styles, all of which are equally likely to lead to children doing well. Think more for yourself. Come up with more of your own answers. Be more confident that you can figure out a good way of handling a situation with your child. You are the best judge of what your child needs. The books and the experts provide recipes to try, but only you can determine which nourishing meal is best for your child and family.

3. *Tolerate ambiguity, uncertainty, and not knowing.* This includes accepting that misunderstanding and conflict are normal and inevitable. By tolerating and accepting these things, parents are less likely to react reflexively or rigidly to situations. As explained in Chapter 2, there is no single truth about what is happening, only various perceptions. Life and human relationships are by their very nature a messy business. We have to resist the urge to immediately try to clean them up.

4. *See the world from your child's perspective as well as your own.* Step into the mental shoes of your child and see the world through their eyes, not just your own eyes. Your child is a separate person with their own separate viewpoint and motivations. Also, a child's mind operates quite differently from an adult's, which is important to take into account in deciding how to respond to your child. Perspective-taking promotes greater empathy in a parent, enables a child to feel understood, and is the cornerstone of a child's ability to develop their own mind.

5. *Be curious, open-minded, and flexible as a person and as parent.* As much as you might wish you knew all the answers, no one can. Additionally, your child doesn't need you to know all the answers. It's OK to have a sense of wonder and question what is going on. Scientists believe people do better in life if they have a variety of ways of seeing the world and a variety of options for how to behave. Since this is a more adaptive way of being, model it for your child.

6. *Regulate children by holding their feelings and holding the line.* Children certainly need parents to help them contain their impulses and soothe their emotions. The best kind of help uses a balanced approach. Parents do this by balancing emotional attunement and sensitivity with setting firm and age-appropriate limits, and by balancing understanding and validation of feelings with establishing boundaries as to how the child can express those feelings.

7. *Teach your child to be competent and resilient.* Ultimately, your child will need to become more and more independent from you. Children make this transition more successfully if they develop competence and resilience. To acquire these traits, first make sure you maintain the attitude that all difficulties can be managed and dealt with and that feelings, even intensely bad feelings, will change over time. Additionally, help your child develop strategies for persevering and coping with challenge, frustration, disappointment, and hurt. In this way, even if a painful situation or crisis knocks your child down, they will be able to get back up.

8. *Be more positive than negative, more optimistic than pessimistic.* Of course, children have their flaws and problems. However, the evidence shows that children do better when their difficulties are minimized in favor of what is good about them. Therefore, emphasize what is right more than what is wrong. Emphasize strengths more than weaknesses. Emphasize that things are likely to get better rather than worse. Notice and praise children's efforts, not just their accomplishments.

9. *Repair ruptures to the relationship if they occur.* Anger and conflict are normal in all relationships. Although it's difficult, children can generally cope well enough with that. What they can't handle at all is when the anger or conflict leads to a rupture in the relationship. This leads to feelings of aloneness and abandonment that are beyond a child's ability to cope with. Therefore, make sure to take the time and effort to repair ruptures when and if they occur.

10. *All kids are unique, so adjust your parenting to your child's specific needs.* No two brains are alike and no two people are alike. Science emphasizes that diversity and variation are part of human life. Therefore, you can't apply the same parenting strategies to all kids. Raise your child according to what best fits who your child is. Of course, all parents

have hopes for *who* their child will be, but it is better to remember that you need to *raise the child you have, not the child you wish you had.*

Remember: The principles are guidelines, not strict rules.

Too often when parents are told that they should "focus on building a strong relationship by following the principles of reflective parenting," they experience it as an extra burden. Their eyes frequently glaze over because they already have too many other things to think about. Some parents say things like, "This sounds like one more issue I have to worry about. Now I have to think about whether I have a *strong* relationship or not?" or "Now I have to worry about remembering the principles. I can't even remember where I left my keys. How am I going to keep all of this in mind?"

To reassure the reader, the principles presented here are only guidelines, not strict rules. The whole point of this book is help parents feel more relaxed and free about their parenting, not more pressured and constrained. These principles are designed to take some of parents' concerns *off* their plate, not add concerns *to* the plate. To say that "the relationship is more important than anything else you do for your child" means that the relationship is more important than, for example, how many play dates your child has, whether your child gets music lessons or plays sports, what type of manners your child should have, or how much electronics your child can use. These are important issues to think about, for sure. However, in the long run of life, most of the choices parents make about these issues come out in the wash, so to speak, as long as the parent is trying to do their best to be reflective and to have a good relationship with their child. The principles remove pressure because they remind parents that a strong relationship is *not* a perfect relationship, *not* a relationship that is warm and emotionally responsive *all the time,* and *not* a relationship where the parent *always* understands the child. A strong relationship is just a relationship that is *on average* reliably warm and responsive and understanding, and one in which, if a parent has difficulty, they are at least trying to get better at it.

Additionally, the guidelines are not just about "What you do for your child?" They are also about "What you do for yourself?" To have a strong parent–child relationship means being comforting, empathic, validating, understanding, accepting, and supportive of your child. But it also means taking this same approach toward yourself! In other words, in order to give your child what they need, you have to give those same things to yourself. In fact, the most common reason for parents to have difficulty with being comforting, empathic, validating, understanding, accepting, and supportive of their child is that they have difficulty being this way in relationship to themselves. For example, parents who can't empathize with themselves will often have more difficulty empathizing with their child. Parents who are harsh and critical toward themselves will often have difficulty being accepting and supportive of their child. A good motto might be, "To be kinder to your child, be kinder to yourself." Think of it as *parent first-aid*. A parent who is feeling overly harsh toward a child's behavior or emotional needs first needs help with being less harsh about their own behavior and emotional needs. This book gives a shout-out to parents: "You are so important to your child that you must take good care of yourself if you are going to be able to take good care of your child."

WHY BE REFLECTIVE?

To better make sense of why it is so important to be as reflective as possible, it will help to understand more of what reflective capacity is all about.

Human relationships operate mind-to-mind.

We humans are hardwired to relate to others as if they have a mind just like ours and to automatically assign *mental* meanings such as feelings and intentions to the behaviors we observe in others. Without reflective capacity, we would not be able to navigate our social world, even with our own children. Because of our reflective capacity, when a person waves in our direction, we assume they are intending to greet us rather than just moving their hand around in a random fashion. When a person smiles, we assume they are feeling happy rather than simply stretching their lips.

Reflective capacity attaches meaning to behavior so that we can make sense of how a person is acting. When we reflect on our own mind, we can make better sense of our own behavior. When we reflect on another person's mind, not only can we make better sense of their behavior, but we are also better able to guide our responses toward them.

When your two-year-old son lifts up his arms or your three-year-old daughter says, "Look at that butterfly!" these are examples of your child's *behavior*. Reflective capacity links the behavior with a meaning or reason for the behavior. Perception of the behavior identifies the *what*. What is the behavior? Reflective capacity is more about perceiving the inner reason for the behavior, the *why*. Why is that person doing what they are doing?

Behaviors exist in the concrete, tangible realm. Meanings only exist in the intangible and abstract realm of the mind. The behavior is specific, but the meanings can vary. Your son's action may mean he is tired and wants you to carry him. It may mean he is curious about what you are saying to your friend and wants you to lift him up so he can be included in the conversation. It might mean he simply needs some closeness. Your daughter's words may mean she wants to communicate her enjoyment of the butterfly, or to show you her language prowess, or to simply get you to look at the butterfly together with her. Being reflective enables you to realize that any of these meanings is possible. This is especially important since your response to your child's behavior will be guided more by the meaning your reflective capacity identifies than by your child's actual behavior.

Reflective capacity is a little like how a cell phone can take a snapshot of another person but can also take a *selfie*. In other words, when we direct our reflective capacity toward our own mind, we can gain access to the memories, motivations, and emotions that underlie our own behavior. This helps a parent better modulate and adjust their responses to their child.

However, like frosted glass on a bathroom window, minds are opaque. We can clearly see the behavior, but the meaning or reason for the behavior is hidden from view. Therefore, reflective capacity is a little bit like the way x-rays allow us to "peer" inside the body. But instead of seeing bones and organs, we "see" beliefs, goals, and needs. Nevertheless, because of the opacity, no matter how reflective we are, we can never be fully certain about our perceptions of someone else's mind. Even when we are convinced we are absolutely correct, we may not be. It's like the way a radiologist looks at an x-ray and says, "I don't think it's a tumor, but it might be." Of course, the radiologist can order a biopsy to find out for certain. When it comes to the mind, for better or worse, all we have is the x-ray. There is nothing physical to take a biopsy of.

Also, lest you think that poor, uneducated parents are less likely to be reflective, it turns out that neither a college education nor affluence guarantees that a person will have good reflective capacity. Reflective capacity is not related to education, socioeconomic status, ethnicity, or cultural background. A poor, uneducated parent is just as likely to be reflective as a college-educated parent raised in a wealthy community.

Reflective capacity is a thinking skill.

Stress can impair complex mental skills such as math or reading. Since reflective capacity is a thinking skill, it also can be impaired by stress. Many of the principles of reflective parenting specifically target this issue, which will be further explored in Chapter 8.

The fact that reflective capacity is a skill also indicates that it operates both consciously and nonconsciously. When you first learn a piece on the piano or first learn how to swing a bat, you have to give it your full conscious attention. Once the skill is practiced and well learned, you can shift into performing it quite well without effort or conscious awareness. If, however, you need to learn a new piece or improve your swing, once again you shift into conscious attention and effort. In turn, when you become proficient at your new skill, you can shift back into nonconscious performance.

Depending on the situation with your child, your reflective thinking skill will need to fluidly shift between these two types of performance modes, nonconscious and conscious. When things are going smoothly with a child, reflective capacity typically operates nonconsciously in the background. The relationship proceeds without effort or conscious noticing. If things get bumpy and confusing, however, shifting into more conscious, effortful reflectivity will be beneficial. In particular, when things go awry and parents are reminding themselves to follow a principle of reflective parenting such as tolerating ambiguity, shifting from a negative to a more positive attitude, or adjusting to the unique needs of their child, it requires their full conscious attention and effort.

Reflective capacity has several steps.

The skill of reflective capacity can be broken down into five steps. Steps 1 and 2 are required only for promoting conscious reflective capacity, whereas Steps 3 through 5 can be either consciously or nonconsciously carried out, depending on the situation. Steps 1 and 2 are especially necessary for times when you are working on improving your relationship or times when you are overwhelmed or simply just confused. It is important for parents to be reflective about their child but also reflective about themselves.

The steps are as follows:

1. Pause and slow down. (Conscious skills take more time than nonconscious ones.)
2. Be present in the moment. (Consciousness takes place only in the present.)
3. Observe the behavior (your child's and your own) and label it with words.
4. Reflect on the meaning of the behavior (your child's and your own).

5. Use the understanding you get from prior steps to guide your response to your child.

Whether these steps occur consciously or nonconsciously will vary according to the needs of the situation. Think about the fact that you have clothes for casual wear and clothes for dressing up. You use the different clothes for different situations. Slowed-down, effortful reflective capacity is for stressful situations or any of the circumstances described in the principles of reflective parenting. The calmer the situation and the better you are at being reflective, the more you will be able to do it without conscious effort. In other words, during periods of uncertainty, stress, or conflict, parents are encouraged to use all five steps. Once you feel more confident about what you are doing or what you have decided, or if the stress has passed or it seems as if things once again are going smoothly, you can allow reflective thinking to return to the background.

A reflective approach helps improve or fine-tune your parenting.

Most of you who are reading this book are already being naturally reflective in your relationship with your child, even if you don't quite realize it. For you, the principles of reflective parenting will serve to *fine-tune* what you already know and give you a greater sense of confidence in your parenting, especially during the ups and downs of daily living. They will also serve as a refresher course, improving your ability to manage the more challenging aspects of raising your child.

Think of eating. Eating is natural, but we don't always eat well. As natural as eating is, there are times—such as when we feel down or stressed—where we need extra reminders and even support systems for maintaining healthy eating habits. In the same way, there are times in parenting when we need the extra reminders that the principles of reflective parenting can provide.

For some readers, being reflective doesn't come as naturally. But take heart! Reflective parenting can be learned, no matter who you are and no matter who your child is. Anyone who puts in the effort and takes the time to practice these principles can modify their parenting style and improve the relationship they have with their child.

Reflective parenting is a lot like having a well-stocked toolbox or a Swiss Army knife of parenting with an appropriate tool for every situation. In this case, the tools include the skill of being reflective plus the skills contained in following the 10 guiding principles. Parents can use the tools of reflective parenting along with other parenting strategies, as reflective parenting is complementary to other parenting approaches. In fact, reflective parenting will help you use those other approaches more effectively.

Finally, the laws of human neurobiology indicate that our inborn genetics place some restrictions on our long-term potential. This means that if you already are a good parent, you can't increase your child's chances even more by being *more good*. All any parent can do, by being reflective, is to help a child achieve their full potential, whatever that may be. Arthur Ashe was known to have said, "Start where you are. Use what you have. Do what you can.". This idea captures the essence of reflective parenting, and is true for your child as well as for yourself.

A reflective approach encourages parents to make up their own minds.

One mother in a reflective parenting group expressed her disappointment about how the group was run. She said she was looking for more didactic information. "I was hoping for more factual information about my child's development. All we do is talk about how we feel and what our kids are feeling. I need to know what to do!" *She is not alone. Some parents wish they could just be told the facts and answers.* This might be easier in the short run. But in the long run, it is better when parents think for themselves and figure out in their own mind what they believe is the best way to raise their child.

As the saying goes, "Give a man a fish and you feed him for a day. Teach a man to fish and you feed him for a lifetime" (Maimonides). A reflective approach to parenting supports parents in using their minds to figure out what is happening between them and their child and in making up their own minds about how to parent their child. In parallel fashion, it also encourages parents to help children to use their minds to figure things out for themselves as much as is age-appropriately possible.

STORIES OF PARENTS AND CHILDREN

- *Principle 1: The relationship is paramount.* John is an avid bicycle rider. Even before his son Phillip was born, John had dreams of taking long rides through the mountains with his son. Phillip liked riding until about age 10, when he started to prefer team sports. John enjoyed the freedom of bike riding and believed it was the best activity for overall conditioning, so he kept asking his son to ride with him. It was painful and disappointing to John as, more and more, Phillip turned down these requests and turned to soccer and baseball instead. However, John could not keep himself from putting pressure on Phillip. His wife finally pointed out to him that Phillip was feeling resentful and guilty about disappointing his dad, but also angry that his dad was being selfish. John started to pay attention and noticed how Phillip acted irritated with him and would avoid conversations together. John resolved to stop the pressure. It was painful for him to give up the dream! But the relationship with his son was more important. *When in doubt, focus on the relationship!*
- *Principle 2: There are no perfect parents and no right or best answers.* One mother, Tammy, asked the caregivers at her children's daycare, "Should my daughters have their own toys, or should toys be shared?" Tammy's two young daughters shared a room, and she decided that the girls' toys should be common property. It was easier for her as a parent to do it this way, and in fact the two girls didn't even seem to notice. They fought and argued about who could play with a particular toy, like all kids do, but it had nothing to do with ownership. Tammy's mother-in-law, however, thought having the

15

girls share all their toys was a terrible idea. The mother-in-law maintained that the girls were not being given "the right to have ownership of their toys and that they would have less conflict if there were some toys they didn't have to share." Tammy felt awful, and her confidence wobbled. She said she didn't want to cause harm to her daughters and therefore wanted to know what was the right way to do it. The people at the daycare, fortunately, were reflective. They told Tammy that there was no right answer and that "any choice you make will have pluses and minuses . . . you can't avoid conflict and problems." At first, Tammy had trouble believing this, but eventually she felt so much better that she was being encouraged to think for herself and to come up with her own answers. *When in doubt, think for yourself!*

- *Principle 3: Tolerate ambiguity and uncertainty.* Sheldon and Marianne's ten-year-old son had just been diagnosed with attention deficit disorder. Although they were relieved to have an answer for why he was not getting good grades in school and why his behavior was so hard to manage, they were also very worried. They particularly feared he would never do well in life because they had heard such bad stories from friends and family about kids with this problem. So they swooped in and did everything imaginable to help him. It all came from caring, but even they could see that all their anxiety was making their son more tense and making him feel like he was a disappointment to them. They said, "We would pull back. We could be calmer if we knew it would all work out in the end. But since we can't know for sure, just to be on the safe side we are going to be on him about his schoolwork as much as possible." All of these feelings are, of course, perfectly natural. The problem was that these parents' inability to tolerate uncertainty was sending them into overdrive, which was not good for their son.

- *Principle 4: See your baby's perspective as well as your own.* Carla's daughter Isabel was a friendly and outgoing 14-month-old girl. When other moms and kids were around, Isabel would easily go up to them to play or to get their attention. Carla was always reining her in, indicating for Isabel to come back and sit down next to her. Carla said, "She will just go up to anyone. It's kind of rude, I think." The other parents in her parent education class thought that Isabel was a lovely girl, and no one was annoyed with her. Despite the group's reassurance that Isabel had good social skills and their encouragement to Carla not to worry so much, Carla was still disturbed by Isabel's behavior. When the group leader encouraged Carla to reflect, she looked inward. She realized she felt embarrassed by Isabel. She also believed others were judging her as a mother for letting her daughter bother other people and that they wouldn't like her daughter for how annoying she was. After a bit more reflection, Carla said, "For me, I'm not outgoing at all. I'm introverted. I feel embarrassed when I talk and ask questions. I would be scared to act the way Isabel does. I guess what I'm doing is trying to get her to behave more the way I do." After reflecting on herself, Carla then reflected on Isabel's perspective. "Isabel isn't scared like me. She is comfortable and enjoys engaging with people. I'm shy, but she's not shy. I want her to feel that's OK too." Carla resolved to try to feel safer and less embarrassed by how Isabel was being with other people. *When in doubt, reflect!*

- **Principle 4: See your teen's perspective as well as your own.** Monique and her 17-year-old son Ezra had been arguing a lot about her texting him so much. Monique defended herself by explaining that the world was not safe and that she was just checking in to connect and make sure he was OK. Ezra defended himself by explaining that he was grown up and that his mother should trust him more. In a mocking and scornful voice, he said, "I don't mind the texting so much; it's that you *always* ask, 'Where are you?' 'Who are you with?' You treat me like I'm still a little kid. Trust me. Stop quizzing me so much!" Monique, irritated with his tone of voice and negative attitude, tried to explain herself yet again. "I trust you. I'm just worried. That means I care about what happens to you." Monique finally realized that they had reached a stalemate and that she needed a different way to communicate. She was able to see things from his

17

perspective when she remembered that as a teenager, she wanted that same sense of freedom and independence. She decided on a plan that would alleviate her anxiety about his safety while at the same time allowing him room to grow up and be separate. She called the plan "Checking in, not checking up." The next time she texted, she asked, "You good?" He replied, "Yup!" Without any further discussion, the conflict resolved. *When in doubt, see it from both perspectives!*

- *Principle 5: Be curious, open-minded, and flexible.* Joelle's rule was that Hannah must clean up her toys before she got a bedtime story. Hannah was an easygoing five-year-old girl and usually did what her mother said. One evening, however, Hannah balked. "I don't want to clean my toys!" Joelle strongly believed kids need to learn to be responsible and followed through on the limits, saying, "No bedtime story until you put the toys in the basket." Hannah asked for help, and Joelle tried to be flexible by helping. Hannah, however, did very little. Joelle found herself putting away almost all the toys. She was a kind and loving mother, but she believed in firmness, so she put Hannah to bed without a story. Things were OK for a few minutes, but then Hannah began to howl and beg for a story. What now? Joelle was kind but firm: "No story because you didn't put away the toys." Hannah continued to cry. Joelle worried that if she gave in, Hannah would only learn that she could get what she wanted without having to be responsible about it. But Joelle could also see that right now Hannah was so upset that she would never get to sleep on time and would be a mess the next day because of it. So Joelle agreed to tell Hannah a story. Hannah immediately calmed down, and right after the story was over she fell asleep without another peep. Joelle, however, was disappointed in herself. She felt she should have kept her resolve to always stand firm on her limits and not wimp out. The truth is, however, that humans are not absolutely consistent. Like the tree that bends in the wind so that it does not crack, parents also have to be flexible.
- *Principle 6: Balance empathy with limit setting.* Six-year old Juno was on the monkey bars at the playground when she shouted to her

mom, Ginger, "Those boys said a bad word to me. Go and tell them to stop!" Her mom sloughed her off saying, "You can deal with it yourself." Juno came down from the play equipment and insisted her mom tell them to stop. Ginger was irritated and said, "No I will not talk with them; you have to learn how to ignore things like this!" At this point Juno starts to sob. Finally Ginger softens. "Okay she says," kindly this time and crouching down to give her daughter a hug. "I know it feels bad when boys talk like that. It hurts your feelings. But the reason I don't want to tell them to stop is that they like it when you get all upset. It stops them better if you just ignore them."

- *Principle 7: Promote coping and competence.* Jeremiah was at the zoo with his parents, his 2-year-old brother Austen, and his grandma to celebrate Jeremiah's 5th birthday. They were just about to visit the gorillas, Jeremiah's absolute favorite animal, when Grandma said she felt faint. Even after she sat down she said she did not feel well and wanted to go home. Jeremiah's parents were very warm, empathic, and understanding when Jeremiah was crying about having to leave the zoo without seeing the gorillas. He was still crying in the car on the drive home. Finally his mom said, "You know, Jeremiah, we all understand how disappointed you are about not seeing the gorillas. But every person has to learn how to get themselves to stop crying even when they are upset, even if it is for a good reason. Your cousin Gregory had to learn it. Dad had to learn it. I had to learn. I think you are old enough to start to learn how to do it. I think it might help if you take five deep breaths. What do you think?" Jeremiah, already starting to contain himself, says, "Will you take five deep breaths with me?"

- *Principle 8: Be more positive than negative.* Gilda said that her 11-year-old son Jacob was a real pill. "He gets upset over everything. He never listens or follows the rules. He is so demanding when he wants something. Something is really wrong with him, because I am yelling at him all the time and taking away privileges for his bad behavior but he still does not act any better. I know I am not doing a good job, but he gets me so wound up, I just lose it with him." When

I ask, "What are Jacob's strengths?" she replies, "His friends' parents like him and think he is really cooperative and polite when he is at their houses. He is a great athlete and he is patient when helping younger kids with sports." Gilda feels better when I say, "Yeah he is a handful. Sounds like he has a difficult temperament that requires you to have to do more work to help contain his emotions and impulses. I am assuming that some of why you punish him so much is because you are anxious and worried about him. So I wonder if it would help for you to pay more attention to all of his good traits, his athletic abilities, his patience with younger kids. What would that be like?" She calms down a bit and smiles, saying, "I am sure it won't surprise you to hear that my mom said I was really a stubborn handful as a kid. He probably just gets some of it from me. He does have a good side. He is more full of life and energetic than the rest of us. I am sure he will love it if I tell him that more often."

- **Principle 9: Repair relationship ruptures.** Gilda's husband Adam complains that Jacob yells all the time. "It grates on me, especially when he screams if you say NO. Like the other day, when he wanted us to take him skateboarding and he threw a giant fit at the dinner table when I said we didn't have time to do that. He ruined dinner for the rest of us. While he was yelling I had to get up from the table and leave the room and told him I was fed up with him. I wouldn't talk with him the rest of the day." When I asked if he knows why Jacob throws fits like that, he said, "He can't handle any disappointment. He gets unglued. I don't like him when he is so weak like that." I ask, "What do you think it is like for him when you write him off like that?" He says, and here a light bulb goes off, "He probably does not like it any better than I did when my mom did that to me. She would literally not talk with me for days if I misbehaved. I was miserable and frightened by that. Ouch. I guess that is what I am doing to him. Okay, I see I should re-connect after we have one of those incidents, even if he has been in the wrong. It's not fair to him if I remove myself so harshly."

- **Principle 10: Adjust to your child's needs.** Abby was helping her

9-year-old daughter Keira with a math project. Keira really worked hard on it for days. Abby believes in "doing things right" so when she notices any mistakes in Keira's work she typically points them out, adding "I don't' like it when people sugarcoat things, so I am not going to do that with her." Abby is a perfectionist and her daughter Keira is not, which causes them to get into quite a few battles over homework, with Keira often digging in her heels and angrily refusing to make any of the corrections that Abby points out. But Abby was recently learning more about Reflective Parenting, so this time she resisted the urge to tell Keira all the sloppy mistakes she can see. Abby reminds herself that Keira is not the detail-oriented person that she is. Shifting her style and being more sensitive to who Keira is, Abby tells her daughter, "I can see how much work you put into it and it looks good." She sees how good Keira feels, but wants to try to find a way to teach Keira how to get better at making corrections in her work. With her new found approach that is more sensitive to the needs of her child, she adds, "You know me, and my pickiness. If you want I could tell you a few areas where you could improve it if you want to." Much to Abby's surprise, Keira, instead of digging in her heels or getting angry, says, "Yeah go ahead and tell me. Then I can see if I want to fix it more."

PUTTING IT INTO WORDS

Here are some ways parents may communicate the importance of the relationship to their kids.

- **Father:** "I realize I've been pressuring you too much to play soccer. However, I can see it's not your thing. I'm sorry it took me so long to realize it. What I really feel is that the most important thing is for you to decide what interests you, and I will do my best to support you in that."
- **Mother:** "We fight every morning about combing your hair before you go to school. I'm not happy about fighting. I don't think you like

it either. Wouldn't it be better for us to figure out another way to deal with the hair situation? Do you have any ideas?"

- **Mother and father:** "We know how badly you want to go Joe's house for a sleepover. with all your friends. But we also love you and want to make sure you're safe, and we aren't sure yet whether the situation at Joe's house is safe enough. We have to get more information and talk more about it together before we decide."

TAKE-HOME LESSONS

- *Practice slowing down and being present.*
  - *Use a mindfulness exercise.* Take some time alone, find a comfortable seated position, and close your eyes. Try to observe the thoughts and feelings that come and go. If you notice yourself becoming caught up in a particular thought or feeling, see if you can gently return to a more observational stance, watching your thoughts and feelings ebb and flow. Continue this exercise for two to three minutes.
  - *Use gestures to remind yourself.* Place your hand on your chest as if you were pushing an imaginary stop button to keep yourself from jumping in too quickly. Clamp your lips together to "bite your tongue" to keep yourself from saying something too hastily. These physical gestures slow down the interaction and give you a moment's pause to calm down and consider the situation more fully before responding to it.
  - *Set aside a time to just be there in the moment.* For at least 15 minutes, turn off all electronics and do nothing except to just be there in the moment with your child. You can tell your child, "I am completely free and available to just be together with you." Of course, make sure your child is available too. Then follow your child's lead and see what happens. Whatever happens is fine. The point is to be available and open in the moment to whatever is going on with your child.

- *Practice tolerating uncertainty and ambiguity.*
  - *Notice a time when you are totally uncertain about how to handle a situation.* Describe how it feels to be uncertain of what to do. For example, are you feeling an emotion? Do you feel something in your body? See how long you can allow yourself to just feel that way before you decide what to do.
  - *Notice a time when the meaning of your child's behavior is ambiguous.* It may be when your child is explaining something to you in a vague way. It may be when you are trying to make sense of their actions but just can't figure it out. Pay attention to how it feels to be confused. Notice how you deal with feeling confused. Think of whether there is another way to deal with it.

In the chapters that follow, the ideas presented about the parent–child relationship, child development, reflective capacity, and the principles of reflective parenting will all be further elaborated on in connection with the science of how the brain operates.

TWO

Your Child's Unique Mind

BRAIN BASICS

The human brain is organized to enable people to relate to one another primarily mind-to-mind, in a way that allows for understanding and misunderstanding.

THE MIND IS THE ARTWORK OF THE BRAIN

The mind plays a starring role in all healthy human relationships and in all healthy child development. The mind is the part of us through which we are aware of and make sense of ourselves, other people, and our physical surroundings. The mind is where our sense of "I" is located; where all of our thoughts, feelings, intentions, goals, and beliefs reside; and the source of meaning for all of our behavior. Although many aspects of how the mind comes to be still remain a mystery, what is generally agreed upon is that the mind is created by the brain and that the nature of the mind is shaped by how the brain functions. Your capacity to understand your child's mind and your own mind are the basic building blocks from which your child develops a mind. Understanding how the mind operates will improve your connection with your child and your ability to respond to your child most effectively.

The very success of Homo sapiens as a species is the result of an especially social nature (Wilson, 2012). It is theorized that the mind evolved to enhance the success of our social relationships and enabled humans to develop language, culture, communities, and civilization itself (Dunbar & Shultz, 2007; Tomasello, 1999). Reflective capacity evolved as a way of perceiving the mind of the self and of other people. A big part of what parenting is about is using your mind to teach your child how to become a competent social person with a well-functioning mind and the capacity to be reflective.

To say that *the mind is the artwork of the brain* means that the physical brain creates the mind. Although the mind is created out of the brain, the mind itself is intangible. Our five senses are for processing the concrete tangibles of life. The mind is for processing the abstract intangibles of life, such as thoughts, feelings, intentions, beliefs, goals, and concepts like freedom, beauty, and loyalty. The brain's creation of the mind can be likened to how an artist works. The artist uses physical things—for example, paint, wood, and metal—but what makes it "art" is not those physical elements. What makes it art is how the artist's mind brings those elements together to express or evoke an experience in the minds of others.

REFLECTIVE CAPACITY: THE BRAIN'S WAY OF PERCEIVING THE MIND

The mind is private and hidden from view. The technical term for what is inside the mind is *mental states*. Reflective capacity operates a bit like x-ray vision or mind-reading, allowing some access to the inner world of others. Reflective capacity causes us to automatically relate mind-to-mind. For example, even though a baby is not born with a mind, parents talk to their newborn *as if* the child already had a fully developed mind. They might say, "I know you're screaming so loudly because I'm being slow in feeding you, and you're trying to hurry me up." Treating the baby as if it has a mind is the first step in the child's beginning to develop its own mind.

The mind is also inherently subjective. Each mind views the world in its own way. Because the mind is both hidden and subjective, even being reflective will not ensure that you will always fully understand your child. When we reflect, all we can really do is make a good guess or inference as to what is *probably* going on inside another person's mind. We may be right. But we are not always right. This is why reflective parenting emphasizes that misunderstanding is possible and common, but by being reflective, a parent is more likely to figure out and clarify misunderstandings when they occur.

THE "YOU-ME-WE" OF THE PARENT–CHILD RELATIONSHIP

Every parent–child relationship involves a *threesome*: a "you-me-we." "You" is the child's perspective. "Me" is the parent's perspective. "We" is the perspective of how the parent and child impact one another. Here is an example:

You (child's perspective): "You are really annoyed because I can't talk with you right now."

Me (parent's perspective): "I am really in a rush, which is why I am not able to talk with you right now."

We (their mutual impact): "When I was in a rush earlier and couldn't talk to you, you became angry and screamed at me. Then I got angry and screamed back at you, and that made you feel terrible, and so you cried."

This "you-me-we" point of view is another way of thinking about the ideas contained in reflective parenting (see Figure 2.1). By employing a "you-me-we" perspective, reflective parents seek to understand their child from the child's perspective (the "you"), understand themselves from their own perspective (the "me"), and also make a point of understanding how they each are impacting or affecting one another (the "we"). The "you" and "me" captures reflective parenting's two-way perspective-taking. The "we" captures reflective parenting's primary focus on the parent–child

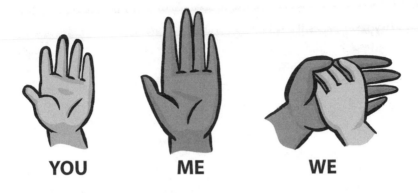

Figure 2.1. You, me, we.

relationship. By always *keeping their eye on the relationship* during the frequently tumultuous process of child-rearing, parents are more able to promote healthy development in all the areas that parents care about, such as social and emotional well-being, behavior and impulse control, cognitive development, and academic accomplishment (Beebe, 2006; Fonagy, Gergely, Jurist, & Target, 2004; Lyons Ruth & Jacobvitz, 1999).

The Role That the Mind Plays in the Parent–Child Relationship

A reflective parent uses language that expresses the role of the mind in the relationship. The "me" of the parent expresses their recognition of the role of the mind by *linking up* the outward behaviors with what is going on internally, inside the mind. In the example given previously, the behaviors are *talk*, *scream*, and *cry*. The mental states they are linked to are *in a rush*, *not able to*, *annoyed*, *feel terrible*, and *angry*. The words the parent uses create a little *narrative*, or storyline, to describe the "we" of the parent and child's mutual impact on each other's mind and behaviors. The mind is always trying to make sense of what is going on. A narrative provides the most coherent way of making meaning out of the events of our lives.

Without any specific instructions, parents transmit their reflective capacity to their child simply by communicating in this reflective way. The child *internalizes* this process into their own mind, and it becomes the child's ability to be reflective.

Raising a Child from the "Baby Room" to the "Boardroom"

Although parenting and corporate business may seem very far from one another, business management consultants frequently recommend an approach similar to "you-me-we" (Goldsmith, 2007). They teach executives and their employees to think reflectively. They encourage all the "you's" and "me's" on the business team to understand where others are coming from and how they all impact each other. They emphasize that everyone brings different perspectives and skills to the team, and that it is how they interact with each other that will determine how well or poorly they do. This same relationship message is the cornerstone of a book about the underdog Washington University rowing team that won the Olympics in 1936 (Brown, 2014).

As a reflective parent, you operate as a team with your child with the common goal of helping him or her develop in the most adaptive way possible. This requires that you recognize and respect the fact that your child has his or her own perspective on the world, even if you don't agree with it. Recognize your own perspective, then work together with your child to understand how you impact one another.

THE BRAIN CONSTRUCTS ALL OF OUR PERCEPTIONS

The mind's subjectivity is a natural extension of the fact that the brain constructs all of our perceptions. It *seems* to us that we simply perceive the world as it really is, but this is not the case. From moment to moment, the brain actively constructs our perceptions for us, which we experience as a flow of reality, much like a video playing in our mind. Our mind experiences it as the real deal, not as the *virtual* reality it is. Just as a video can be edited, so too are the final perceptions that our brains construct edited by our emotions, beliefs, and assumptions.

Research indicates that children do better when they *perceive* the parent–child relationship to be safe, connected, understanding, supportive, and accepting. Children also do better when their parents perceive them in a more positive and optimistic way. Knowing that your brain constructs all of *your* experiences and that your child's brain constructs all of *his or her* experiences can help you realize that perceptions are malleable and can be reedited if necessary.

THE BRAIN IS LIKE A GIANT LEGO SET

The whole brain is made up of many billions of individual cells called *neurons* that are linked together. The neurons are clustered into areas or

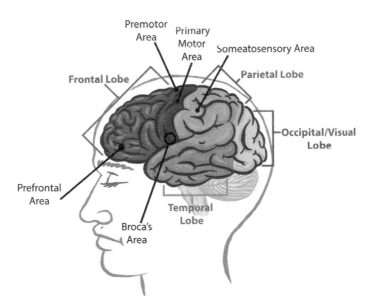

Figure 2.2. Brain lobes and areas of the cortex.

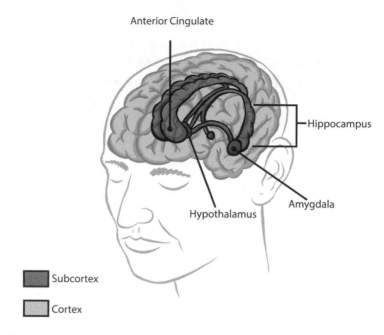

Figure 2.3. The cortex and subcortex.

regions throughout the brain that are specialized for different brain processes. The outer rind, or cortex, of the brain has specialized regions for
vision, hearing, and touch, for example. The deeper parts, or subcortex,
have specialized regions for memory, emotion, and habit formation,
among other things. The cortex and subcortex are highly interconnected
with one another (see Figures 2.2 and 2.3).

Neurons and How They Are Connected

A neuron is a cell that can transmit an electrical signal. Each neuron
has branched fibers called *dendrites* and *axons* that connect it to other
neurons (see Figure 2.4). Dendrites transmit the signal toward the cell.
Axons transmit the signal away from the cell. Along the dendrites and
axons are many contact points called *synapses* where the fibers of one

Synapse

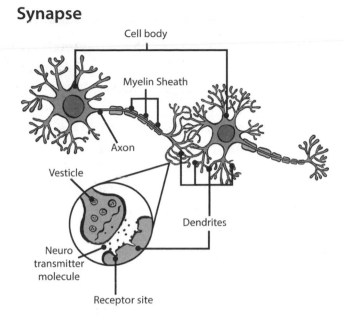

Figure 2.4. Neurons and synapses.

neuron connect with fibers on another neuron and where the signal is transmitted from one neuron to the next.

When an electrical impulse reaches a synapse, a neurotransmitter chemical is released and crosses the gap, like a ferry crossing a tiny river. When the neurotransmitter arrives at the other side of the synaptic gap, it activates an electrical impulse that allows the information to travel along that neuron. The more often a signal moves across a synapse, the stronger the connection between the neurons becomes. Eventually, in this way, many neurons get "wired" together into brain circuits. The relationship you have with your child is what wires the circuits of your child's brain.

Perceptions Are Inferences

The brain contains roughly between 86 billion and 200 billion neurons, and each neuron has between 5,000 and 60,000 synapses. The total number of synapse connections is approximately 10^{27}, or 10 with 27 zeros after it. Out of all these neurons and synaptic connections, a truly vast number of patterns of interconnected neurons are possible—in the range of 10^{million}, or 10 with one million zeros after it. Think of a Lego set in which the little pieces can be connected into many different patterns or configurations so as to create many different types of structures.

Here is an oversimplified description of how the brain creates all of our perceptions (Llinas, 2001; Pally, 2001). The brain sits deep inside the head and is not directly connected to the outside world. The *only* information that reaches the brain from the outside environment comes in the form of bits and pieces of sensory information detected by the sense organs—for example, the eyes, ears, and skin. The bits and pieces of data include such elements as colors and contours, sound frequencies and volume, and tactile pressure. This incoming information activates neurons in the various sensory areas of the brain, such as the visual, auditory, or touch centers. The brain puts together all these bits and pieces of sensory information together to create whole objects, people, and scenes by linking the neurons into patterns of interconnected neurons. The brain then uses the patterns of interconnected neurons to draw an inference as to the outside source of the sensory inputs—in other words, what objects, people, or scenes those inputs were coming from. This hypothesis or guess can be altered if new information becomes available, but each perception is the best guess for that moment in time. Once the brain makes a conclusion, we experience that conclusion as a perception.

You Can't Always Trust Your Brain

The world is indeed out there. However, we perceive only our brain's *interpretation* of what is happening out there. Each person's view of reality is not *the* fact or *the* truth. Each person's view of reality is a personal perspective created by their brain. Other people create their own reality, their own perspective, which feels like the fact or the truth to them. An example is how in the U.S. we see a man's face in the moon. In Mexico they look up at the same moon, but they perceive it differently. They "see" a rabbit (Drake, 2014).

The genetic code includes a large number of innate brain blueprints or rules for how to structure particular sensations into perceptions. For this reason, most of us tend to create similar perceptions. When there is a tree in the meadow, we all usually perceive a tree. This is also why a baby right from birth is oriented more to faces than to anything else (Frank, Vul, & Johnson, 2000). The baby is born with a genetic blueprint for putting dots and curves together into a face pattern.

But the blueprints are not complete and the rules don't cover every situation, leaving the brain susceptible to making perceptual errors. Think of *optical illusions*, such as the mirage effect of seeing water on a hot desert road. Think of driving and perceiving a dead animal on the road ahead, only to pass by it and realize it is just a pile of rags. Here the brain receives visual sensations but *guesses* wrong, and an incorrect perception is formed.

When it comes to perceptions about the mind in the context of relationships, we are even more prone to wrong guesses. We not only must perceive another person's outward and tangible actions and words but also must perceive the inward, intangible elements in their mind. It is proposed that the *mentalization system* evolved in humans as a brain region specialized for perceiving minds (see Chapter 4). Like all perception, our reflective capacity involves guesswork. The result is that even in our most precious relationships with our children, we sometimes create *mental illusions* or perceptual errors about what is happening with them.

A few other situations illustrate that we do not perceive a true reality because it is our brain that creates our perceptions. For example, a part of the brain can be directly activated during brain surgery, or indirectly activated by delivering an electrical or magnetic signal through the skull. Although the source of brain activation is artificial, the person nevertheless has a very real perceptual experience. It may be of seeing an object, or feeling their body move, or of vividly recalling an event from several weeks ago.

Phantom limbs are another example. Patients with an amputated limb may still *feel sensations* in the lost limb because the brain region that was connected to that limb is still intact. Another example is that we use the same part of our brain to perceive shapes made from 'squiggly lines' such as we see in the clouds, or on the moon, as we do when we perceive the objects they resemble (Voss, Federmeier, & Paller, 2011).

INFLUENCES ON THE BRAIN'S PERCEPTUAL PROCESS

Many factors influence what perception the brain creates. As a reflective parent, you will often have to assess what influences may be affecting your perceptions of your child.

Emotion and bodily drives shape perceptual experience.

Inputs from emotional centers in the brain, such as the *amygdala* and *hypothalamus*, become integrated with the neural patterns from the sensory inputs. In this way, emotion will affect the final perception. For example, when we are frightened, we are more likely to perceive events as dangerous and faces as more sinister. The emotion of fear biases our perceptions toward danger in order to boost our fight-or-flight system so that we can more readily protect ourselves from harm. Similarly, our need states shape our perception. Hunger, for example, will bias us to perceive food as more appetizing.

Memory shapes current perceptual experience.

The author William Faulkner was talking like a neuroscientist when he wrote, "The past is never dead. It is not even past" (Faulkner, 1951; Act

1, sc. 3). Whenever a situation occurs, the same neuronal pattern that forms the perception of the situation also gets stored as the *memory of that experience*. The recall of a memory is the activation of the same pattern that was activated in the original experience. The more often an experience occurs or the more significant the experience is, the stronger the connections in the pattern are, the stronger the connections in memory will be, and the easier it will be to recall that memory. To speed up the perceptual process, the brain uses patterns stored in memory as a shortcut. Rather than waiting for the long, slow process of all the inputs coming in and activating the whole neuronal pattern underlying the particular experience, the brain gets a hint from memory. As the pattern is forming, the brain matches the incoming pattern with patterns already stored in memory. When it finds a *similar-enough* match, it "declares" the current situation to be identical to the one in memory, and a perception forms. Take, for example, when we read. The brain scans the beginnings and ends of words and matches the corresponding neural patterns with ones stored in memory for a similar context. When it finds a similar enough match, the brain *fills in* the rest of the word.

You have heard the Revolutionary War saying "Don't fire till you see the whites of their eyes." The brain uses an opposite philosophy: "Run as soon as you hear a rustling in the grass." Treat the sound as if it is a snake and react accordingly.

Expectations and assumptions shape perception.

In its zest for using shortcuts, the brain anticipates the future and uses that prediction to shape current experience (Fuster, 1998; Llinas, 2001; Pally, 2007). This is why our minds are forever filling in what someone else is about to say. Expectations and assumptions are closely connected to memory. Our memory libraries already contain many possible sentences the person may be trying to say. As the person utters the first few words of their sentence, our mind predicts the rest of the sentence. The brain uses the prediction as the perception and uses that to figure out

SCIENCE SAYS

The Placebo Effect and How Predictions Impact Perception

A group of subjects in a scanner were told that a medicated cream rubbed into their skin was an anesthetic and that they would feel no pain when they received a tiny pinprick. Although, unbeknownst to them, the cream was just face cream, most subjects reported no pain. We know that pain activates the brain's pain center, the *anterior cingulate cortex*. Subjects who reported no pain showed less anterior cingulate activity than the subjects who did experience pain. The placebo effect was caused by the prediction that the cream would prevent pain. The prediction became the perception of "no pain" by inhibiting the activity of the anterior cingulate (Wager, et al., 2004).

how to respond instead of waiting to hear and perceive what the person *actually* says. As a result, we are more likely to *see what we expect to see and hear what we expect to hear*. And, as we engage in conversation, much of the time we have already prepared our response even before the other person has finished their sentence. If they say something different than we expected, our response will probably not make sense to them.

To perceive consciously or nonconsciously:
That is the question.

When your colleague asks, "How do you like my new glasses?" do you reply, "I didn't even realize you wore glasses"? Almost 99 percent of our brain activity remains nonconscious. Certain processes, such as the regulation of our blood pressure and digestion, can happen only nonconsciously. Other processes, such as perception, emotion, and memory, can operate either nonconsciously or consciously. Conscious processing is much slower and demands more resources than nonconscious processing. Therefore, for all familiar situations and well-learned tasks, the brain opts for nonconscious processing as much as possible. This is the basis for all the rote behaviors and habits we engage in without even being aware of them. Think of when you take a walk or a drive. You may be consciously focused on listening to a podcast on your smartphone, not conscious at all of your actions or the world around you.

However, because conscious processing allows for greater accuracy and flexibility, it kicks in on an as-needed basis. Like all perception, reflective capacity can operate nonconsciously as well as consciously. Generally, we make inferences about people's minds without even being aware we are doing it. However, if a conflict or misunderstanding arises as you are parenting your child, I encourage you to shift into conscious reflection. When parents are consciously reflective, they can actively consider whether their first conclusion about their child was accurate and whether certain emotions they feel or past experiences they may have had are shaping—or misshaping, if you will—their understanding of what is going on in their child.

IMPLICATIONS FOR REFLECTIVE PARENTING

Neuroscience explains that all our perceptions of the outside world and of the minds of others are simply our own subjective perspective on what is going on, created by our own brain. Our perceptions can be created entirely outside conscious awareness when we are functioning on autopilot. The bad news is that this causes us to have lots of misunderstandings and conflicts with other people. The good news is that perceptions are malleable and that our brains are fully capable of altering perceptions if we put our mind to it. Reflective parenting encourages parents to look inside themselves—to their own emotions, bodily needs, expectations, and even their childhood memories—in order to have a greater ability to recognize when these may be shaping their perception of their child.

Misunderstanding is normal and frequent.

Many misunderstandings occur simply due to the limitations of our brain's perceptual system. So much of life is like the game of telephone. You whisper something into the ear of a person sitting next to you, their brain shortcuts and passes on the misperception to the next person, and so on down the line. Now the message is totally garbled. Too often we take misunderstandings to mean something personal or worrisome. Often, it is better to accept that they just happen and need clarification. For example, you might say to your child, "Please feed the dog." Your child says, "I'll do it! Promise," and yet you may *hear* "I did it. Promise." You see the bowl is empty, assume your child is lying, and shout "Get in here right now!" Your child now screams, "Why are you getting so angry? I said I'll do it!" While it's always nice to apologize, you can also use an incident like this as a reflective teaching moment by saying something like, "These things happen. People just misunderstand each other lots of times."

Reflective parents must take the slow lane.

Correcting the misperceptions that result from the brain's use of shortcuts takes slowing down, being curious, and questioning the original perception. For example, perhaps you are disappointed in your son. It appears to you that he didn't work hard and that that's why he failed the test. This will probably lead you to be less empathic about his upset feelings. But if you want to make sure your original perception of the situation is correct, you need to slow down, step back a bit, and wonder if your experience of him is accurate. This requires looking at other details that may alter how you perceive the situation—such as recalling that he asked you some questions about his schoolwork. Maybe he is not as zealous as you wish he were, but it helps when you recognize that he did put in more effort than you were giving him credit for.

Misunderstandings can result when parents have bad childhood memories.

Misunderstandings frequently result when a parent has a history of being emotionally or physically wounded in childhood. These memories can have a powerful impact on how the brain shapes their current perceptions, without the parent realizing it. For example, one father, whose own father was abusive, says, "I've got an aggressive little one on my hands" when he talks about how often his infant daughter pulls on his beard. One mother, whose father abandoned the family when she was young, complains, "My daughter could care less about me. When I pick her up after school, she doesn't even want to talk with me in the car on the way home."

What makes it so hard for parents is that once our brain creates a perception, we experience it as an accurate depiction of the situation. This means that if the parent perceives their child as aggressive or uncaring, the parent will believe it is the truth about the child. But what if it isn't the truth? How will the parent ever know? It takes courage for parents to look inside themselves and consider whether their own past may be influencing how they perceive their child. It takes bravery for a parent to admit that some of their own pain may be having a negative impact on how they parent. The first step in becoming a braver parent is learning not to blame yourself.

This is why a core feature of reflective parenting is to be nonjudgmental toward both yourself and toward other parents. The brain is wired so that powerful childhood memories leave long-lasting effects on a parent's way of experiencing their child. For example, in the case of the father, it took a while for him to trust that he would not be blamed or judged by a parent group leader for what he thought about his daughter. Eventually he felt safe enough to talk about how traumatic it had been for him with his father and how he was starting to see the ways in which that experience distorted how he saw his daughter. The mother, too, was supported in a nonblaming way. As a result, she was able to talk about how her father's abandonment left her vulnerable to perceiving her daughter as uncaring.

Conscious awareness can take effort.

Reflective capacity operates nonconsciously as well as consciously. For example, one mother was consciously aware that she perceived her son as immature because at seven years old he was not yet picking out his own clothes. However, she was unaware of the nonconscious level. When she was encouraged to consciously reflect to see if there might be anything she was not currently aware of, she initially resisted. She said it was too much extra work and that she already had enough on her plate to deal with. Finally, though, she made the effort to look deeper inside herself. She discovered how irritable and impatient she was with her son's slowness. She could see that he hadn't learned how to pick out his own clothes because she hadn't been calm enough or patient enough to let him do it. She realized it had been so much easier for her to pick out his clothes herself in the morning rush of getting out of the house.

Another challenge for parents is recognizing that conscious awareness requires the effort of paying focused attention to a situation. For example, you tell your child to get ready for bed. Your child doesn't move. You get annoyed that your child is ignoring you. The dilemma is that for the brain to perceive words *consciously* requires focused attention on them. Even when your child is sitting right next to you, they literally may not hear you if they are focused on the computer screen. Yes, technically they are ignoring you, but ignoring occurs naturally when we are engaged in a task we are motivated to be involved with. Recognizing this can help parents reduce their irritation about being ignored.

Be a real and authentic person.

There are so many cultural myths and stereotypes about how parents *should* be: "Parents should always be patient and calm when dealing with their children's behavior." "Mothers are supposed to always enjoy playing with their children." "Parents should always be interested in what their child is talking about." Science, however, maintains that every brain is wired differently and comes with different preferences, talents, and interests. Therefore, we are inevitably going to be different from one another. The truth is that *real* parents do not fit these myths and stereotypes. Real parents can get impatient and lose their temper. Children's games can sometimes bore parents. Sometimes parents may find that what their child is talking about is dull as a doornail. Parents are people, and the brains of people don't always operate in the most adaptive ways. Therefore, all people, including the most reflective of parents, have strong emotions, are not always in control of themselves, are not always interested in their kids, and do not always enjoy their kids.

Fortunately, a child needs a relationship with a real person, not a stereotype of a person. It is the real *you* that your child wants and needs, warts and all. Stop trying to be perfect. It is not a good message to send to your child, because no one is perfect. A reflective parent follows the mottoes "Raise the child you have, not the child you wish you had" and "Be the parent you are, not the parent you think you should be." When parents are honest about having a flaw rather than being defensive about it, they provide a great role model for their child.

Being "real" does not equate to a free-for-all on behavior or mean that it's okay to hit or insult your child. It doesn't mean you share *all* your personal history with a young child or tell them about *all* your flaws and weaknesses or *always* give your honest opinion. We have to protect our children from harm and respect what they can handle and what they can't. But as long as we avoid the extremes and place certain limits on ourselves, depending on the age of our child, we should aim to be as real as possible.

Each parent will be real in a different way. One parent may be fine about sharing their ice cream with their child; another parent won't like to share. One parent will enjoy giving expensive gifts; another will be more economical. One parent will hate TV and believe children shouldn't watch it; another will enjoy TV and not mind so much if their kids watch. One parent will be a late riser, another an early riser. One parent will love to celebrate and decorate for the holidays; another will prefer something quieter and more subdued. Remember that there is no right way to be. Your child simply needs to know which way *you* are.

Knowing who you are helps them make sense of how you act. It also helps them to feel that it's OK to be honest about one's feelings and opinions and even one's flaws.

STORIES OF PARENTS AND CHILDREN

- Nina complains that her nine-year-old daughter Shawna is messy, saying that she drops her clothes and towels all over the place and doesn't always brush her hair. Nina says, "I kinda feel like she is a slob and that it's my responsibility to teach her properly, and so I am on her all the time to be neater. She hates it when I do that, and I wish I didn't feel this way about her." Nina is encouraged to think about how she interprets her daughter's behavior as being so negative. Nina says, "I guess another way to interpret it is that she is freer than I am in many ways. I am on the very neat side. I can see that sometimes her comfort with messiness is really good. She can go hiking and explore nature, even if it's wet and muddy. She really enjoys those kinds of things. I don't like getting dirty. I think she will be more adventurous than I am, and that's a good thing."

- A. J., the divorced father of a 12-year-old boy named Shane, tells the story of how he misinterpreted the meaning of a question his son asked. "Shane told me his mom was dating, and didn't I think that was awful? I interpreted this as him asking if it was OK with me for his mom to date. So I said I was fine with it and thought it was perfectly normal for her to start dating other men. But he still kept going on and on asking if I didn't think it was awful. Then I realized I had missed the boat. My interpretation was wrong. It wasn't that he wanted me to reassure him that I was OK with it. He was asking me for permission to be upset about it himself."

- Eleanor, mother of 19-year-old Shelby who is away at college, gives a wonderful illustration of the power of misperception: "When Shelby doesn't call me for a week or so, I create a whole story in my mind— that I offended her, made her angry with me, and now she is giving me the silent treatment. My made-up story feels real, and I have real feelings about my imaginary story. I feel guilty for offending her and irritated with her misunderstanding of me. The urge to call and find out if she's angry with me and to ask for forgiveness can be powerful. At times the urge to call and chide her for misunderstanding me can also be powerful. My reflective mind works hard to remind me and reassure me that most likely she didn't take offense, and to remember that if she did, she usually gives me a pass, knowing I'm just being a mother. This calms me down and quells the urge to call. I'm usually glad I didn't burden her with my unnecessary worry, because in a day or so she will call me all bright and chipper."

- Jane and Peter discover that their 14-year-old daughter Natalie has posted a message online about how sexily she plans to dress for a party. They are frightened, believing that their sweet, lovely daughter has turned into a sexually provocative teenager. So Jane immediately goes into Natalie's room to scold her and teach her a lesson. "I saw what you posted. Are you an idiot? Don't you know how provocative that sounds?" Natalie screams, "Shut up! Get out of my room! You don't know what you're talking about!" Despite how upset she is, Jane takes a reflective moment and realizes that maybe she didn't perceive the situation clearly because of her own feelings of fear and protectiveness. This allows her to talk more calmly with her daughter and find out why her daughter made the post. Natalie explains that she was just fooling around with her girlfriends. Her intention was not to be provocative with boys. She reassures her mom that she knows it's stupid to be provocative. Jane calms down, and the two of them have a good discussion about the problems with posting things online.

PUTTING IT INTO WORDS

- "I guess I heard you wrong. You are sure you told me you didn't have any homework. I thought you said you *had* homework."

- "I anticipated that you were going to give me a hard time about doing your chores, so I was already in high gear to have an argument with you, although in fact you were totally cooperative. But I guess that's why I pounded so hard on your door. Sorry!"
- "I didn't realize that my face looked like I was angry. I am not angry at you, but I guess since I'm still angry about something that happened at work, my face is still expressing that."

TAKE-HOME LESSONS

Practice noticing misunderstandings and the ways in which you and your child can have different perspectives on the same situation. Remember that there is no right way to do the exercises and that there are no right answers. Just do them your way.

- Notice a time when you have jumped to the wrong conclusion about what your child was saying or doing. Become an investigator. Spend some time piecing together all the influences that might have led you to misperceive what was happing with your child. There is no right answer and no blame. Just notice and then be curious. Was it simply because you were in too much of a rush? Was it the mood you were in? Was it some expectation about how your child would be? Was it something in your own childhood?
- Focus on the relationship you have with your child during two or three specific activities, such as getting ready for school, eating dinner, or going to bed. Think about what words you would use to describe the relationship, such as *connected, loving, hurtful, conflicted, smooth, rough, pleasant,* or *unpleasant.* It doesn't matter what words you use. The point of the exercise is just to notice the relationship and to realize that it can be described and that it can change character during different kinds of activities and different times of day.
- Take a common daily routine you have with your child, such as dropping them off at school, helping them with homework, or hav-

ing them do their chores. Then see the routine from the "you-me-we" perspective in regard to perceptions, feelings, goals, and intentions. For example, if the routine is getting your child out of bed, you may feel anxious or rushed. Your child may feel irritated or indifferent. Your goal may be to get your child out of bed as quickly as possible, and your perception may be that your child is lazy or disobedient. Your child's goal may be to stay in bed as long as possible, and their perception may be that you are uncaring. Think about how you and your child are impacting one another.

THREE

The Brain's Mirror System

Wired for Empathy

BRAIN BASICS

Social relationships are so important to human beings that the brain dedicates a full third of its real estate to this purpose. The brain areas that enable us to form attachment bonds and to understand, empathize with, cooperate with, and collaborate with others are collectively called the social brain.

IT'S ALL ABOUT BEING SOCIAL

Have you ever wondered why your baby loves looking at you? Or how your child knows how to speak even though you've never explained to her how to move her mouth to form words? Have you ever wondered why very young children imitate everything you do? How your toddler knows exactly how to use your iPhone and iPad even though you've never explained it to him? Why schoolchildren spend so much time discussing the rules of the game, sometimes even more than they do actually playing the game? Have you ever wondered why your teenager is so obsessed with her friends? The answers to all these questions lie in the organization and function of the *social brain*, which is specialized to engage in social relationships.

Biologists conclude that human beings are the most social creatures on earth (Wilson, 2012). Child development specialists have come to understand that "nurturing, stable and consistent relationships are the key to healthy growth, development and learning" (Shonkoff & Phillips, 2000, p. 412). Therefore, one of your most important roles as a parent is to help your child become a social being, and you can do this only by having a social relationship with your child.

WHY BABIES ARE BORN SO IMMATURE

Human beings are the most cognitively advanced and behaviorally flexible of all animal species. Instead of being born with a limited number of behaviors and a limited environmental niche that they can survive in, as occurs in other animals, humans are born to be highly adept at learning a multitude of behaviors and adapting to whatever particular environment they are born into (Meltzoff, 1999). You can find humans from the Arctic to the Equator, from sea level to 10,000 feet above sea level, from the desert to the tropics. You can find them eating beetles or eating hamburgers, spearfishing or shopping in supermarkets, wearing clothing made of fur or clothing made of cloth, speaking Hungarian or speaking English. To achieve this amazing capacity for adaptive variation, evolution arrived at the unusual "trick" of having the human infant born totally immature and helpless (Bruner, 1972; Meltzoff, 1999). Although other animals can manage on their own relatively quickly, the benefit of such immaturity and helplessness in humans is that infants and children learn what to do from the people around them. In this way they can acquire the specific skills they need to survive wherever and with whomever they are born.

The social brain enables parents to care for their immature and dependent children in the emotionally sensitive way that we know fosters healthy brain development, learning, and well-being in offspring. Similarly, the social brain in the developing infant and child makes it possible for them to feel safe, cared about, and supported, and to learn how to be social within the group they are part of.

THE PARENT–CHILD RELATIONSHIP
AND THE SOCIAL BRAIN

Social learning is the first kind of learning an infant does and continues to be an extremely important form of learning throughout development (National Scientific Council on the Developing Child, 2004; Olson, 2012; Shonkoff & Phillips, 2000). Even the learning of nonsocial behaviors, such as how to eat, dress, read, and study, happens in the context of being social. This is why a child's academic performance can be influenced by the nature of the social relationship between parent and child. This is supported by anthropology, which states that *all societies use the parent–child relationship as the basic system for teaching a child how to be social* (Quinn, 2005). Children need to be taught the specifics of how to be social within the family and wider culture they are born into; namely, the social rules, customs, and belief systems of *their* family and *that* culture. This social learning is filtered through the parents, who teach their child their personal interpretation of what is most important for the child to know. The parent's mind is the storage space or warehouse for what is to be taught, the parent–child relationship delivers the goods, and the child picks up what they need to know.

Cultures change over time, and social behaviors
much catch up.

There is such a rapid pace of cultural change in modern times that a parent is raised in one culture while their child grows up in a different one. It is as if *every parent is an immigrant in the culture of the new generation.* Since, typically, you were born some 20 to 30 or even 40 years before your child, you are currently raising your child in a culture you are not as familiar with and, in many respects, not as comfortable with. Much of what you know from your generation still holds up for the next generation, but not all of it. We are not raising our children to fit the society we grew up in. We have to raise them for the society *they* are growing up in. This is a big reason why parenting practices change so much over time. We are trying to catch up with changing times and never quite fully getting there. An obvious example is the rapidly changing technologies of electronic communication that are flooding our lives and the rush for parents to learn how to meet these challenges. A parent–child relationship holds the seeds for managing this intergenerational flux when parents are open-minded, valuing and holding on to *what is good about the old* while making room for *what is good about the new.*

Being social is not about how many friends you have.

Our sociable human nature does not necessarily mean being outgoing and gregarious. It means being able to engage with and relate to other people. It is not about the numbers of people you engage with; it is about how you relate, in terms of empathizing, being cooperative, and considering other people's point of view. Even a shy child who is slow to warm up or an introverted child with only a few friends can nevertheless be socially competent, while a talkative child may lack social skills.

Social skills promote achievement.

Long-term achievement and success depend strongly on a child's *executive functions*—the set of mental skills that enable us to inhibit impulses, control behaviors, focus attention, establish priorities, plan ahead, and solve problems (Diamond, 2013). The parent–child relationship contains all the elements necessary for a child to acquire these skills. A focus on having a social relationship with your child is the optimal way for your child to develop their executive functions (Shonkoff & Phillips, 2000). A child is developing their executive skills every time a parent says, "You have to stop playing now and get ready for bed," "No, you can't have a cookie now because it's too close to dinnertime," "Do you want to come to the market with me or stay home with Grandma?" or "You seem to be having a hard time getting ready on time for school in the morning. Can you think of any way to make it go more easily?" The self-control, cooperation, and priority-establishing skills your child develops with you are exactly the same skills she or he will need to sit still in class, pay attention, follow directions, and accomplish what is expected in school, on the team, on the job, or in the community. By learning these executive skills within the relationship, the child is more prepared for academic learning. If the academics are presented before the skills are achieved, the child will not learn as well.

Achievement needs to be balanced with healthy development.

Parents need to balance their desire for their child to achieve with recognition that healthy development is not about how much you achieve, what educational degree you hold, or the amount of money you make. Successful development involves reaching one's *potential* to achieve while also being socially competent, being responsible for oneself and others, feeling satisfied with one's life, and being connected to the community within the constraints of one's strengths and weaknesses, resources, and needs (O'Connor et al., 2011).

Learning occurs through internalizing the relationship.

Children learn not what their parent *tells* them, but how the parent *relates* with the child. The *relationship is the lesson* to be taught! One example is how the baby learns that social relationships operate in a *serve-and-return* manner, like a tennis ball going back and forth. The mother acts. The baby responds. Mother reacts, baby reacts, back and forth, over and over. Serve-and-return is so embedded in what the child assumes relationships are all about that when someone does not *return their serve*—for example, when a mom does not smile back when the baby smiles—it leads to distress in the baby (Beebe, 2006).

Some elements of the social brain are online right from birth, so that infants can communicate their distress and be aware of cues in their environment that signal social information. However, for the most part, the social brain gets wired in the course of child development.

HOW THE SOCIAL BRAIN WORKS

The *social brain* is an interconnected collection of brain circuits that are all involved in being social. The activity of the social brain makes it possible for us to successfully navigate our social relationships—to form intimate loving bonds, to be empathic, to share, to take turns, to engage in conversation, to play, to cooperate, and to collaborate.

Self and Other: Two Sides of the Same Coin

The social brain treats the self and others as two sides of the same coin. Our brain uses what are referred to as *shared circuits* to re-create the experience of others using the same circuits in our brain that we use for our own experience. The shared circuits for touch, pain, emotion, and behavior, are described in this chapter. Chapter 4 discusses the shared circuit of mind.

The Social Brain

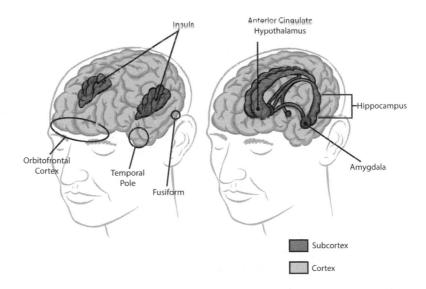

Figure 3.1. The social brain.

Here is an example of shared circuitry. In the film *Dr. No*, James Bond has a tarantula crawling on his shoulder. As you watch, the same brain circuits are being activated in your brain, as if *you* had a tarantula crawling on *your* shoulder, causing you to feel a creepy tingling on your skin and a sense of emotional dread.

The brain's shared circuits activate experiences in us even when they are not actually *our* experiences but rather someone else's. We are that connected to others! With respect to the parent–child relationship, shared circuits enable parents to understand and empathize with their children, explain why children imitate their parents, and explain why children can feel so deeply what their parents are feeling.

We preserve a sense of separateness because the brain circuits we activate for self-experience are *not totally identical* to the ones we activate for the experience of others (Keysers et al., 2004). Thus we know what others experience but also retain the distinction between ourselves and others. Children need their parents to *balance* promoting closeness and encouraging separateness. The brain's shared circuitry helps parents maintain this balance by recognizing the self as being both like others and different from others.

Shared Circuitry for Touch

Being touched activates our *somatosensory cortex* (see Figure 2.2). Watching someone else being touched also activates our somatosensory cortex, but to a lesser degree than when we are being touched ourselves (Keysers et al., 2004). This is why stroking your child's head may also feel good to you.

Shared Circuitry for Pain

Shared circuitry also occurs with pain. The *anterior cingulate* is where we experience our own pain. This same pain region is also activated when we observe someone else experiencing pain, although to a lesser degree. The shared circuitry of pain is how we empathize with the pain of others (Keysers, 2011) (see Figure 3.1).

Moral Behavior and the Shared Circuits of Pain

People will go into a burning building to rescue another person. Less heroic forms of moral behavior occur daily as we avoid bumping into people and try not to hurt their feelings. Morality and moral decision-making involve some degree of rational thinking, but for the most part involve the ability to feel the emotions and distress of others (Keysers, 2011). Much of our moral behavior relates to preventing pain in others and relies on the brain's shared circuitry for pain and emotional distress. When people have their brains scanned while they make difficult moral decisions, one of the regions activated is their anterior cingulate cortex—the region where we experience pain. This implies that part of teaching children to be moral and inhibit their hurtful or selfish impulses involves helping them be aware of and feel the hurtfulness their own behavior can cause others. This is why parents will often say things like, "I want you to think about how hurt Devon was when he was visiting and you didn't want to play with him." As with everything else in this book, it is always recommended that you maintain a balance. You want to promote empathy by activating your child's shared pain circuitry, but not too much. If a child feels too much pain it impairs learning.

Remember that every child is a bit different. Some kids need some extra help empathizing, while some feel other people's pain too strongly, which can interfere with their social functioning. For example, a child may allow a friend to hurt her because she is afraid of hurting the other child's feelings by getting angry at him or not wanting to play with him. As much as we strive to help children be empathic, sometimes we also have to help them be less empathic so that they can take better care of themselves.

SHARED CIRCUITRY FOR BEHAVIOR: THE MIRROR SYSTEM

The *mirror system* is a shared circuit for behavior (Iacoboni, 2008; Keysers, 2011). When we observe another person performing an action, we re-create their action in our own brain. Our brain matches what others are doing *as if* we were performing the same action they are performing. This action-matching underlies our ability to recognize what a person is doing, as well as a little bit of why they are doing it and how they are feeling doing it. The mirror system supports a very physical sense of connection. We feel we are doing what others are doing. And because our mirror system communicates closely with our pain and emotion centers, we also will feel any of the pain or emotion of others that is being expressed by their behavior.

The mirror system recognizes what a person's behavior is.

When you watch your child pour milk from a carton, your own brain is activating your milk-pouring circuits as well. You know what she or he is doing because you know what you would be doing if you were performing that action. The mirror system also matches behaviors we hear, even if we don't see them. This is why you have a good idea of what your child is doing in the next room when you hear a ball bouncing.

You might be thinking at this point, what's all the fuss about? I know what my child is doing when I see her or him doing it. It's right there in front of my eyes. But, in fact, although it may be happening right in front of you, you don't know what your child is doing unless your mirror system informs you.

The mirror system recognizes why a behavior occurs.

Whenever a person performs an action, there is always a reason *why*. There is always some intention or purpose underlying the action. As important as it is to know *what* action a person is doing, it is even more important to know the intention or purpose of that action. Think about a friend reaching toward you, holding an apple in their hand. You recognize the action as "holding an apple in their hand." You need to know the reason why they are holding that apple, because your response will be based on your assessment of their intention. You will respond differently to the very same action depending on whether you assess their intention as wanting to share the apple with you, wanting to show you what a beautiful red apple it is, or wanting to bluff you into believing they want to share it with you.

Reflective parenting emphasizes that we react more to *how we interpret the intention or goal* of our child's actions and words than to the actions and words themselves. This is one reason that the parent–child relationship can get so messy. Remember that we can see the behavior, but can't see the intention or goal. It takes a bit of guesswork. Let's say your two-year-old pulls your hair. You will react differently if you interpret this as a normal sign of poor impulse control in a toddler versus evidence that your child is *trying* to hurt you.

The mirror system is smart, but only when the answer is fairly obvious.

The mirror system can figure out intentions only as long as they are relatively easy to determine from the observed behavior, such as picking up a glass of water with the obvious intention of taking a drink. However, if there is no obvious intention—for example, the person lifts the glass of water to their nose—the mirror system may not even be activated by the behavior. If the intention is intangible, such as trying to make someone laugh by being silly, interpretation will require the addition of the shared circuit of mind, the mentalization system, which is discussed in Chapter 4.

Fortunately, you needn't think hard to figure it out every time. The mirror system works automatically and without effort, so that for fairly familiar and routine behaviors, you will generally understand your child's intentions without thinking about them (Cattaneo & Rizzolatti, 2009; Iacoboni et al., 2005).

Your child assumes you understand her or his intentions.

The connection between parent and child operates in a lock-and-key fashion. When the child performs an action, she or he *expects* their parents to understand the message they are communicating by their actions. Because young children don't yet have a mechanism for realizing that their parents can't read their mind, a young child will become upset or angry when a parent doesn't understand. The mirror system of even the most loving parent will not always be accurate. This is because, when we match another's behavior to understand their intention, we rely on our own intention as a guide. You can see how this might lead to misunderstanding between parents and children.

To fully appreciate how hard it can be for a child when you don't understand their intentions, think about how you feel when your own intentions are misinterpreted. Take, for example, a time where you were intending to be helpful and someone didn't recognize your intention and got annoyed with you for interfering. How did you feel? These kinds of situations can feel very hurtful and upsetting even for adults. Imagine what they do for children.

One father described how he had to give his two-year-old daughter some horrible-tasting medicine and actually had to hold her down while she cried and fussed. His eight-year-old son pushed his dad out of the way and told his dad he was doing it wrong. The dad yelled at him for interfering, "Can't you see I'm having a hard enough time with your sister? I don't want to also have to deal with you pestering me!" The boy cried. The mom comforted the boy and later suggested to the dad that the older son was caring about how upset his younger sister was and was trying to help his dad. The dad apologized to his son, thanked him for trying to be helpful, and empathized with how hard it must have been for him to watch his baby sister cry.

The mirror system helps to predict what a person
is likely to do next.

The brain operates as a prediction machine, doing its best to anticipate and know ahead of time what people are most likely to do in the near future (Pally, 2007). This allows the brain to prepare to respond most adaptively when the person does the expected thing. By predicting people's upcoming actions, we are more successful in dealing with each

SCIENCE SAYS

Context influences the mirror system. For example, experiments have shown that the mirror system responds differently to the action of a person holding a cup if the context is setting the table versus clearing the table (Iacoboni et al., 2005).

other. This is why having a good sense of a person's current intention is so important. Not only does it help us make sense of the person's actions so that we are more able to respond appropriately, but also it assists us in being able to predict what a person is likely to do in the very near future. For example, when you see your toddler run toward a ladder, you automatically have a sense that their intention may be to climb the ladder. This prepares you to take action if necessary. Although you allow your child the freedom to explore and run close to the ladder, you are fully ready to stop her from climbing up if she tries.

The mirror system's response to context has influences on parenting.

The fact that the mirror system is sensitive to context has implications for reflective parenting. For example, suppose your child grabs a toy from another child at preschool. Is the intention of the grabbing to be selfish, or is it to hurt or retaliate, or is it to try to hold on to as many resources as possible? It could be any of these, depending on the context. Try to puzzle out what the context is and how it may be influencing what intention you assume about your child's behavior. A child who has recently experienced the birth of a new sibling or the loss of a loved one may be trying to hold on to anything and everything possible because they don't feel in control of their environment. Although what they are doing may look selfish and hurtful, that may not be the goal they are working toward.

IMITATION AND THE MIRROR SYSTEM:
CHILDREN SEE, CHILDREN DO

One of the most startling findings about the mirror system is that children learn *how* to behave primarily through imitation. Children learn more from imitating the social and nonsocial behaviors of others than they do from instruction and being told what to do. Your child will observe you and copy almost everything you do, both your nonsocial and social behaviors. This is the way children learn *nonsocial* behaviors, such as how to open the refrigerator and get the milk out, how to put on their socks, and how to use a smartphone or the TV remote. It is how they learn social behaviors, from waving, clapping, playing patty cake, sharing, and taking turns to a whole array of mannerisms, gestures, facial expressions, and cultural practices of the adults around them. If you hug or shake hands or kiss once or three times, your child will automatically learn the custom you follow. If you light candles as part of your religious practice, kneel to pray, or bow your head, your child will automatically learn that practice through imitation.

Children are such powerful imitators because their mirror system translates the observed action into a performed action. Their mirror system re-creates the actions of others in their own brain. Then their *ventral prefrontal cortex* automatically signals the *primary motor cortex* to turn on the muscles to move. This is why kids are such copycat machines. When you clap your hands, your 14-month-old will clap his hands. One toddler plays with a cup; the other toddler grabs the cup to play with it. Two 4-year-olds can drive their parents nuts as they copy each other's silly noises and facial expressions. When a six-year-old mimics everything her four-year-old sister says at the dinner table, it's enough to try the patience of even the most reflective parent. Even teenagers will copy the gestures, vocal patterns, and walking style of their peers, much to the chagrin of their parents.

Children are so much more prone to imitate than adults are (and the younger they are, the more prone they are to imitate) because their prefrontal cortex is less developed and they lack sufficient inhibitory control over mirror system activity. While adults make an internal copy of the other person's behavior, inhibitory areas of their prefrontal cortex block the signal so that it is not sent to the motor cortex to initiate an action. When you consciously decide to imitate, however, your prefrontal cortex does not send its inhibitory signal. Children, on the other hand, are imitating *involuntarily*, because their prefrontal cortex is not yet mature enough to inhibit the action.

The upside to children's lack of inhibitory control over the mirror system allows them to copy whatever others are doing in a highly efficient manner that does not require conscious effort or instruction. They *automatically* pick up how to speak and behave in the culture they are born into. Although it is not appropriate as an adult to imitate your dinner guests, it is appropriate for a young child. This is how the child will learn how to eat, how to behave at the dinner table, how to open and close a door, how to turn on the dishwasher, how to put away their toys, and even how to use the coffee maker. In cultures where fishing is the main source of income, very young children automatically learn how to throw out the fishing nets. This is why your one-year-old knows how to turn on the TV remote or dial your cell phone, even if you have never shown him how. As development of the prefrontal cortex catches up, children are more and more able to inhibit themselves from always copying what they see others do.

It can be puzzling and even irritating to parents when their child knows perfectly well how to tie their shoes, how to make their own breakfast, or even how to share and take turns but does not always do so. The reason kids are so inconsistent is because their prefrontal cortex is still too immature to contain their impulses, especially if the child is fatigued, stressed, or upset or if the impulse is really strong. They know *how* they are supposed to behave, but because of their immature prefrontal cortex, they can't always conform their behavior to what is desirable or to what they are capable of. Try to remember that they are probably not being willfully disobedient so that you stay calmer as you step in and assist them with nonverbal gestures and verbal instruction.

Children imitate their peers.

One underappreciated fact is that not only do children learn from their parents and other adults, but children learn a lot from other children. For example, toddlers in daycare bring home new skills they learned by watching other toddlers in daycare. One reason that children will often behave better at school than they do at home is that they are going along with the behavior of other children. When your child copies silly or even "bad" behavior, it may help you stay calm if you keep in mind that copying other kids' behavior is part of the important lesson of learning how to be part of a group. Be patient. It will take time for your child's prefrontal cortex control centers to kick in and enable her or him to better inhibit undesirable behaviors. In the meantime, your child will continue to need your gentle reminders.

Children imitate intentions, not just actions.

The mirror system enables children not only to imitate the actions they see, but also to imitate the intentions underlying those actions. For example, a child is shown several behaviors, all with the same intention. When asked afterward to imitate each of these same behaviors, the child may simply do one of the actions. This is because the developing brain prioritizes learning the intention over learning to exactly copy an action (Cattaneo & Rizzolatti, 2009). The ability of children to prioritize intention learning contributes a lot to creativity and innovation in children. Since their mirror system enables them to know the goal or intention of your actions, they can also creatively modify an imitated behavior by keeping the same intention but adjusting the behavior in a way that works better for them or by applying it to a situation they have never encountered before. What this implies is that parents must leave plenty of room for their child to find her or his own way of doing things.

Imitation is a form of connection and a way
to develop agency.

Children are aware when others are imitating them (Meltzoff & Decety, 2003). Babies enjoy being imitated just for the fun of it as well as for the learning it provides. Young babies express this by increasing the behavior they are doing when a parent imitates it. Older infants respond to being imitated in a slightly different way. They will often switch to a new behavior as if they are "checking" on the parent to make sure the parent is following them. The older infant is developing an important sense of agency by experiencing a little bit of control over their environment as they get their parent to imitate their new behavior. These imitation games, while good for children, should not be imposed on the child if the child is not interested.

A tiny bit of imitation can promote social understanding
and connectedness.

Overt imitation decreases over time as children develop. However, even in adults, without realizing it, there will be times that prefrontal control centers allow a tiny bit of mirror matching to be expressed overtly. We are more likely to *overtly* match someone's behavior when we are particularly emotionally involved. This is why without your

SCIENCE SAYS

Overt matching between adults can enhance social rapport. Experiments show that the more two people who are total strangers overtly match each other's behaviors, even if they have no awareness of doing it, the more they report a sense of affiliation and empathy for one another (Hove & Risen, 2009).

realizing it, when you see your child's head nod up and down, your own head is very likely to nod as well. Or picture your eight-year-old son or daughter playing soccer. As you watch him or her kick the ball, if you pay attention to it, you will notice your own leg actually moving a bit or even a lot. Without your even trying to do it, your mirror system is automatically overtly matching your child's movements. This explains why, when your toddler is playing with a new puzzle and having difficulty moving a piece into place, you may sense your own hand "wanting" to move it into place, or perhaps even twisting in the correct direction a little bit.

THE MIRROR SYSTEM AND EMPATHY

People's emotions are outwardly expressed as behaviors, such as facial expressions, gestures, posture, and direction of eye gaze. When we observe these emotional behaviors of another person, we not only re-create them within our own mirror neuron system, but we also re-create the whole emotional experience of the other person inside ourselves—the emotional feelings such as sadness and joy, along with the sense of pain or pleasure and the bodily changes that correspond to those emotions, such as an increased heart rate or stomach contraction. The mirror system makes empathy possible through its links to emotional centers and pain centers in the brain.

More-empathic people feel what others feel more readily, because they are more likely to match and imitate other people's behaviors (Chartrand & Bargh, 1999). We automatically switch on our mirror system empathy circuits more for people we know well and care about, and switch them off or dampen them for people we do not know as well or don't care about as much (Keysers, 2011).

Mirroring enhances empathy and social competence in children.

By about 10 years old, children have the same mirror neuron activity as adults (Iacoboni & Dapretto, 2006). As with adults, when children observe the facial expressions of other people, their mirror system's behavioral matching of the facial movements is linked to the experience of the emotion the face is expressing. The higher the responsiveness, the greater their empathy and social competence.

Empathy should be expressed in just the right amount.

The mirror system is involved when a parent uses empathy to calm their child's distress. It goes like this: A child expresses emotional distress. The parent's mirror system re-creates the child's behavioral expressions of distress. This activates the parent's emotional centers, so the parent then feels some of the distress the child is feeling, but less than the child. The parent expresses the child's emotional distress in this reduced form. The child now mirrors the parent's reduced level of emotional distress, and the child's inner distress lessens.

In what might be called the Goldilocks effect, too little empathy is not good and neither is too much empathy (Decety & Ickes, 2011; Decety & Jackson, 2006). Remember "Goldilocks and the Three Bears" and how Goldilocks finds bowls of porridge on the table and tastes them? "This porridge is too hot. This porridge is too cold. But this porridge is just right." Too little empathy makes children feel they are not cared about or insufficiently soothed and comforted. Too much empathy can exacerbate a child's emotional distress. If a parent doesn't match the child's distress enough, their face, voice, and body won't express their attunement with the child's experience. The child won't feel understood, so the distress will not abate. If, on the other hand, the parent matches the distress too much, they will express a high state of distress in their face, voice, and body. The child's mirror system matches this high state of distress, and although they may feel understood, they will also feel more distressed rather than feeling soothed.

The point is for a parent to empathize with their child to the amount the child needs and benefits from. Some kids want more overt empathy than others. Some do better with empathy that is more understated. Therefore, how you empathize will differ depending on who your child is.

Why Some Parents Overempathize or Underempathize

Sometimes overempathy is a matter of temperament—just how a person is wired. Their emotional systems have their volume turned up high, and so they feel other people's feelings louder. If your overempathy is too much for your child, as a parent you probably have to find a way to tone down your natural tendency. Another reason for overempathy is that sometimes a parent has experienced a lot of pain in their own childhood, and when they are connecting to their child's pain it activates the deep pain from their past. In this case, a parent has to really pay attention to where their overempathic feelings are coming from. The parent can't eliminate their painful feelings, but they can reduce them somewhat by separating themselves a little from their child and trying to recognize that their distress is more than their child is actually experiencing.

Underempathy can also be a matter of inborn temperament, and parents with such a temperament may need to find a way to increase the volume on their empathy circuit. Childhood pain can also lead to underempathy. When a parent with a lot of pain from their past empathizes with their child's pain, it may surpass the parent's ability to cope. This can cause the parent to withdraw from a child or dismiss a child's distress in order to reduce their own pain. These parents may appear as if they are being insensitive or as if they don't care. Inside, however, their child's distress causes them to feel more pain than they can tolerate. These parents need extra support and empathy for how difficult it is for them when their child is upset. In many respects, they are having a kind of posttraumatic reaction to their child's distress. These parents may consider seeking professional help.

When kids are distressed, empathy is not always needed.

There are times when empathy is not what is needed and where it can even impede resilience. Often, a slower, wait-and-see approach is in order. Suppose your child falls down while playing or running. You don't always have to say, "Oh, that must have hurt!" On some occasions, you may say that in order to empathize and validate your child's experience. But it would also be fine to say, "Oopsy daisy, you fell! But you're OK!" Being reflective means being flexible and trying to get a sense of how upset your child is and what they really need. Both messages are very valuable, but use them according to what you believe the situation calls for. Empathy is more for situations where you want to make your child feel connected, soothed, and understood. The response "You will be OK" is for when you're trying to support more resiliency. Saying "It's OK" doesn't mean you're being insensitive to your child's pain. It can be like the placebo effect that actually reduces their pain. If a child is really upset, validate, soothe, and empathize, of course. If they pick themselves up right away and seem fine, you may not even need to say anything. In this way, the child learns to take things in stride and to not always need support. Remember, it's all about reading your child's cues and responding to what you think your child needs in the current situation.

REFLECTIVE PARENTING:
MAKING LINKS AND LINKS BETWEEN LINKS

One thing that we know about the mature brain is that it is highly integrated (Tononi & Edelman, 1998). This means that the various areas of the brain are highly connected and linked to one another. An important aspect of reflective parenting is for the parent to make links between different simple elements of a child's experience and to link those together with even more complex elements of experience.

For example, a reflective communication from a parent to a child often narrates to the child what the child is doing, why the child is doing it, and what the child may be feeling while doing it. The ability to integrate these elements of the child's experiences is based on knowledge the parent gains from the activity of the parent's mirror system. For example, a parent might say, "You are giving Mommy a piece of bread to share your food and let Mommy know you love her." At the level of the brain, when the parent verbally makes links between a child's actions and their associated meanings, their intentions and goals, their emotions, and their communicative elements, it wires the relevant brain structures and also strengthens the child's ability to eventually self-regulate. Making verbal links is helpful, but don't do it all the time. Too much verbal linking or empathizing makes the relationship stilted. Aim for somewhere in the middle.

STORIES OF PARENTS AND CHILDREN

- *A case of matching a child's behavior too overtly.* Crystal sits on the floor with her 12-month-old son Gabriel, who is playing with a shape-sorter toy. Gabriel is trying to put the round peg into the triangle-shaped hole. It's not working, but Gabriel keeps at it. Crystal feels bad for him, and so she takes the peg and shows him how to put it in the round hole. Gabriel squawks. He turns away and tries the square peg in the round hole. Again Crystal shows him the right way, and again he squawks and turns away to look for another shape to try. When it is pointed out to Crystal that her son was just fine when he was trying to do it on his own and that when she helped he got irritated and turned away, Crystal sheepishly says, "Oh, I guess it was hard for me to watch him struggle. I can see now he was doing fine without my help. He is a really persistent little guy. He wants to succeed at it himself."

- *A case of misinterpreting a child's intentions.* In a parenting group, Collin complains that his 14-year-old daughter Hailey has a bad attitude and is intent on ignoring what her father says to her. He explains, "Hailey makes an annoyed face or gives only one-word answers to any questions I ask or comments I make, and she might even leave the room in the middle of my sentence." He says this makes him feel angry because his daughter is being rude, and it makes him feel responsible to teach his daughter not to behave this way. "I mean, aren't I allowed to ask questions? I'm just trying to have a good relationship. And isn't that what we're supposed to do as parents, teach them how to behave properly?" Collin is asked if perhaps he also feels something besides anger, and he immediately relates how rejected and disrespected he feels when Hailey ignores him. The other parents empathize with Collin about how hurtful it can feel to have someone ignore your questions. Then he is asked if he can imagine what Hailey is feeling. Collin ponders a bit and has an "aha" moment, recalling how he and his friends felt the same way with their parents. "I hoped it would be different with my children. I am so much more understanding and empathic than my parents ever were. Doesn't that count for something?" He is told that of course it counts for a lot and that most likely his daughter appreciates it, but that Hailey is a teenager, which means she is in the time of her life when breaking the closeness with her parents is important for development. Collin promises himself that he will try harder to understand this, adding, "Deep inside, I'm glad she can separate from me and not always have to answer my dumb questions."

- *A case of too much empathy.* Rita sits with her six-year-old daughter Tracy in the waiting room of a lab where Tracy is about to get some blood tests done. Tracy is anxious and crying. When her name is called, Tracy runs out of the room, saying she "hates needles." Her mom brings her back, but no amount of soothing or cajoling by Rita or the lab personnel can calm the girl down. The lab technician tells Rita to leave the room, saying, "She will be fine." Rita is feeling so distraught herself that she can't tolerate one more second of her daughter's crying. Much to the shock of the lab techs, Rita takes Tracy in her arms and walks out. Is this mother being irresponsible? No! Is she spoiling her daughter and giving in too easily? No! She is just overempathic and is literally as upset as her daughter. It should be no surprise that this mother had many hospitalizations as a child and *hates blood tests too*. Being a responsible mom, she sends the dad in with Tracy the following week. He doesn't feel these things as strongly.

PUTTING IT INTO WORDS

The following examples illustrate ways that reflective parents can communicate their understanding of their child's intentions and also teach their child how social relationships often require the child to regulate her or his emotions and inhibit his or her behaviors and impulses. These are just examples. You should use your own words.

- "I know how badly you want to talk with me. I can see you are upset. I will be right with you. Right now I'm on the phone and you have to wait a bit. You will be OK. I trust that you can calm down and wait."
- "I know how hungry you are, but dinner isn't quite ready yet. You have to wait a bit. I hear you screaming how hungry you are. It's going to be ready pretty soon, but screaming won't make it go any faster."
- "Dinner is ready. Time to sit down. I know you are playing, but now you have to stop playing and go and wash your hands and come to dinner."

TAKE-HOME LESSONS

- Take the time to closely observe a few of your child's behaviors, such as when he or she is getting dressed, eating breakfast, playing with another child, studying, or playing a sport. Try to pay attention to what is happening in your own body. You may notice sensations in various body organs, such as your stomach churning or your lungs breathing deeply. You may notice sensations in your muscles or even little movements of your muscles. Notice whether your child's behaviors have any similarity to your own behaviors. Perhaps he or she uses the same gestures or the same voice intonation or the same words.

- Notice the links between your mirror system and your emotional system. When you observe each behavior of your child, what emotion do you notice yourself feeling? Consider whether the emotion you are feeling is empathy for whatever you think your child is feeling at the time. Consider whether what you are feeling may have another source. For example, you might see your child cry on the baseball field, but rather than feeling empathy for your child, you may feel irritation or anger or embarrassment. Think about what might be the source of those kinds of feelings.

- Practice fostering creativity and innovation. For example, when you show your child how to tie their shoe, do a puzzle, do a math problem, make their bed, or greet their grandparents, observe exactly how they do it. Is it an exact copy of what you showed or told them to do or something different? Allow room for it to be different.

- The game Simon Says provides practice in strengthening the mirror system as well as inhibitory control over it. However, remember that although teaching and practicing strategies for self-control can help, sometimes all you can do is be patient and wait for the prefrontal cortex to mature.

- As much as possible, behave the way you want your child to behave. Think about a behavior in your child that annoys you. Now think about whether your child is simply imitating what you do. Of course, some behaviors are appropriate for adults but not for children. These behaviors in your child will require limit-setting. But what if the behavior is answering your cell phone at the dinner table or not cleaning up after yourself or yelling a lot? You have choices now. You can either accept the behavior in your child, or you will have to modify these behaviors in yourself.

FOUR

The Brain's Mentalization System

Wired for Reflection

BRAIN BASICS

The human mind is not just the product of a single brain, but results from the interaction of the minds, bodies, and brains between people. The brain has a special circuit for perceiving the minds of the self and of other people. This perceptual ability is called reflective capacity.

REFLECTIVE CAPACITY IS HOW
WE PERCEIVE THE MIND

You are trying to be a sensitive and responsive parent. But try as you might to understand your child, it can often be a confusing and sometimes impossible process. This is because a big part of the information you need is hidden from view, inside your child's head. It is also because children's minds are less developed and they tend to see things in a different way than adults do. You do get some insight automatically from your mirror system. But when things are really complex, the mirror system isn't enough. The social brain's other shared circuit, called the *mentalization system*, comes into play when the situation is not so obvious.

The mentalization system is a shared circuit of mind. It uses the same brain areas to understand one's own mind and the minds of others. It is this system that underlies reflective capacity[1] and facilitates our being able to form deep emotional bonds by understanding and taking an active interest in what is happening on the inside of us and of our child; our being wise enough to realize we can't always know for certain; and our being humble enough to accept that we are sometimes fooled (Fonagy & Target, 2006). Neuroscientists coined the term *mentalization* system because it is all about what is going on in the *mental* world. It takes outward behavior and *translates* it into its underlying mental processes: intentions, goals, beliefs, meanings, and emotions.

Strictly speaking, the mirror system is *pre*reflective because it understands only what is fairly obvious about the mental processes underlying behavior. Reflective capacity, on the other hand, is about being able to "see" what is not so obvious from the situation. It gives us a more nuanced and abstract understanding. Because the brain is an integrated system, the mirror system and the mentalization system usually work together to maintain a person's adaptive functioning (Sperduti, Guionnet, Fossati, & Nadel, 2014).

ANATOMY OF THE MENTALIZATION SYSTEM

The MENTALIZING SYSTEM includes three main regions, each of which plays a somewhat different role in our overall ability to understand the mind, have a sense of self and, to modulate our emotions and impulses. The regions are VENTRAL-MEDIAL PREFRONTAL CORTEX (VMPFC), POSTERIOR CINGULATE CORTEX, and PRECUNEUS (Figure 4.1) (Lieberman, 2013; Takahashia, 2015; Buckner, Andrews-Hanna, & Schacter, 2008). The importance of the mentalization system to the quality of our social relationships is illuminated by the roles each of these areas play. The ventral-medial prefrontal is involved in social-emotional decision making. Examples

---

1 Many child development experts use the terms *mentalization* and *reflective capacity* interchangeably.

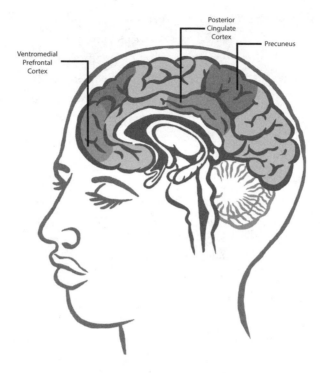

Figure 4.1. The mentalization system.

include: moral decision making; anticipating the future consequences of one's decisions; assessing abstract intentions (e.g., generosity, selfishness); and in guiding decisions based on the emotions of guilt or envy. Abstract intentions play an enormous role in parenting. For example when your child is playing with a friend and you say things like, "*share* your toys" or "remember to *be fair* and take turns," *share* and *be fair* are abstract intentions that can only be understood through the reflective capacity of the MENTALIZATION SYSTEM. The posterior cingulate and precuneus are both essential for conscious self-reflection.

WHAT EVOLUTION CAN TEACH US ABOUT REFLECTIVE PARENTING

The shared circuitry of the mirror system is something we have in common with our closest primate relatives, the chimpanzees. It is important for our relationships but only enables us to understand the here-and-now, more-obvious actions or experiences of other people. It does little to help us understand ourselves or figure out what's going on when relationships get complicated.

Scientists propose that when Homo sapiens arrived on the scene about 200,000 years ago, genetic mutations led to the growth of new brain circuits, which made possible new abilities that permanently changed not only human beings but the whole world as well (Klein, 2002). These changes increased the complexity of the prefrontal cortex. Scientists believe these changes are responsible for the fact that roughly between 100,000 and 50,000 years ago, human beings started to show evidence of having a mind capable of abstract, symbolic thought and creativity. This is difficult to prove: You can find a skull or an arm bone in the fossil record, but you can't find an abstract thought there. Therefore, scientists rely on several indirect pieces of evidence to support their theory that a mind capable of representing intangible and abstract ideas emerged around this time. One line of evidence is cultural artifacts that show up in the archeological record during this period, such as decorated stones, beads, cave paintings, and signs of ritual practices. Another is that the human larynx (i.e., the voicebox) is lower in the throat, which enables people to better articulate specific sounds and communicate through speech—presumably to communicate about these new abstract and symbolic ideas they were having (Hauser, Chomsky, & Fitch, 2002).

Something is abstract or symbolic when it both constitutes a physical thing itself and also represents other things at the same time. By definition, something that is abstract is intangible and does not physically exist in the here and now. For example, an apple is an apple. But an apple can also be an abstract symbol with multiple meanings, as in "an apple a day" or "the Big Apple." Words are actually abstract symbols. They refer to both the sound of the word and the meaning of the word. The sound is physical. The meaning is abstract. The word *brain*, for example, is associated with certain sounds and also several different meanings. It can mean the actual physical brain. It can mean intelligence, as in "He really has a brain." It can also mean common sense, as in "He is really using his brain." Concepts, by definition, are abstractions.

A Really Successful Strategy for Social Relationships

Abstract thinking ability means being able to think about symbols and other intangible concepts. Successful relationships require the ability to communicate our abstract thinking with one another, as we do when we relate to one another mind-to-mind (Baron-Cohen, Tager-Flusberg, & Cohen, 2007). If you want your child to successfully become a member of society, it will be your role to make sure that they master mind-to-mind relationships as much as they can.

Reflective Parenting: Because We Are
Symbolic Creatures

When your child communicates in the form of behaviors, it is like a symbol for what is going on inside. When a parent sees their child's behavior, they recognize that there can be many possible meanings to the behavior. It does not mean you will always respond in exactly the right way. But the point is that you "get" that whatever is going on could and most likely does have multiple meanings.

For example, your 12-year-old son comes home from school and throws his books on the floor. What do you do? If you are stressed and not very reflective at the moment, you are likely to operate in reflexive mode and scold your son for mistreating his books. But let's say you are in a really reflective frame of mind and you know better. Now what do you do? The behavior is the behavior, but it also represents an emotion and a communication, maybe more than one communication at a time.

SCIENCE SAYS

The mentalization system is activated when we use abstract symbols as indicators of mental states. When subjects are shown a *neutral* face with little circles on the face representing tears going down the cheeks, it activates the mentalization circuits and subjects are more likely to interpret the face as expressing sadness (Takahashi et al., 2015). The circles are the *symbol* for the real tears.

Suppose that in this case, it turns out that his aggressiveness with his books was his way of expressing feeling angry, frustrated, and defeated all at the same time: "I want you to know how annoyed and upset I am!" together with "Don't come near me or ask me anything about it!" The mentalization system plays a role in this kind of abstract thinking and understanding in social situations.

ABSTRACT SYMBOLS: THE CURRENCY OF THE MIND

The mind operates only in an abstract and symbolic way. This is the reason for so much discussion about abstract symbols and ideas in a book about parenting. Because it is in the mind, the meaning of your child's behavior is not a concrete fact, and it can have more than one meaning at a time. If you can accept that whatever meaning you ascribe to your child's behavior may not be the absolute truth and that there can be other ways of thinking about it, you are well on your way to being a highly reflective parent.

Every time you engage in a conversation about abstract ideas, you are exercising the muscles of your child's developing mind. To be clear, abstract thought and mind-sharing need not involve a high or sophisticated level of thinking. Discussions can be as ordinary as talking about such concepts as *yesterday* or *tomorrow*, or about superheroes and their superpowers. These ideas are abstract and symbolic because they do not actually exist in the here and now. The point is to not get too bogged down in focusing on what is true and factual when having a conversation. It's about sharing ideas, which by definition are intangible and abstract.

THE MENTALIZATION SYSTEM CAN'T HELP BUT BE SOCIAL

Scientists have identified that social cognition is the default mode of how the mind operates (Mars et al., 2012). Social relationships are so vital to our well-being that the mentalization system grabs every quiet moment it gets to focus on them (M. D. Lieberman, 2013). When we get together with other people, we talk a lot about our kids, our friends, and all the people we are involved with. But even when we are alone and seemingly doing nothing at all, our minds typically fall into an active mental reverie that wonders about, assesses, and evaluates what is going on between us and other people. This mental reverie about social relationships corresponds to activity in the mentalization system.

Imagine you are waiting in line at the supermarket, not doing anything in particular. Your mind automatically starts to wander in a free-floating way. You think about the party you went to last night and regret not talking to more people. Your mind jumps to the recent gossip at your office about your new boss. You end up thinking about how it went for your daughter at school today because she had a test. You quickly snap out of your reverie when the checkout clerk says, "That will be forty-five dollars."

When we are *at rest*, not doing anything else, our mind engages in an internal reverie that wanders across past, present, and future and thinks about social relationships from different perspectives. During rest, activity in the mentalization system is *high* while activity in task-related areas is *low* (M. D. Lieberman, 2007, 2013). When we engage in external tasks, such as paying our bill at the supermarket in the above example, activity in the mentalization system immediately becomes *low* while task-related brain areas show *high* activity. When we engage in reflective thinking, that is, directed thinking about what is going on in our own mind or the minds of others, mentalization system activity goes up even *higher* than when we are at rest.

Being in "Task Mode" versus Being in "Reflective Mode"

Because doing externally directed tasks lowers activity in the mentalization system, being too busy with activities may interfere with your ability to understand your child. On the other hand, *too much activity in the mentalization system* can reduce activity in brain systems involved in doing external tasks, which can interfere with task performance. This is why when we are engaged in tasks, the brain tends to reduce activity in the mentalization system, and social processing diminishes. This can have psychologically adaptive value. A purposeful activity, like a workout at the gym, can get our mind off worrying about our relationships. Self-help books for people who worry too much often recommend going out and doing some type of exercise in order to feel better (Korb, 2015). It's not just because exercise itself calms anxiety and improves mood; it's also because focusing on some external task—it could even be gardening, cooking, or cleaning for that matter—gets your mind away from your worries.

Reflective Capacity Links Minds and Bodies

Being reflective happens on multiple levels. It means not only realizing that there is a link between your child's behavior and their inner feelings or intentions, but also making multiple links, such as between your behavior and your mental state, between your child's mental state and your mental state, and between mental states. The more links a parent makes when talking about their interactions with their child, the more reflective that parent is said to be.

Take, for example, the situation where a parent picks up their 10-year-old daughter after school and she doesn't want to talk. A not-very-reflective parent might talk about the situation this way: "When she gets in the car and doesn't talk, I just say, 'Cat got your tongue?'" The parent is aware of the behavior but doesn't link it to anything internal in the child. A parent with a little higher but still quite low reflective capacity might say, "When she's upset, she won't talk, so I just don't talk to her; that teaches her how it feels." This parent makes only a small link between feelings and behavior, but not in a way that promotes empathy or understanding. A reasonably reflective parent might talk this way: "I could see from her face that she seemed angry, so I figured that was probably why she wasn't talking. I felt a little rejected, so I stayed quiet too." This parent makes more links—linking the child's behavior with the child's mental state and with the parent's own behavior and mental state. A highly reflective parent will make even more links. For example, they might add, "I feel rejected, but I also know she doesn't mean this personally, and that thought helps me feel less rejected. I also sense that she feels glad that I allow her to be quiet until she's ready to talk, and that makes me feel good." Here the parent makes links between their two different mental states and also makes links between the child's mental state and the parent's mental state.

This example also illustrates that being reflective can mean just thinking about what's going on. It doesn't always require sharing with your child what you're thinking. In this case, suppose that once they get home, the girl tells her parent what happened earlier in the day. "I was really angry at Miles today because he tried to cheat off my paper during the test. I was so angry because the teacher noticed and she thought I was trying to help him." Now the parent has to choose whether or not what their reflective mind was thinking about earlier was helpful. One parent might decide to say, "Yeah, I kind of had the idea that you were upset about something, and I figured if you wanted to tell me, you would when you felt ready." Another parent may decide not to share that. The point is, a parent need not share every reflective link they think of. It is the reflecting in the first place that supports a strong relationship, and the parent being able to determine how much to share or not. But lest you worry about having to be a perfect "10" at reflecting, it turns out that just being average—being a "5" at reflecting—is good enough.

REFLECTION CAN BE CONSCIOUS OR NON-CONSCIOUS DEPENDING ON THE SITUATION

Often when parents first learn about reflective parenting, they think it just means more work for them. "I don't have the time to always stop and think about what's going on. Between work and taking care of the kids and maybe getting some exercise, I don't have the energy to be reflective all the time." Therefore, it should reassure you to know that the majority of the time, reflective thinking operates outside conscious awareness, as do most aspects of brain function (Pally, 2007, 2010). Nonconscious processing works well for highly practiced, familiar, clear, and expected situations. For example, when you pick up your daughter after a sleepover and she dawdles, your nonconscious reflection can let you automatically know that she needs a few minutes to say good-bye to her friends before she can leave.

The benefits of nonconscious processing are that it operates without effort or paying attention and is quick, smooth, and fluid. The downsides are that it tends to be inflexible, habitual, and not as precise or accurate about details. This is why we never forget how to ride a bike once we have learned how to do it. But it is also why we tend to think, behave, or feel as we have always done in the past.

So why be consciously reflective at all?

The answer is that all conscious processing, including conscious reflective capacity, allows for more flexibility, greater accuracy about details, and improved regulation of emotions and behaviors. However, since conscious processing is slower and takes more effort, for the sake of efficiency, the brain opts to rely on nonconscious processing as much as possible. The brain uses conscious processing only on an as-needed basis. As a parent, you need to make the effort to consciously reflect only when the situation is unfamiliar, ambiguous, or uncertain or when you sense a conflict or misunderstanding. If your nonconsciously operating reflective capacity comes up with a response that is off base, you can repair the situation by shifting into a more conscious reflective mode, slowly pay attention to the precise details of what is going on, and correct whatever needs correcting.

We shift between nonconscious and conscious reflection.

For example, suppose Martin's eight-year-old daughter Phoebe asks for a little more TV time before going to sleep. Martin is fine with that, since he can use a few more minutes to finish his emails before reading a bedtime story to Phoebe. He doesn't have to consciously reflect on what the request means. Nonconsciously, he assumes it's just a normal request. If things go smoothly, Martin won't have to do any conscious reflecting at all. But it turns out that after the few minutes are over, Phoebe keeps bugging her dad for more TV when he says it's time for bed. Now Martin is annoyed and says, "It's late, and I don't want to argue with you about this." Phoebe keeps pressing him. He gets really angry with her and she cries. But he is still not consciously reflecting; he is just getting angrier at her for being demanding. At some point Martin realizes he needs to shift into conscious reflection. This helps him realize that he's angry with himself for having said yes to more TV in the first place. He also realizes that Phoebe probably just needs a little more transition time before going to bed and that he riled her up by being so angry with her when he set the limit. This helps Martin's anger subside, and he says, "Hey, Honey, instead of more TV, I will read you a little longer story when I put you to bed."

Conscious reflection supports self-regulation.

When a parent is emotionally distraught and overly reactive toward their child, conscious reflection can help the parent gain control. In turn, parents can teach their children to consciously reflect as a means of self-calming. For example, a parent might say this to an 11-year-old daughter who is anxious about going to a birthday party where she doesn't know anyone: "If you are uncomfortable at the party, remember it means that you feel anxious when you don't know people at first, but then you usually calm down. Also remind yourself that it's normal; lots of people feel anxious at parties where they don't know anyone." This conscious reflection brings in the brain's memory system knowledge to further support emotional control. Additionally, the mere act of putting feelings into words helps to calm the feeling.

Conscious reflection helps you recognize the impact
of your child's behavior on you.

As already mentioned, we respond more to what a child's behavior *means* to us than to what the child is actually doing or intending. Suppose that a child says hurtful words to another child. The impact of this action on

SCIENCE SAYS

Neuroimaging studies show that reflecting on one's feelings and putting them into words is an effective strategy for regulating negative emotional responses (M. D. Lieberman, 2013). Feeling intense emotion or viewing emotionally evocative images is associated with increased *amygdala* activity; reflection on the feeling or verbally describing the emotional image reduces amygdala activity.

the parent will differ depending on whether the parent takes this to mean that their child is an uncaring person or takes it to mean that their child has simply not matured enough to fully grasp that their words can hurt someone. In the first case, the impact on the parent might be that the parent feels angry and responds harshly to their child. In the second case, the parent may feel embarrassed but respond more neutrally and provide guidance as to how to properly behave. Only by consciously reflecting on what we feel and what meaning we've assigned to our child's behavior can we better navigate our responses to our children.

For example, Anna, a mother in a reflective parenting group, complained how unpleasant it was when she played with her daughter, 14-month-old Julia. She explained that when Julia was frustrated with a toy she would cry; but when Anna tried to help her, Julia continued to cry. "It's so irritating. She cries for me to help her but then rejects the help." Anna's initial, nonreflective assumption was that Julia was crying because she wanted her mother to help. It was a perfectly natural and understandable assumption, but it wasn't working. Another mother in the group offered that maybe Julia was crying but not asking for help. Anna consciously reflected, "I think I'm hurt because I assume Julia wants help but is rejecting *my* help." Consciously reflecting opened up her ability to take perspective, and she saw that it was *not* personal. It was not a rejection of her. Julia was crying simply because she was frustrated, but she wanted to work it out on her own. By not taking Julia's frustration so personally, Anna was able to enjoy playing with her daughter more.

Conscious reflection helps you recognize the impact of your behavior on your child.

Of course, you also have to recognize the impact your behavior has on your child. For example, Andre, a father in a reflective parenting group, felt that he and his son, 12-year-old Jayson, were not getting along well. He complained that his son kept to himself and didn't talk much. Tearfully, he explained, "Jayson doesn't seem to enjoy being with me." He felt jealous of his wife, with whom Jayson was much more talkative and animated. When asked to describe his behavior toward Jayson, Andre explained, "I try hard to be a good father. I teach him how to be a responsible man, to do his schoolwork well, to improve his basketball game, to make sure he speaks well and is polite to other people." Andre was clearly being a better dad than his own father, who he recalled as being detached and uninvolved. So what was going on? The answer appeared when Andre was asked, "What impact do you think your behavior has on Jayson?" A light went on. "It must be a drag to have your dad always correcting and teaching you how to improve." Andre decided to stop all the teaching business, to start hanging out together more, and to be more conversational about whatever his son wanted to talk about. Things soon improved greatly.

Reflectively narrating experience is calming.

Because it can integrate the past, present, and future, reflective capacity enables us to put events into a storyline. With younger children, reflectively narrating the child's experience often involves describing what the parent assumes is going on inside the child's mind as the child engages in behavior. With an older child, it may involve going back over a challenging situation that occurred earlier. Narrating has many benefits for the child. It helps the child make links between behavior and mind. Narration communicates a parent's understanding to the child, which makes the child feel that their experiences makes sense and that their parent is right there with them in the experience. Narration is also a means of building up the child's reflective capacity, because it models being reflective and engages the child in a reflective process. In fact, the ability to create a coherent narrative about one's life is considered a sign of good reflective function (Slade, 2006). If you practice reflective narration with your child, your child will be more likely to be reflective about his or her own life when he or she becomes an adult.

When kids are scared, it is often enough to just say something reassuring like, "Everything's OK" or "You're all right. Nothing to worry about." But sometimes that isn't enough. Narration can serve as an additional tool for calming and reassuring your child. Let's say your seven-year-old son falls down at school and cuts his knee. The school nurse takes care of it and he is fine. But when you arrive to pick him up in aftercare at the end of your day at work, he bursts into tears and is inconsolable about how badly his knee hurts. This is when you can reflectively narrate his experience. You might say, "You were playing in the school-yard with your friends when you fell and got a bad cut. It was scary to bleed so much and you had to go to the nurse. You were upset because you didn't get to finish the game you were playing with your buddies. And then you had to wait a few hours before Mommy could come and pick you up. Days like that are really difficult, aren't they?" You never said a direct word like "You will be OK" or "Stop crying; Mommy is here now." But the effect of your narration is that your child stops crying and is ready to go home. Narration communicates, "I can understand. Your experience makes sense to me." That is what is calming.

Narrating your child's experience can calm you down as well.

Reflective parenting is as much for the parent as it is for the child. It is just as important for the parent to feel they understand their child as it is for the child to feel understood. Sometimes the mom or dad just needs to say the storyline silently in their own mind and not even share it out loud with their child. Let's consider a dedicated father reading a book to his three-year-old daughter before bedtime. The girl gets restless, rubs her eyes, and loses interest halfway through the short book. Now what does the dad do? He's dedicated and knows how important it is to read to his daughter, and he hasn't been reading that long. So he is determined to finish the book. As he is reading, however, he starts to narrate silently to himself, "We had a long day . . . lots of activities . . . she's extra-tired tonight and wants to go to sleep already." The narration is for the dad, not the girl. In fact, when he says out loud, "Honey, we had a long day; you're tired and want to go to sleep," his daughter sits bolt upright and says, "I'm not tired! I don't want to go to sleep!" The dad's silent narration to himself works better in this situation. It helps him to get out of the fixed mindset that he must read a book to his daughter and into a more flexible mindset where he can just follow his daughter's nonverbal cues. The next time his daughter rubs her eyes, instead of saying anything he scoops her up and lays her gently down on her bed, and without a peep the girl closes her eyes. He even inhibits his urge to say, "I knew you were tired."

Narrating can actively engage a child in trying to cope with difficulty.

Narration can sometimes be interactive. For example, suppose that a dad realizes that all his efforts at soothing his six-year-old son's fear of the dark as he tries to put him to bed are not working. The son, James, refuses to let his dad leave the room. Steve, the dad, is getting impatient that it's all taking so long. At first Steve considers using a tough-love approach and insisting that James will have to stay in his room even if he's scared. But on second thought, he opts to give narration a try. "James never likes the dark. He's begging his daddy not to leave the room tonight. Even when his daddy tells him it's safe and that there aren't any monsters under the bed, he still doesn't like the dark and won't go to sleep. Oh, boy, is his daddy confused. Usually he's good at calming James down, but tonight nothing is working. It's making him impatient with James. He doesn't like it when he's impatient with James. And James doesn't like it either! His daddy wonders what he should try to do next."

Wow—that narrative had a lot of really high-level reflective linking going on! To the dad's relief, James pipes up, "You can give him a tummy rub. Maybe his tummy hurts when he's alone in the dark." The narrative interaction helps Steve realize that the real issue is not the dark. The issue is separation anxiety, which can be a perfectly normal thing even for a six-year-old to feel at bedtime. The narrative interaction helps Steve to better understand the situation and helps James to express his need for connection. Steve says, "Hey, how about if I rub *your* tummy and kiss it three times?" Afterward, James says he is ready to go to sleep.

The point is that narration is part of a reflective process. It can work, as in this case, even if each person is a little unclear about what is actually happening. This is the value of stories—they function at both the concrete level and the abstract level. The concrete is tummy rubbing; the abstract is separation.

A REFLECTIVE PERSPECTIVE: TWO MINDS EQUALS TWO POINTS OF VIEW

If there were one concept that most encapsulates what it means to be a reflective parent, it would be two-way perspective-taking. Perspective has to do with the *meanings* and *interpretations* that each person's mind infers from a situation (Buckner, Andrews-Hanna, & Schacter, 2008; Lieberman, 2003). If you pat your son on his head, he will respond differently depending on whether he takes the pat to mean encouragement or takes it to mean that you're being dismissive of him. Or suppose that it's raining and you remind your teenage daughter to take her umbrella, to which she replies "Whatever!" Your response to her will depend entirely on how you interpret the meaning of her words. Is she being derisive or nasty? Or is she just trying to show she is separate from you? Two-way perspective taking enables you to recognize that you and your child may each interpret or understand a particular situation in a different way (Figure 4.2). It also means that you and your spouse may each have a different perspective about what is going on with your child (Figure. 4.3).

PASS IT ON! TEACH YOUR CHILD TO BE A REFLECTIVE THINKER

We know children are not born with the ability to think reflectively because they do not have a mature mentalization system. They are born

Figure 4.2. Two-way perspective taking.

Figure 4.3. Each parent may interpret the child's behavior differently.

SCIENCE SAYS

*The Mentalization System Accomplishes
Two-Way Perspective-Taking*

Subjects in a scanner were shown people's faces and asked to
think about what the other person was feeling, think about what
they themselves were feeling when looking at the face, and make
a judgment as to the person's personality. These perspective-
taking tasks activated their mentalization system (Gusnard,
Akbudak, Shulman, & Raichle, 2001; Ochsner et al., 2004).

only with the ability to *learn how* to think reflectively. And they learn
how only if they are related to in a reflective manner by people who are
reflective thinkers. A big part of being a reflective parent means building up your child's mentalization system. It means passing on the reflective baton from parent to child. When parents use reflective thinking to
calm themselves down, they are a role model that the child internalizes,
and thus the child acquires the ability to regulate his or her distress.
When a parent uses reflective language when talking with their child or
encourages the child to come up with reflective ideas of their own, this
teaches the child how to be a reflective thinker.

The Learning Arc of Reflective Thinking in Children

Becoming reflective is a slow process, because it takes time for prefrontal
cortex elements of the mentalization system to mature. Some rudimen-
tary reflective ability can be seen as early as the first year of life (Kovács,
Téglás, & Endress, 2010). At first, a baby is interested only in action.
When the mother or father points at an object, a seven- or eight-month-
old baby looks at their finger and not at the object being pointed to. Typically, by 12 months or as late as 18 months, the first glimmer of mind

awareness is evident in that instead of looking at a parent's finger, the baby now looks to what the parent is pointing at (Tomasello, Carpenter, & Liszkowski, 2007). This is called *joint attention*. The parent points to what he or she wants the baby to look at. The baby infers the parent's intention and looks at what the parent is looking at. From this point forward, the child is able to infer more and more meanings from the parent's pointing (Tomasello et al., 2007). The parent may point to indicate where a toy is hidden or where the child should place an object, and the child will follow the nonverbal instructions. At around this same age, babies begin to point as well. Their pointing can also have different mental meanings. The child may be trying to get the parent to look at an object they are pointing to, get the parent to give them what they are pointing to, or get the parent to name the object they are pointing to.

What a discovery! The baby has learned that "Mommy has a mind that she wants to share with me" and "I have a mind and I want to share it with her." Recognizing that people have minds and that minds can be shared is what makes it possible for the baby to eventually develop all those other fancy social abilities such as empathy, taking turns, and cooperation.

Being truly reflective requires recognizing that minds are separate and can be different from one another. It is not until children are around four to five years of age that they learn that every person's mind has a different perspective, meaning that not everyone sees the world in the way the child does. As the mind grows and matures, the child's recognition of separate minds improves.

Does Your Computer Really Have a Mind of Its Own?

Being reflective is so important for social functioning that the brain goes overboard, especially in young children, treating almost everything as if it has a mind (Epley, Waytz, & Cacioppo, 2007). This is why children will attribute intentions to all their toys, to characters in a book or movie, or to the family pet. A child will happily talk to a stuffed toy or even a sock if it is presented like a puppet *as if* it had a mind.

As adults, we ascribe intentions to our cars and gadgets. "My computer has it in for me today. It doesn't want to let me finish my work." "My car is so happy because I took it to get washed and waxed today." The difference between the child's mind and the adult's is that adults at least understand that *things* do not have minds. There is a virtue to a child's less-developed mind in not making these distinctions. Children learn an enormous amount about how the mind operates by talking about the minds of their toys or the characters in books they read with their parents. It's all exercise for the reflective brain circuits.

THE VALUE OF DOING NOTHING

The mentalization system's love of daydreaming and mind-wandering are not given the full respect they deserve. Unfortunately, our modern society is too task-focused, whether we are at work, at school, or doing extra-curricular activities. The science indicates that too much task focus is not good either for the brain or for the person whose brain it is.

Children need downtime to daydream.

To be awake, perchance to daydream! The relatively unfocused mental reverie associated with high levels of activity in the mentalization system has a number of benefits. It provides time for the brain to do some necessary social "bookkeeping." Daydreaming and mind-wandering flow fluidly from topic to topic, considering alternative outcomes, perspectives, or possibilities. "If only I said yes instead of no when my boss asked me out to lunch. Maybe he would have given me the raise I asked for." Or "I wonder what Noreen thought about my presentation. I imagine she liked it, but it's possible she thought it was too technical." Or "It would probably have been better to realize my child was exceptionally needy this morning and not get so angry about having to help him get dressed. I wonder if it's best to apologize or just let it go."

As a parent, you want to make sure that during their awake time your child has enough downtime to daydream and let their mind wander. This will strengthen their mentalization system, because it will give them a chance to see and hold on to alternative possibilities.

REFLECTIVE STRATEGIES FOR REGULATING YOUR EMOTIONS

Children activate intense emotions in their parents. Parents need these emotions in order to be responsive to their child's needs and actions. However, overly or "underly" intense feelings can be problematic.

Strategies for Regulating Empathy

Regulating empathy involves teamwork between the mirror system and the mentalization system (Herbet et al., 2014; Sperduti et al., 2014). The brain shifts back and forth between the two systems as parents utilize different strategies to regulate their empathy level—ratcheting it down or amping it up. The mirror system understands other people from more of a distance, more from the outside looking in. It is not as connected to the self of the other person or the self of the person doing the understanding. The mentalization system, on the other hand, is the basis for having a sense of self in the first place. It uses one's sense of self to understand the self-experience of others. This is why the emotional empathy that results from the mentalization system can be more intensely experienced.

Distancing Strategies to Decrease Your Empathy Level

If a parent feels their child's distress too strongly, it can cause the parent to overreact. If you sense yourself being in too much pain when your child is upset, you can use your mirror system to distance a bit by focusing more from outside what is going on. "I am going to focus only on my child's action of stamping around. That way I'll know what she feels but not feel it so much myself." You might shift from a self to an other focus. Imagine how you would feel if it were someone else's child who was upset.

Integrating Strategies to Decrease Your Empathy Level

Imagine seeing your daughter cry as you drop her off at preschool. Perhaps you feel so distressed for her that you can't leave even though you will be late for work. Try using your mentalization system to integrate the past and future with the present situation. Maybe you reflect on the past and realize that it's your childhood experience of your parents not caring how you felt that is causing you to overidentify with your daughter's distress. But you are a caring mother or father, so your daughter is not having the same experience you had. You reflect on the future and remember that the teacher told you that your daughter stops crying as soon as you leave and happily joins in with the other kids. These integrating reflections calm you enough to say comforting and confidence-building words to your daughter. "I know you are upset now. But you are going to be just fine. Remember how you cried yesterday but were fine when I left and you had lots of fun with the other kids? That is exactly what is going to happen today. I love you, and I will pick you up in the afternoon." Your daughter may still be a bit tearful, but you will both feel more confident about separating.

Imagination Strategies to Increase Empathy

When children express strong emotions, most parents can at least name or label the emotion. This *knowing* what the other feels is a function of the mirror system. But knowing is not empathy. Knowing is frequently not enough to help a parent regulate their child's emotions. Sometimes when parents can't adequately empathize—can't actually *feel* their child's emotions—it can ramp up the child's emotions, because the child will be trying to express what they are feeling more strongly to try to get their parent to "understand." To increase empathy, try using an imagination strategy. Imagine a situation in which you might feel what you think your child is feeling. This will activate your mentalization system and enhance your ability to feel inside yourself what your child is feeling inside their own self.

Strategies for Regulating Anger and Hostility

All parents at times get angry and even feel hostile toward their child. Being a reflective parent requires you to try your best to keep your emotions from getting the better of you. But you don't want to eradicate these feelings entirely. We need these feelings. Feelings serve as important signals to ourselves about what is going on inside us and how others are impacting us. But too often parents try to ignore their feelings of anger and hostility because they believe they are not supposed to have these feelings. Unfortunately, this can prevent them from setting appropriate limits. If a parent ignores an angry feeling for too long, it can sometimes erupt so powerfully that it frightens their child and interferes with the parent's role in regulating the child's emotions.

Use anger as a "note to self" and not as a weapon against your child. Anger serves as a *signal* to you that things have gone too far—that a boundary has been crossed. As a parent, it serves as a little note that your child has overstepped your limit or pushed on one of your tender spots. For example, suppose a toddler keeps throwing food on the floor. The mom gets that it's a fun game for the baby. But she must also get in touch with a little anger if she is to deal with the situation appropriately by telling the child to stop and removing the food.

For the anger to serve as an effective signal to the parent, however, it has to be regulated. If there is not enough anger, the parent will avoid setting a limit. If it is expressed too harshly, it can make the situation worse. To keep anger regulated, the reflective parent checks in with their own perspective (e.g., "I don't like this behavior!") but also checks in with the inner perspective of their child (e.g., "I'm exploring how to assert my autonomy. I'm just a child and I don't yet recognize what the limits are"). This two-way perspective-taking activates the mentalizing system, which contains self-regulatory centers that will help a parent to modulate their anger so that they can set the limit in a more neutral and therefore more effective way.

Externalizing as a strategy to regulate anger: It's not all about you!
When your child is upset with you, taking it too personally can make you overly angry with your child. For example, if you interpret their distress as meaning that they don't like you or something is wrong with you, it can make you feel hostile and defensive. Try externalizing. Use you mentalization system to shift more to their inner world than yours, and use your mirror system to realize that it's more about them than about you.

MINDFUL AWARENESS IS DIFFERENT FROM REFLECTIVE CAPACITY

The use of *mindfulness* (aka *mindful awareness*) is quite popular. Often, people confuse mindfulness with *reflective capacity* (aka *mentalization*). Both are helpful tools for parents because they can reduce stress, enhance empathy and compassion, and increase a sense of well-being (Grossman, 2004). However, mindfulness and reflective capacity are different and rely on different brain circuits. Mindfulness uses a heightened present-moment conscious awareness that involves intentionally observing and paying focused attention to the immediate *now* of what is going on in one's mind in a nonjudgmental, dispassionate way (Kabat-Zinn, 1994). By contrast, reflective capacity can operate with or without conscious awareness, pay attention to one's own mind and the mind of another person, and step in and out of the present moment.

Mindfulness decreases the stress and emotional reactivity of the present moment that can interfere with a parent's reflective capacity, but it does not replace it! Reflective capacity, grounded in the mentalization system, is for figuring things out and making sense of the back-and-forth of interpersonal interactions *over time*. Reflective capacity is actively curious, is open to multiple possibilities, and shifts between your own perspective and your child's and between feeling emotions more deeply and feeling them in a more detached way. Reflective capacity is especially good for figuring out misunderstandings and repairing ruptures in the parent–child relationship, because the parent is able to talk about or narrate what was going on during their conflict.

Remember, you are the parent!

The parent's capacity to be reflective is higher than the child's for a very long time! Therefore, it is more the parent's responsibility than it is the child's to keep the relationship strong. It may not feel fair to always have to work harder than your child does to keep the relationship strong, especially when your child is a teenager or even a young adult. This isn't a matter of fairness, however; it's just how the brain operates. Your child's reflective capacity fully matures only late in his or her 20s.

STORIES OF PARENTS AND CHILDREN

- *Use your reflective capacity when there is a conflict.* Miranda is always rushing in the morning and becomes extremely harsh and irritated with her daughter, Stephanie. She does not recognize that Stephanie's goal is to continue playing with her Legos. To resolve the conflict, Miranda first must be able to consciously identify and label the situation as a normal *conflict of interests.* This will help her to stop shouting "Come on! Hurry up!" again and again. It will help her to downshift and show that she understands what Stephanie's goal is. "I know you want to finish what you're working on, but we need to get to school. I will make sure that when you get home, you have time to finish what you're making."
- *Use your reflective capacity to regulate emotional distress.* Katrina is a mother in a reflective parenting group who typically downplays emotional distress in herself and in her three-year-old daughter, Mila. One mother encourages her to notice that downplaying is not

working to calm her child but is instead leading to greater distress. The group leader encourages Katrina to reflect on her feelings and her thoughts about them. Katrina says it makes her very anxious if Mila is upset. "I immediately *feel* I have to fix it." She believes that is what a good mother ought to do. Other parents in the group reassure Katrina that they can't always fix it when their child is upset. No parent can! Once Katrina stops expecting herself to always keep Mila calm, she gets more comfortable acknowledging Mila's feelings and tolerating Mila's distress, and this actually makes her more successful in calming Mila down.

• **Use your reflective capacity to adapt your parenting to your child's needs.** Hannah is worried that her shy and introverted 10-year-old son, Cal, doesn't have the social skills he needs to do well. She is always pushing him to talk more and assert himself more. Not only is this not working, but she's starting to feel as if she's not being the best mother for him. When she takes the time to reflect on who Cal is as a person, she realizes that he has a few friends who really like him, but he's not going to be one of the popular kids and that popularity is actually overrated. She reminds herself that his inborn traits are part of who he is and are great for the kinds of things that seem to interest him, like doing engineering projects at home. This reduces her worry about him and makes her focus on herself. "Now it's up to me to stop pushing him."

PUTTING IT INTO WORDS

• *A simple narration.* A father is feeding his 14-month-old son applesauce: "You were really hungry. You were having a hard time waiting, so you were yelling. But now that Daddy is feeding you, you are happy."

• *A more complex narration.* A mother is teaching her three-year-old son not to be so aggressive with his younger brother, Timo. Repeatedly she tells him, "Cut it out! You are hurting Timo and being too aggressive." But it doesn't work. So she creates a reflective narration: "I think you like to wrestle with Timo. You are trying to be a good older brother and play with him how older boys play. But then what happens is he cries. That's probably because he's just a little guy and gets hurt easier than you. I wonder if, as his older brother, you can think of a softer way to play with him until he gets bigger and can handle the rougher stuff?"

- **Sharing your reflective mind with your child.** A dad says, "All your arguing with me is making me too overwhelmed to think. I love you, but right now I'm too upset to respond appropriately. I need to take a little time out and collect my thoughts. When I calm down, I will be able to talk again."

TAKE-HOME LESSONS

- If you find yourself unable to reflect because you are under too much stress or are too upset, take a little time to do a mindfulness exercise. For example, try simply paying attention to your breathing. Try noticing the flow of your thoughts without judgment. Mindfulness will help reestablish your emotional equilibrium so that you are more able to be reflective once again. You can even be quietly mindful when the dinner table gets too chaotic for you or when helping with homework is pushing all your distress buttons.

- Practice being curious. When your child learns some new information, encourage him or her to explain it to you. Be curious and ask them what their opinion is about what they learned. When a public event happens—perhaps something they hear on the news or at school—find out your child's point of view about the event. Be curious about what they think happened and why it happened. Remember when flexing your child's reflective muscles that there are no wrong answers! Anytime they express their opinion or point of view, they are strengthening their mentalization system.

- Practice noticing how you feel when you set limits. Notice whether you tend to feel guilty or if you overidentify with your child. These feelings may make you more tentative about how you set the limits. Notice whether you feel like a bad parent. This may make you look to your child for reassurance that you are not bad, such as insisting that they agree or understand your reasons for setting the limit. Not allowing your child to be annoyed or grumpy when they abide by your limits can make your child feel resentful that you do not allow them enough separateness of mind.

- *Practice repair.* Notice a situation where too much conflict happens. Perhaps you and your child have a fight that causes a big rift in the relationship. Wait until the heat dies down. Be reflective to figure out what you think caused the fight. Think about what was happening inside your child. Think about what was getting triggered in you. Think about the impact you had on each another. Then go to your child and tell him or her you want to be close again. If you got too angry, apologize for overreacting. If it was just a misunderstanding, say so. You might share some of what you reflected on and ask your child to share what they think might have happened. The point is to get past the rift and be close again. It's not a time for blame or finger-pointing. It's a time to explain that people can get really mad at each other and still love each other and come back together. Kids really need this kind of thing. And, in truth, so do parents.

FIVE

The Brain and Maternal Care

Wired for Motherhood

BRAIN BASICS

The human brain is highly plastic, meaning it gets wired in response to the individual's environmental experiences, especially their social interactions with other people.

THE TRANSFORMATION OF A WOMAN INTO A MOTHER

Becoming a parent brings about a major transformation in one's life. It's a bit like growing a new arm. It takes time to learn what to do with it, how to take good care of it, and how to integrate it into your sense of self. Of course, as a parent, you are growing a whole new person, not just an arm.

Being a new parent is like being given a black box and told you must figure out what's inside. With a real box, you could open it up and look at the contents. As a parent, all you can do is make a very good guess as to what's inside the black box of your child's mind.

Being a new parent is also like training for the Olympics. It is stressful and requires extra resources to care for the baby and a shift in focus to prioritize the baby over everything else.

The saying "Babies don't come with an instruction manual" is only partly true. There is a genetically programmed set of changes in the mother's brain that activate *maternal care* and guide her through the initial few months of her baby's life until she has gotten more experience under her belt. This chapter focuses primarily on maternal care during the first few months of life. This is a unique but rather brief phase of parenting that serves as the launching pad for becoming a parent and sets the stage for what is to come later on. Although times are changing, most of the research on parenting infants and toddlers still focuses primarily on moms. Research on fathers, still in its "infancy," is included where possible.

WHAT IS MATERNAL CARE?

Maternal care refers to the characteristic set of behaviors and mental states a mother employs to ensure the safety of her baby, promote closeness between herself and her baby, focus her attention on her baby, heighten her empathy and her nurturance toward her baby, and provide herself with sufficient motivation to be successful at motherhood (Leckman et al., 2004; Swain, 2011a; Swain, Lorberbaum, Kose, & Strathearn, 2007).

Maternal care begins in the last trimester of pregnancy with the cleaning and preparation of the home for the baby's arrival. As soon as the baby arrives, the mom exhibits heightened attention to all things concerning the baby. She repetitively checks, inspects, and grooms the baby's body; keeps the baby and the area where the baby is especially clean, and stays close to her baby by feeding, changing, dressing, and playing with her or him.

The mental state of a new mother is called *primary maternal preoccupation*, in which moms show a heightened anxiety about the well-being of their new baby (Leckman et al., 2004; Swain, 2011a). Thoughts, worries, and concerns about the baby intrude frequently throughout the day. The mom is hypersensitive to detecting any sounds or movements coming from the baby. There is an excessiveness about this preoccupation with the baby that most mothers recognize as too extreme, but they are impelled by it anyway. It's more than love. It's a compulsion driven by the mother's brain. Moms of new babies sometimes get a bad rap for being too emotional and too worried about the baby. Nature has designed it this way for the survival of our species. The helpless baby needs at least one person to be especially attuned to her or him, and nature opts for it to be the baby's mother, at least in the very beginning.

This stage of heightened emotional sensitivity and preoccupation peaks in intensity when the baby is about three months of age and diminishes by about six months of age. This period of maternal care involves a strengthening of the mom's reflective capacity, as her heightened sensitivity to her infant's cues and needs enables her to put herself more in touch with the perspective of her baby. Her heightened emotional state becomes a source of greater empathy for her child's state of mind.

However, this is also a time of high emotional risk for a mother, and she is prone to conditions such as the "baby blues" and the more serious postpartum depression (Wisner, Parry, & Piontek, 2002). Women during this period need lots of support, because heightened stress can increase the likelihood of developing postpartum depression, especially for women with a prior history of depression or with a family history of postpartum depression. With all the extra attention being paid to the needs of the baby, the needs of the "mommy" are too often forgotten. In Western industrialized countries, the increased incidence in postpartum depression is probably due to the fact that these countries do not prioritize maternal care and the needs of the mother. Non-Western, nonindustrialized cultures give moms a time of rest after the birth of a child. The mother's primarily responsibility is to nurse the baby as other women pitch in to help her with chores and caring for her baby. This is not a trivial matter of cultural differences. Postpartum depression has serious consequences for the health and well-being of the baby. Our culture is in need of improvement in this area.

MATERNAL BRAIN CHANGES

There is a common belief that motherhood is natural for women and that mothers always feel devoted to their children. It turns out that motherhood is not natural, because caring for a baby requires such a major dedication of physical and emotional resources and attention that the average person is not normally up to the job. So nature intervenes. A mother must develop a new way of seeing, listening, and responding in order to form the kind of relationship her developing child needs. The research shows that this is exactly what a new mom's brain is being rewired to do.

Brain rewiring is partly driven by genetic influences.

A mom must be prepared and *ready to go* as soon as the baby arrives. Therefore, it is built into the human genetic code to biologically and automatically initiate maternal brain rewiring late in pregnancy and continue it during labor, delivery, and nursing. These preparatory brain changes make possible a greater ability to notice and be responsive to the appearance of the baby, the noises of the baby, and the movements the baby makes. This is why if your baby cries in the middle of night, you immediately get up and go find out what's the matter, even if before you had a baby nothing could rouse you out of a deep sleep. The genetically determined brain changes have a short-term and a long-term function. They ensure the newborn's immediate survival. Also, because they turn up the volume on the mother's perceptual and emotional systems, she is more sensitive and attuned to her child for years to come.

Brain rewiring is also driven by experiential influences.

A mother's brain is also getting wired in new ways, experientially. It is a "rule" of neurobiology that experiences that really matter become written into the wiring of the brain. For this reason, the very act of caring for the baby and of being exposed to the baby's sights and sounds leads to

SCIENCE SAYS

Each Mom Is Attuned to Her Own Baby

• When the mother of an infant has her brain scanned, her brain reacts more to the sound of her own baby's cry than to the cry of another baby (Swain, 2011b).
• Being exposed to the baby's odor activates growth of dopamine neurons in the mom's reward system (Lundström et al., 2013).

increased growth of neurons in the mother's brain. The growth in each mother's brain is specifically geared to interacting with her particular baby.

> The amount of growth of these circuits has
> predictive value.

The amount of growth of new circuits in the mother's brain is predictive of the quality of maternal care. The greatest increases are seen in mothers who show high levels of maternal care behaviors and positive perceptions of their baby (P. Kim et al., 2010; Swain, 2011a). A greater amount of growth in a *mom's* brain is predictive of a better long-term outcome in her *child*.

THE CHEMISTRY OF MATERNAL CARE

Oxytocin: The "Calm, Care, and Connect" Hormone

Toward the end of pregnancy and during labor, delivery, and nursing, increased amounts of the hormone *oxytocin* are released by the hypothalamus. Oxytocin's reproductive role is to stimulate uterine contractions and produce milk. In its parenting role, oxytocin supports nurturing maternal behaviors, causes the mother to prioritize care of her baby over all other interests, increases her understanding of her baby's signals, reduces her stress, promotes attachment, and fosters empathy (Domes, Heinrichs, Glascher, et al., 2007; Domes, Heinrichs, Michel, et al., 2007; Ebstein et al., 2009; Leckman et al., 2004; Macdonald & Macdonald, 2010; Swain et al., 2007).

Maternal care, mother–infant touch, and the baby's sensory cues of social bonding all stimulate oxytocin release (Leckman et al., 2004; Swain et al., 2007). When a newborn infant is placed on its mother's chest, its hand movements and suckling stimulate oxytocin release. Mother–infant skin-to-skin contact immediately after birth elevates maternal oxytocin levels, as do breast pumping and breastfeeding. The infant separation cry can trigger an increase of oxytocin receptors in the mother's brain, which prompts the mother to relieve the child's distress (P. Kim et al., 2010). On the other hand, prolonged separation from the infant can downregulate oxytocin activity in the mother's brain (Swain et al., 2007).

Oxytocin improves maternal care by increasing calmness and reducing anxiety, stress, aggression, pain, and even depression (Domes, Heinrichs, Glascher, et al., 2007; Domes, Heinrichs, Michel, et al., 2007).

Fathers also produce oxytocin, but less than mothers. Note, that the same hormone causes mothers and fathers to parent differently. Oxytocin in mothers tends to wire them to be more emotionally responsive and sensitive, whereas in fathers it wires them to be more physical, rough-and-tumble, and to encourage their children to explore the surroundings. These differences sometimes bring up conflict between moms and dads. The science, however, indicates that kids need both of these!

Mothers who describe a good attachment bond with their own mothers prior to the birth of their child (as most mothers do) have higher oxytocin levels in the presence of their baby, do better on tasks that require reflective capacity, and are more motivated to relieve their child's distress when they see their baby looking sad than moms who describe an insecure attachment (see Chapter 6) (Fonagy, Bateman, & Bateman, 2011; P. Kim et al., 2010). Interestingly, when the moms look at the sad face of their baby, those with higher oxytocin feel the sadness and the motivation to relieve the baby's sadness. By contrast, those with lower oxytocin also feel the sadness, but they are not as motivated to relieve the baby's sadness.

The higher oxytocin that most mothers have starts them out with a higher level of motivation and sensitivity and a lower level of emotional distress in their mothering role. The good news is that mothers with lower levels of oxytocin can be helped to improve their reflective capacity and maternal care if help is given nonjudgmentally and with compassion.

Dopamine: The Neurotransmitter for Reward and Motivation

The *dopamine system* is made up of neurons that release the neurotransmitter dopamine in certain sections of the brain. Dopamine plays a role in all forms of pleasure, excitement, and reward. There is a long list of its roles in parenting. Dopamine underlies the positive experience of caring for a child and the desire to do so. It promotes rewiring of the mother's brain in response to the appearance and expressions of her baby. It provides the sense of purpose and focus a mother needs to devote so much of her time and energy to the care of her baby. It gives her a sense of pleasure and reward for all her hard work. It provides the motivation for mothering and the determination to do *whatever it takes* to soothe and care for the baby. It reinforces all the behaviors she uses to care for her baby, which is why caretaking gets easier the more she does it.

Dopamine also plays a role in reducing the stress of caretaking. As a result of dopamine, the infant's cry, which would otherwise be stressful, now activates the reward system instead. This enables the mother to be less stressed and more able to persist in trying to calm and soothe her baby. Your baby can't say, "Thank you, Mommy, for taking care of me." Therefore, nature makes sure that when your baby looks at you, smiles at you, or even cries, your brain is bathed in the reward and perseverance chemical dopamine.

When a mother makes her baby happy, it increases activity in her reward circuitry. If a mom makes her baby *unhappy*, it stimulates her stress system (Mayes et al., 2012). Reflective parenting reassures parents that it's normal and natural for what a mom does to sometimes make her baby upset. This is really important for moms, because if a mom feels too stressed by making her baby upset, it can interfere with her reflective capacity, empathy, and sense of confidence in her role as mother.

Mothers who are emotionally responsive have greater activity in their dopamine reward system when interacting with their baby, whereas mothers who are emotionally dismissive are more likely to activate brain regions associated with pain (Strathearn, 2011). In other words, emotionally responsive mothers have more reward than pain in their role as parent, whereas it is the opposite for mothers who tend to dismiss their child's emotional distress. Scientists propose that one reason for such mothers to be dismissive is that they are trying to get away from what is causing them pain. These mothers can be helped by someone who understands and empathizes with their pain.

*Babies differ in how well they activate
their mother's reward system.*

Dopamine is a mother's gift from her baby for all her hard work. When babies smile, coo, and laugh in response to their mother's caretaking, the

SCIENCE SAYS

It Feels Good to Mother

• A mother's dopamine system is activated when she sees her baby smile, hears her baby cry, or plays with her baby and makes her or him happy, with the greatest increases being in mothers who are highly maternal and have positive perceptions of their baby (P. Kim et al., 2010; Mayes et al., 2012; Strathearn, Fonagy, & Montague, 2008; Swain, 2011a).

extra dopamine released in the mom's brain makes it feel good to mother and provides her the motivation to keep at it, even if it is hard and stressful (Strathearn et al., 2008; Swain et al., 2007). Unfortunately, some babies are not as able to make their moms feel good. Babies born prematurely, or who are ill or who have a difficult temperament, will not be as good at giving their mother the positive cues she is looking for that stimulate her dopamine reward centers. They may not be able to smile as much or to calm down as easily in response to her efforts at making them happy. In the short run, this lack of stimulation to a mother's reward system can deprive her of feeling good and in the long run may even decrease her motivation and caregiving behavior. Therefore, a mother with such a baby is more vulnerable to feeling distressed, angry, or even detached from her baby. She, too, is a mother who will need compassionate and nonjudgmental support and assistance.

Don't blame the mother!

To reiterate, some mothers naturally feel pleasure in comforting a distressed child, which allows them to be empathic and emotionally responsive. Some mothers, however, such as those with poor attachment to their own mothers, may experience pain and stress that make it difficult for them to be emotionally responsive. Some mothers have babies that are easier and therefore more likely to activate a feeling of reward in them. Some mothers, on the other hand, have more difficult babies that make it harder for them to be emotionally responsive. Blaming moms for not being emotionally responsive enough is like blaming a short person for not being able to reach something on a high shelf. Moms who have difficulty in the role of mother need help, not blame; support, not criticism; and empathy, not judgment.

Cortisol: The Hormone for Dealing with Stress

Although it sounds paradoxical, the stress hormone *cortisol* is a key player in preparing the new mother to be able to take on her new role.

SCIENCE SAYS

The Loving Side of Cortisol

First-time mothers with high levels of cortisol can better identify their own infant's odors and engage in higher levels of affectionate contact with the infant.

The release of cortisol heightens her sensitivity to her new baby so that she can be ready at a moment's notice if her baby needs her (P. Kim et al., 2010; Swain, 2011a). Cortisol works in tandem with oxytocin. Stress releases cortisol, which keeps the mother on high alert, and the oxytocin calms her down a bit so that her stress doesn't go overboard.

Unfortunately, chronic stress, such as poverty, family discord, or prolonged illness, impairs cortisol regulation and causes mothers to have reduced sensitivity to the changing states of their baby (Dias-Ferreira et al., 2009). Mothers with postpartum depression have impairments in cortisol and oxytocin production and regulation that result in a reduced investment in forming a relationship with their infant (Swain, 2011a). In fact, if stress is excessive or support is insufficient for any reason, even previously healthy mothers may be prone to developing postpartum depression.

Reflective capacity has a protective effect during times of stress. In the stressful situation of having difficulty soothing a baby, mothers with high reflective capacity persevere in trying to comfort the baby longer than mothers with low reflective capacity (Mayes et al., 2012; Rutherford, Williams, Moy, Mayes, & Johns, 2011). This is because mothers with high reflective capacity have a higher tolerance for stress.

Too many mothers have the misguided impression that they should be able to remain cool and collected when their child is acting up or being difficult. This is a myth. Many parents say things like, "I look around. No one else seems to be having such a hard time." This is simply not true. Neuroscience demonstrates that being stressed is adaptive as long as it is not too extreme. The truth is that all mothers experience stress, even if you can't see it.

PARENT, BE SENSITIVE TO THYSELF

Mothers are people too! They don't do well if they don't get enough rest and food and time to go to the bathroom. Nature understands that even parents of little babies can be grumpy and irritable at times and are sometimes preoccupied with adult issues. The genetic code is organized for dealing with the generally expected environment. The usual environment, even for a tiny baby growing up in the best of circumstances, is not expected to always be perfect. For this reason, embedded within the child's developing brain is the capacity for managing even if a parent is not always exactly, perfectly sensitive all the time. There is some leeway in the baby.

The infant brain is designed to actually function better with some degree of misattunement along with attunement. Some degree of maternal disinterest or boredom or even annoyance is not going to permanently harm a baby. In general, a mom's heightened sensitivity to what is going on with the baby will be enough to smooth over moments of insensitivity, as long as they are not extreme.

The neurobiology of maternal care launches a mother into her new role. But, after that initial boost, she must take an active role in sustaining a basically warm, sensitive, and empathic attitude toward her child. As a parent, you will be in a much better position to sustain this attitude if you take the same attitude toward yourself. Yes, of course, as a parent you may interrupt your sleep but not your child's sleep. You will interrupt your meal in order to feed your child. You will defer the vacation you prefer for one that works better with kids. These things are part of what parents do. But the point is that you will do this better if you also have a kind and caring attitude about your own emotions and your own needs. It will help you be more able to reliably provide kindness and caring to your child.

Parenting, despite all the hype, is not supposed to be a totally selfless endeavor. One of the most common reasons for parents to have difficulty with being comforting, empathic, validating, understanding, accepting, and supportive of their child is that they have difficulty being this way in relationship to themselves. Parents who have rejecting, critical, harsh, or judgmental attitudes toward their own emotions are more likely to have difficulty when it comes to their children's emotions. The words of support these parents need are "Be kinder to yourself!" You might call it *parent first-aid*. The parent who is feeling overly harsh in regard to a child's behavior or emotional needs first needs help being less harsh about their own behavior and emotional needs. Parents, you are so important to your children that in many respects you must take as good care of yourself as you take of your child.

REFLECTIVE CAPACITY FOR
ALL YOUR RELATIONSHIPS

Using your reflective capacity is not limited to being a reflective parent. All your relationships will be smoother if you can see the other person's perspective as well as your own. Couples raising a child together have to be extra reflective with each other. In most cases, both parents care equally about the child and both have a vision of how things are supposed to go. However, usually both bring a slightly different approach. Parenting couples have to try as hard as they can to see the other's point of view. Too many happy and loving marriages and other parenting partnerships end up having so much extra conflict because each partner gets bogged down in thinking their own perspective is the right one or the best one. Parents don't have to see eye to eye on everything, but they do have to see where the other person is coming from and to respect and value their viewpoint. Generally, parent couples are better able to compromise and find agreement if each parent feels understood by the other parent.

New parents attract the attention of everyone around them. It seems that everyone has an opinion about how you should parent. Whether what others offer is out of caring and helpfulness or out of criticism, it is best not to let what others say make you start to doubt yourself. Sometimes even the most caring or loving friend or family member can make you feel judged, misunderstood, or anxious. This is where reflective capacity can assist you. Remember that everything a person does or says is connected to something going on inside their mind. This means that, very often, what other people tell you is more about what is going on inside them and less about what would really be right for you and your child. They are not trying to be unhelpful or hurtful. It is just that babies have a way of heightening everyone's inner emotions. Your parents, the baby's grandparents, will have their needs; your friends will have theirs; and your siblings will have theirs. All these inputs and reactions from other people can be hard to juggle. Parents do need help and advice; they have never done this before, so some of the input is welcome. But by remaining as reflective as possible, you will be able to maintain a good balance between following what you believe and taking advice from others when it makes sense to you. You are the best expert on your child.

STORIES OF PARENTS AND CHILDREN

- Alisha and her husband Oliver waited a long time before they decided to have a baby because they were so focused on their busy careers. Alisha worried because she didn't particularly enjoy her friends' babies and was concerned that she would be bored to death staying at home all day. Her plan was to go back to work as quickly as possible. But much to her shock and amazement, when her son Marcus arrived, she was smitten and totally devoted to him. Oliver, who was also in love with and devoted to his son, actually began to worry a bit. It seemed to him that his previously intelligent and interesting wife had disappeared and had been replaced by a woman who could talk about diapers, sore nipples, and the pros and cons of sleep training for hours on end. But all that had really happened was that Alisha's brain was aglow with oxytocin and dopamine. She was in a passionate love affair with her baby and a fierce mother lion protecting her cub.

- Meagan was looking forward to motherhood and envisioned herself as a loving and devoted caretaker. When her daughter, Nicki, had difficulty with breastfeeding and did not seem to be gaining enough weight, Meagan threw herself into getting help with nursing. It was not clear whether Nicki was having difficulty with suckling or whether Meagan was simply not producing enough milk. No one really could figure it out. But in the end, when Nicki was seven weeks old, the pediatrician recommended that Meagan supplement the breast with a bottle after each feeding, "just to be on the safe side." Nicki quickly lost interest in nursing and hungrily devoured the bottles. Meagan's husband and family were relieved to see the baby start to gain weight, but Meagan became depressed. She felt like a failure and started to withdraw from the baby, finding all kinds of excuses to have her husband or her mother do the feedings. Probably Meagan's natural sources of oxytocin and dopamine were reduced. Fortunately, Meagan and Nicki were lucky. Meagan's husband and sister were quick to reassure Meagan that she was not a failure and that she was a wonderful mother and that Nicki adored her. Meagan came around. She was able to see that her daughter was flourishing on the bottle and needed her to see it as a positive thing. Her perspective became more optimistic and her mood once again became exuberant and loving.

- Rhonda gave birth to fraternal twin boys, Duane and Colton, who arrived one month prematurely but had no other medical problems and thus went home from the hospital quickly. Duane was a calm, easy-to-please baby and Rhonda got a great deal of pleasure from caring for him. Colton, on the other hand, was very irritable and difficult to soothe. Rhonda felt rejected by Colton, who made her feel inadequate. When Rhonda talked about Colton, she described him as a burden and was not sure she even loved him. It is likely that the premature birth interfered with the usual late-pregnancy burst of oxytocin. The fact that Colton did not signal positive responses to his mother's efforts also deprived Rhonda of sufficient dopamine when caring for him. At first, Rhonda rejected getting any help because it only made her feel as if it was all her fault and as if she was a failure as a mother. But, fortunately, a highly sensitive pediatrician was able to explain that Colton had a really difficult temperament that would test any mother's maternal instincts. In a reflective parenting group, Rhonda reflected on the fact that she had felt rejected by her own mother, who was critical and hard to please. The emotional pain of rejection from the past was reactivated in the present in Rhonda's relationship with her baby. Rhonda was told that her infant son's nervous system was wired in a way that made it harder for him to be comforted. This helped Rhonda to stop taking it so personally when her baby cried as she tried hard to soothe him.

PUTTING IT INTO WORDS

- **A mother talking about her new baby.** "I didn't think it was possible for me to love anyone like I love my baby. All I think about is her. All I want to do is be with her. Nothing else matters."
- **A new father talking about his new baby.** "I love her so much that it shocks even me. She is so tiny, but I just love jiggling her or holding her up in the air. It upsets my wife. It makes her anxious, but I want to protect her as much as my wife does, and I know I will never let her fall. My wife sometimes complains that all my playing with her is preventing her from falling asleep at bedtime. But I think babies need some energetic play. It's good for them."
- **A mother being woken out of a sound sleep by her crying baby.** "The baby is crying. Darn! I am so tired. I really don't want to get up! But the poor little thing needs me. I better go and find out what's the matter."

TAKE-HOME LESSONS: JUST STARTING OUT WITH A NEW INFANT

- Whenever you start to worry that you don't know what you're doing, remind yourself that nature doesn't require you to be skilled at parenting right away. In fact, nature kicks in just enough instinct so that you're on the right track most of the time. Remind yourself that the rest of what you need to know about your baby will develop over time as you learn about who this new person is, what their unique personality and needs are, and what works and doesn't work for them. Your brain connections will build up as you learn.

- If you feel overwhelmed, notice whether you are accepting or judgmental of yourself. Do you feel silly for getting overwhelmed, or are you able to look for and receive support? Most parents are shocked at how much time and energy is required to take care of a new baby. This is not the time to prove what a good mother you are by doing it all yourself. And if you notice yourself getting depressed, don't try to hide it. Let others in and be open to getting professional help if necessary.

- Practice establishing your family boundaries. You may disappoint people. Everyone wants to see you and the baby, and you want to be nice to everyone. But you need to protect yourself from doing too much and getting spread too thin. You can be kind and gracious toward people who offer to help, but if their help is not helpful, it's OK to decline. If they get their feelings hurt, you can say that you didn't mean to be hurtful or rejecting but that right now you need to do what's best for you and your baby. Grandparents can be especially sensitive. They can easily feel left out or be annoyed that you don't want all of their "amazing help." It's an adjustment period for all of you. It's important to set your boundaries as the parent, but also to accept that it will take all of you time to learn new ways of interacting with one another. You will probably do better at establishing your boundaries if you do it by also being empathic about where the grandparents are coming from.

- Practice accepting that sometimes babies are just fussy and there isn't much you can do to soothe them. Yes, usually their distress signals mean that they are tired or hungry, need a diaper change, want to be held, want to be rocked or soothed, or want to be a little social and look at you. But sometimes it takes a while to figure it out, and sometimes nothing works. Eventually you will get better at reading their cues. Even when babies are fussy and you can't do anything to soothe them, there is something you can do. You can tolerate their fussiness and let them know that you are there and trying to be of help and that they will get through it. Nature leaves room for babies to be fussy. Just don't take it personally or think it has anything to do with you not being a good parent.
- Remember that primary maternal preoccupation is a real thing. Being in the throes of primary maternal preoccupation is a bit like being in an altered state of consciousness. Try to remember that nature has put you there for a reason. Try to reassure yourself and everyone else that you will come out of it, but that for the time being people have to be supportive and patient with you.

SIX

The Brain and Attachment

Wired for Connection

BRAIN BASICS

The more an experience relates to survival, the more frequently it occurs, and the earlier in life it happens, the better its chances of becoming deeply encoded into the wiring of the brain. Attachment is such an experience. Therefore, the circuitry of attachment will have a profound—even lifelong—impact on a person.

WHAT HAPPENS WHEN MOTHERS AND BABIES INTERACT

The bond of attachment is not present either at birth or even within the first few months of life. On average, it takes about nine months to fully develop. Basically, attachment is the result of how well the mother can reliably keep the baby well regulated. *Regulation* means being responsive to the baby's needs in such a way as to keep the baby's body physiology and level of arousal in a state of equilibrium. It takes time for the bond to develop because it takes time for the baby to learn what to expect. Is the mother a reliable source of regulation or not? If she is reliable enough, what is called a *secure attachment* bond emerges that provides the baby with a sense of safety and comfort and the knowledge that there is always

SCIENCE SAYS

Attachment Makes People Feel Safer and Feel Less Pain

When subjects view an attachment figure during a threatening experience like physical pain, they report feeling less pain than when they are not viewing the attachment figure. Their brain scans show increased activity in regions associated with safety signaling and decreased activity in regions associated with pain processing (Eisenberger et al., 2011).

someone to turn to in times of need (Ainsworth, Blehar, Waters, & Wall, 1978; Waters, Hamilton, & Weinfield, 2000). *Reliably* means "often enough" or responsive most of the time. It does not mean perfect! In other words, the baby learns that the mother is basically dependable, even if she messes up a bit now and then (Fonagy & Target, 2007).

Not coincidentally, the attachment bond appears just at the time the baby becomes more mobile and interested in venturing out to explore a wider environment. At this point, the baby needs to know who they can count on if they need help—who is the safe harbor to return to if they venture too far. A secure bond of attachment provides a safe haven from which the child can explore and to which the child can return when they need to reconnect. The secure attachment is the starting point from which a child feels safe and confident enough to launch out into the rest of life. A secure bond is elastic in that it supports the baby's dependency and holds mother and baby close but also can stretch to allow for independence and separateness. Secure attachment gives a child an inner sense of well-being, grounding, worthiness, and being understood. Attachment is the feeling that there is a safe haven to return to in times of need, that one is not alone, and that others can be depended on to help. It also fosters the child's zest, curiosity, and resiliency in growing up.

Here is an illustration of secure attachment: After Dorothy has her adventures in the Land of Oz, the good witch reassures her that all she has to do is click her ruby slippers together and say over and over, "There is no place like home. There is no place like home!" When she opens her eyes, she is back in Kansas with her loving Aunt Em and Uncle Henry.

Attachment is not about making sure your child is happy all the time. Children don't need to be happy all the time! Children get upset, distressed, disappointed, and sad. They need room to have their feelings. Emotions are just as much a part of us as our arms and legs. If a child's negative emotions are too big and overwhelming, of course you want to help your child reduce them. But acknowledge the feelings *before* you try to help them modify their feelings. They need to know that *you know* what they feel. It helps them be more open to calming down. The attachment bond is the child's template for how relationships in general can be expected to go. With a secure attachment, a child will develop a basic sense of trust in others, which will enhance their ability to form positive relationships with other people.

REGULATION

Regulation means keeping the baby's behavior, body physiology, and emotional arousal within a healthy range of equilibrium most of the time. Regulation is a dynamic process. Think of a boat swaying from side to side. As the boat sways to one side, regulation means bringing the boat more upright so that it does not tip over. To be regulated does not mean the boat is always in an upright position. It means that the boat can sway from side to side and that with each sway, the captain of the boat brings it back toward the midline. Another example is a thermostat set to 70 degrees. When the room temperature goes above 70 degrees, the thermostat turns *on* the air conditioner, and when the room temperature goes below 70 degrees, the air conditioner turns *off*.

Right from the beginning, mothers and babies work together to keep the baby regulated (Beebe et al., 2010). For example, when a baby is hungry, the mother feeds the baby. When the baby is sated, the baby pulls away from the nipple. Social engagement between mothers and their babies is another illustration of this co-regulation process. Mothers and their four-month-old babies love to look at each other, smile and "talk" or vocalize to each other, and share their positive emotion with each other. During these emotional exchanges, they synchronize the pitch and frequency of their vocalizations and synchronize how they move, such as how they touch, how big they smile, and how wide they open their eyes. When the emotional excitement goes up too high, the baby turns his or her gaze away from the mother as a signal to the mother to stop stimulating the baby. The emotionally responsive mother reads the cue and turns her gaze away as well. In this way, the mother regulates the baby by bringing her baby's arousal state back down to equilibrium. Mothers and babies do this co-regulation dance over and over. They go up. They go down. Up and down.

As a result of these co-regulated interactions, infants gradually learn to independently regulate their emotions (Beebe et al., 2010; MacLean et al., 2014). The ability of a baby to synchronize with her or his mother in infancy correlates with better self-regulation at two, four, and six years of age. Children learn to regulate themselves as their mother once regulated them. The attachment bond mediates the mother's provision of regulation for the child and becomes the template for the child's eventual self-regulation.

Match-Mismatch-Repair

When scientists look really closely at how moms and babies interact, they observe that regulation proceeds in a somewhat bumpy fashion. Moms go through regular cycles of emotional attunement, misattunement, and reattunement with their baby. There are regular cycles of matching each other's nonverbal expressions, mismatching them, and repairing by rematching them again (Beebe et al., 2010; Tronick, 2007). When moms are too often out of sync with their babies or too often in sync with them, the security of the attachment can be compromised.

It should relieve parents to know there is a "rule of thirds" associated with a more secure attachment style and greater resilience in babies. Securely attached mothers and babies are in sync only about a third of the time, out of sync a third of the time, and trying to get back in sync a third of the time. As a parent, you don't have to be attuned to your baby all the time. You can't. No one can. And it wouldn't even be good to try. The fluid shifting between states of match-mismatch-repair is what nature has designed as best for children. But if you and your child have a big rupture in your relationship, for whatever reason, it is essential to find a way to repair the bond. It doesn't have to happen immediately—just relatively soon.

PREDICTABILITY

When a mom is reliable in providing emotional responsiveness, the baby learns to predict that the mom will be responsive. For example, a baby learns to *predict* that "if we are smiling happily together, Mommy will keep smiling with me until I let her know I am ready to stop" (Tronick, 2007). If what the baby predicts doesn't occur, the baby becomes upset. This is painfully illustrated by the "still face" experiment with babies three months, six months, and nine months of age. The moms are told to play with their babies as they would at home. Then the mother is told to keep her face perfectly still. The baby nevertheless still *expects* the mother to be responsive, as evidenced by the fact that the baby keeps trying harder and harder to reengage the mother. If the "still face" goes on for too long, the baby gives up and may lapse into despondency and immobility. It is a very hard experiment to watch, and certainly don't try this at home!

Babies don't require parents to be perfectly predictable. In fact, when moms move in and out of sync with their baby, it provides a learning experience for the child that builds resiliency. For example, some infants are not as distressed by the "still face" as other infants. It turns out that these babies have mothers who not only are more responsive to the baby but also have more times when they are repairing an emotionally mis-matched state with their baby. With some degree of fluctuation in responsiveness, babies learn that there can be new and different ways to connect with the important people in their life. They learn to trust that in important relationships, it is OK if anger, conflict, and miscommuni-cation happen and that repair is possible. Having enough of the repeated *match-mismatch-repair* with their parents as youngsters makes people more resilient to the reality that out in the world, not everyone will always be perfectly attuned with them and not everyone will repair the misattunement. It is as if these early experiences of match-mismatch-re-pair are creating a protective shield against the slings and arrows your child is bound to experience in life.

What is called *stranger anxiety* is not so much about the person being a stranger as it is that they are unpredictable, and this makes the baby upset. They don't have the predicted face. They do not engage with the baby in the way the baby has come to expect. This "violation" of predict-ability causes distress in the baby, which is what makes the baby very cautious in the presence of unfamiliar people and what makes the baby hold on to the source of good predictability, that is, the primary attach-ment figure. Once the "stranger" becomes familiar and predictable, the child is then perfectly happy to play.

Attachment identifies you as your child's guide.

The child's attachment figures are the main people the child looks to for empathy and understanding, for clarification about what is going on, and for guidance as to what the child should do in response to what is going on and who to trust in the absence of the parent. In times of separations, such as going off to kindergarten, the child will look to the parent for signs of guidance, such as "Is this a safe place?" "Am I going to be OK here?" "Who should I go to if I need help?"

When attachment kicks in, some children may seem
more difficult.

It can confuse parents when an infant who previously was completely at ease with unfamiliar people, would go eagerly into new situations, or would go to sleep with ease is now showing signs of hesitation, caution, or even fear. This is because, along with their new motor prowess in crawling or beginning to take a few steps, they also have a new awareness of what being separated from Mommy and Daddy actually means. Reflective parenting encourages parents to look for the positive side. In this case, the new caution or hesitancy is a positive sign of the growing infant's greater maturity.

HOW MANY ATTACHMENTS
DOES IT TAKE?

Babies can form a number of attachments. However, babies tend to select a *primary attachment figure*. This person will be the one the baby tends to strongly prefer to help them in times of distress. They can still be cared for by a number of people and do fine, but there is nevertheless typically one person that is their go-to person, especially when they are sick, cranky, tired, or distressed.

When a baby is sick or very tired and Daddy and Mommy are both there, the baby may want to reach out only to Mommy—or sometimes it might be Daddy. The other parent can mistake it as meaning they love one parent more than the other and experience it as a personal rejection. For the baby, however, attachment is *not* about love! No one should take it personally when the infant prefers the other parent in times of distress. It should be taken as a sign of growth, of the child's having learned that people are different in how they manage his or her distress. Sometimes it's about knowing who is around more or who is more at ease calming them down. Sometimes it is a mystery, such as when both parents work and both parents are involved in the care of the baby.

Sometimes moms feel hurt if the baby shows signs of distress when making the transition from their nanny or childcare provider back to her when she comes home, even if she is the primary attachment person. Moms, dads, babysitters, grandmas, and grandpas all need to learn not to take any of this personally. It may feel painful, for example, when the baby looks sad when the nanny goes home. But remember that it has nothing to do with the baby loving the nanny more.

ATTACHMENT FLUCTUATES FROM BACKGROUND TO FOREGROUND

For the most part, the attachment system is always there but remains quiescent, in the background, somewhat the way a floor holds you up without you even noticing it. When the baby is comfortable and calm, the baby's background attachment provides a sense of ease that is unobtrusive. With that emotional floor in place, babies are free to play, socialize, look around, and explore. It is only under threatening conditions of some sort that the attachment system gets activated and moves into the foreground. Common examples are bedtime and other times of separation, when unfamiliar people are around, and being in new surroundings. Attachment returns to the background once the child feels safe. This is why, if your child is calm and content, they don't need constant attention or reassurance that you're there. Even young babies need some downtime to just *be*—time to just look around or explore their fingers. If they do feel distressed or threatened, their attachment system will kick in and they will signal their need for you.

The attachment bond continues throughout childhood and adolescence and into adulthood. But as the child gets older, it comes into the foreground less frequently and with less intensity.

SOMETIMES ATTACHMENT GOES AWRY

If there is difficulty in the attachment process, it isn't always clear what the source of the difficulty is. Sometimes the parent is not able to provide adequate and reliable comfort and soothing to the baby during times of distress, making it less likely that the baby will feel safe enough to move out into the world and explore. Sometimes factors on the baby's side may be the source of the difficulty. Some babies are more sensitive and reactive or more irritable and difficult to soothe. Sensitive, reactive babies may need more comfort, soothing, and patience from the parent than the usual baby. Irritable babies have a harder time using the parent as a source of safety and comfort. These babies often require a parent with greater-than-average perseverance and tolerance in the face of distress. Often, in these cases, the parent must be even more reflective than usual.

We are wired for life to our early attachment figures. If you had difficulties with your own parent, even if you feel you have overcome them, you may to this day find yourself influenced by old feelings from your childhood. For example, you may experience feeling harshly judged or inadequate and be more susceptible to feeling overly concerned about what others think—even your child. These leftover feelings from the past are normal and common but require reflective capacity to keep them from spilling over too much into your relationship with your child. Let's say your parents made you feel unlovable. You can use your reflective capacity to pay more attention to your child's cues that he or she loves you and wants you.

Some parents feel ashamed that the past still has a grip on them. Yes, the past was long ago, but the attachment process gets deeply carved into a person's brain circuitry. It is just how brains get wired. Don't be ashamed about it. You can use your reflective capacity to modulate and try to counteract your feelings from the past. But don't expect to totally extinguish the past.

Attachment Styles

Parents and babies tend to fall into patterns of how they relate to one another when the infant is distressed. The pattern is called the *attachment style*. The mom's attachment style is related to how emotionally responsive she is to her child's distress. The baby's style is related to how much he or she is able to use the mother as a source of comfort. A mother's attachment style will be influenced by her psychological makeup and her own experiences as a child. The baby's attachment style is colored by the baby's temperament and the baby's ability to adapt (Lyons-Ruth & Spielman, 2004). The brain is organized for adapting. Even a little baby's brain can adapt to some degree to these kinds of differences in moms. As long as parents avoid the extremes, such as being way too emotional or harsh or detached, things tend to go well and parent and child form a healthy attachment.

The majority of moms and babies have secure attachment. A smaller number have a type of insecure attachment. An even smaller number have disorganized attachment. The mother's attachment style has some influence on the baby's attachment style.

The Adult Attachment Styles

A parent's attachment style can be measured in a structured research interview, called the Adult Attachment Interview (Fonagy et al., 2011), in which the parent talks about their relationship with their own parent.

Secure Attachment in the Mother
A *securely attached* mom is reliably responsive to her infant's distress and is competent at soothing her baby. She will be more likely to have a baby who also has *secure attachment*.

Insecure Dismissive or Preoccupied Attachment in the Mother
A *dismissive* mother is less emotionally responsive—even somewhat distant or rejecting toward her baby's distress. She will tend to downplay

the infant's distress or try to get the child not to show distress. We all do this kind of thing from time to time, but it can be problematic for kids when it is a regularly repeated pattern. These moms are more likely to have babies with *insecure avoidant attachment*.

Preoccupied mothers are responsive but have a regular pattern of being anxious about their child's distress and as a result can have more difficulty soothing the child. These moms show distress when the baby is distressed, both because they are anxious and also because that is how they express their empathy. Because these mothers are overly anxious and emotional, that can be intrusive in their child's life, such as swooping in too quickly to "fix the situation" before allowing the child any time to manage on their own. They are more likely to have babies with *insecure ambivalent attachment*.

While both of these types of insecurely attached moms generally need some extra help, they should not be blamed or shamed for how they are being. More often than not, they are parenting the way they were parented. They typically have difficulty tolerating their child's distress. Dismissive moms use distance to manage the child's distress, and preoccupied moms use overprotection and overresponsiveness to try to make the baby's distress go away. Both types of moms can be helped, but only when others are compassionate and understand where they are coming from.

Disorganized Attachment in the Mother

In secure attachment and even in both types of insecure attachment, how the parent behaves tends to be highly predictable. Even if the mother is emotionally less than or more than what the baby needs, at least she is less or more in a predictable way. Even with an insecurely attached mom, her predictability at least creates some degree of security for the baby. Therefore, the baby knows what to expect and can develop some type of coping strategies for dealing with her typical responses.

Moms with *disorganized attachment* will unpredictably vacillate between positive and negative emotions, between being loving and being hostile, between drawing the baby in and rejecting the baby—and sometimes will do both at the same time. This lack of predictability is harmful to the baby. Moms with disorganized attachment tend to have a history of trauma—perhaps the early loss of a primary attachment figure or some type of abuse that they have not yet worked out or recovered from. These are the parents who are most difficult to help, and they typically need the most services. But they can be helped. That's the good news.

The Benefits of the Insecure Attachment Styles

In the long run of life, even kids with parents who are dismissive or preoccupied can do well as long as the parent is not too extreme. The truth is that there are benefits to the dismissive and the preoccupied parenting patterns. Preoccupied moms are really good at expressing caring and closeness, whereas dismissive moms are really good at promoting resiliency and self-sufficiency. A reflective approach emphasizes that as long as they aren't going to extremes, parents can feel good about their parenting even if they have features of being dismissive or preoccupied.

Infant Attachment Styles

An infant's attachment style is measured using a research protocol called the "strange situation," during which a baby is first separated from and then reunited with his or her mother on two separate occasions (Waters et al., 2000). Infants show different patterns in how well they use their mother as a source of safety, soothing, and comfort. Their attachment style is based primarily on their behavior and emotional state when they reunite with their mother.

Secure Attachment

A baby with *secure attachment* is distressed when their mother leaves; when she returns, they are positive and happy and go to her. They are easily soothed by her and are soon ready to get down from her lap and start to play again. The moms of these babies tend to easily empathize with their child's distress, but they are able to remain relatively calm themselves as they express their empathy and try to soothe their child.

The mom is reliable as someone to reach out to and get help from, and the baby feels free to express distress. It is proposed that these babies do better in life because they form a view of others as being helpful while viewing themselves as worthy of being helped (Jacobsen & Hofmann, 1997). Most babies are securely attached.

Insecure Avoidant Attachment in the Infant

Approximately 15 percent of middle-class, home-reared one-year-olds are categorized as having an *insecure avoidant attachment*. These babies show hardly any *outward* sign of distress when their mother leaves, and they are less likely to seek her out for comfort when she returns. Their moms are often the dismissive type who either overly downplay or do not respond to their infants' open expression of distress. It is as if, because the mom is not a reliable comforter, the baby is not as free to openly express distress and resorts to dampening down his or her emotional needs. The theory is that these babies are adapting to a mom who is not warmly expressive and may even be uncomfortable with the open expression of emotion. As a result, they use a coping strategy of pushing down and holding in their feelings more. Thus, these babies have learned how to not need someone so much and therefore don't look bothered when they are separated. It is proposed that these kids can have more difficulty in life because they tend to think of themselves as unworthy and unacceptable (Larose & Bernier, 2001).

Insecure Ambivalent Attachment in the Infant

Babies with *insecure ambivalent attachment* show signs of intense distress when their mother leaves. When she returns, the baby approaches her but resists contact and may even push her away. Sometimes the baby goes to the mom but then withdraws from her, hence the term *ambivalent*. These babies have difficulty being soothed and comforted and often cling, reluctant to do any further exploring. They may continue to cry despite the fact that the mom is back and trying to be comforting. It can take them a while to settle back down. The theory is that these babies have developed a coping strategy for adapting to

SCIENCE SAYS

The Long Run of Life Is More Difficult If You Start Out Insecure

• Children who have an insecure attachment do not tend to do as well over the course of their life as do kids with a secure attachment. For example, a baby categorized in infancy as having an insecure attachment is more likely to have a larger *amygdala* in adulthood, which can cause him or her to be overly fearful (Moutsiana et al., 2015).

• Babies with avoidant attachment show little to no signs of distress outwardly, but inwardly, at a biological level, they show a high state of arousal (Gander & Buccheim, 2015). This suggests that it is more adaptive to allow children to show their distress, at least to some degree, so that they can develop skills for calming their bodies.

who their mom is. These moms connect to their babies through anxiety and distress. Therefore, the baby also connects to the mom through anxiety and distress. In a sense, it is what these moms are more comfortable with, but the side effect is that their babies take a little longer to calm down. It is as if these babies know their anxious moms are going to make them feel anxious too. They need her, but it's not always so *comfy* being close to her. Ambivalent children tend to have a negative self-image and exaggerate their emotional responses as a way to gain attention (Kobak, 1993).

Disorganized Attachment in the Infant

Moms with a history of unresolved loss or trauma are more likely to have an infant with disorganized attachment. These babies show conflict around closeness and distance, often flipping back and forth between approach and distancing behaviors or even doing both at the same time.

This is a high-risk and serious situation. The moms and babies will need lots of extra help. Fortunately, this category is the smallest, but these parents and children probably are the most costly for society in the long run. These are the kids who are more likely to go on to develop major psychological, social, and academic problems and are more likely to become involved with the law and to have difficulty becoming employed. They are the most difficult to treat. Intervening early in these cases is also costly, but it probably saves society money in the long run in the form of reduced mental health, welfare, and even prison costs (Shonkoff & Phillips, 2000).

Outside the Neat Categories

A baby can be secure with one parent and insecure with another. Attachment security can also change with circumstances. An extremely stressful situation can overwhelm a securely attached parent's resources so that they no longer can provide the reliable emotional responsiveness they once were able to. Some parents can be warm and responsive to positive emotions and rejecting only of negative ones. Some parents are better with babies and some with older children. In fact, in some cultures it is more the norm for a parent to have a somewhat dismissive style.

The role of personality or temperament can influence attachment security, especially if there is a strong contrast between the baby's temperament and the parent's. A highly gregarious parent may be more disappointed or impatient with a shy baby who is slow to warm up, whereas a shy parent who is slow to warm up may be more irritable or anxious with a highly gregarious baby. Fortunately, for long-term health, babies need only one secure attachment. If the baby is insecure with the mom or the dad, the other parent can fill in. Finally, many parents show a mixture of styles depending on the situation.

THE NEUROBIOLOGY OF ATTACHMENT

A primary purpose of the brain is to meet our physical, emotional, and social needs. At its most basic, the brain's attachment system is designed to keep mothers and babies close together so that the mother can meet the baby's needs, as well as her own need to care for her baby, in a tender, nurturing way (Lyons-Ruth & Spielman, 2004). For the most part, the brain regions and mechanisms involved in maternal care are also involved in attachment.

Dopamine: Reward-Seeking and Motivation

Dopamine is what gives us the oomph to get off the couch. It provides the motivation to seek out *rewards*, or anything that meets our needs (e.g., food, sex, achievement, social connection) and makes us feel good. Dopamine is released by the reward itself, but it is released even more during the search for the reward. That's why it feels good not just to eat or achieve, but also to make the effort to obtain food or achieve. Dopamine underlies the formation of the habits we form to fulfill our needs.

Dopamine provides the urge for mothers and babies to be close to each other, and it's why they eventually form regular habits, or "styles," of how they stay close. Dopamine is what makes moms hurry to get home from work and babies to race across the room to greet her when she arrives.

There are dopamine differences between moms who are securely attached and moms who have insecure, dismissive attachment. Securely attached moms tend to have *higher* dopamine reward activity when they interact with their babies, whereas moms with dismissive attachment have *lower* activity in dopamine circuits. As a result of their higher dopamine activity, moms with secure attachment tend to feel and express more pleasure and show higher levels of motivation than do moms who have a dismissive style of attachment. Securely attached moms demonstrate this higher dopamine not only when their baby is smiling, but also when the baby is crying! This gives them more stick-to-itiveness in trying to soothe their crying infant. By contrast, moms with a dismissive style also respond to their baby's smile, but in a more dialed down and rational way, presumably because of their lower dopamine response.

SCIENCE SAYS

Brain Differences and Attachment Style Differences

• When secure moms see their baby smile or cry, they have higher activity in their dopamine reward, mentalizing, mirror, and limbic systems (i.e., the emotional centers). Moms with an insecure dismissive style show higher activity in the *dorsal prefrontal cortex*, a part of the brain associated with rational thinking.

• When moms with secure attachment play with their baby, they show higher activity in their *hypothalamus* (which produces oxytocin and is a stress regulation center) and *nucleus accumbens* (a dopamine reward center) and release higher levels of oxytocin into the brain and body. On the other hand, moms with an insecure, dismissive style of attachment show lower levels of activity in all these same regions when they play with their baby.

Cortisol: Coping and Resilience

Cortisol is called the *stress* hormone. It should be called the *coping* hormone, however, because it provides the brain and the body with resources for managing stress.

When a mom and her baby are separated, the cortisol-producing system in each of them activates feelings and behaviors of distress and releases the energy they will need in their efforts to reunite. It is cortisol production that causes both the baby's cry of distress and feelings of distress in the mom when she hears the cry. When the separation distress is relieved, cortisol production shuts off in both of them. Although no one thing ensures that a child will do well in life, your ability to help regulate your baby's emotions and stress builds your child's resilience and plays a very big role in his or her ultimate well-being.

Endorphins: Pain Relief and Comfort

Endorphins are best known as the brain's natural pain reliever, because they work the same way as opiate drugs like heroin and morphine. Endorphins are released whenever a person achieves or consumes a pleasurable reward, such as eating ice cream, having sex, or swallowing a Vicodin (Panksepp, 1998). If dopamine provides the oomph and excitement in seeking out rewards, endorphins provide the relaxed satisfaction of partaking in them. In parenting, endorphins are released during nursing and whenever a mom and her baby are reunited after a separation. The endorphins released in the mother's brain and in the baby's brain when they are reunited after a separation are the basis of what is referred to as *reunion comfort*. Once the pair are reunited, the endorphins shut off the dopamine system. Endorphins are also released when the mom and baby express physical affection toward one another. In other words, the comfort of reunions and affection causes moms and babies to literally become addicted to one another, but in a good way.

Endorphins enhance memory and learning about *what* is rewarding and *how* and *where* to obtain rewards (Panksepp, 1998). This is why moms and babies become so adept at knowing how to make each other feel good. When babies are with their moms, endorphins create a library of "emotional memories" regarding what their body feels like in terms of things like heart rate, respiratory rate, and tension, shaping the baby's expectations regarding comfort and well-being in relationships in general. Dopamine and endorphins lay the groundwork for what infants come to expect from other people in the future and contribute to the habits they will form in responding to emotional and physical situations.

Infants who have mothers who are sufficiently affectionate, who are able to soothe and comfort them during times of distress, and who are effective in managing separations and reunions with them are much more likely to trust other people and expect relationships to be positive. When babies don't get this, they are less trusting and tend to expect relationships to go poorly.

SCIENCE SAYS

*Dads with Higher Oxytocin Levels Are More
Socially Interactive with Their Babies*

The benefits of higher oxytocin levels apply to dads as well. When oxytocin is administered to dads, they show an increase in key parenting behaviors, including more touching and social reciprocity. Interestingly, this results in higher oxytocin levels in the babies as well (Wiseman, Zagoory-Sharon, & Feldman, 2012).

Oxytocin: Caring and Connecting

Oxytocin plays an important role in attachment (Fonagy et al., 2011). Moms with higher oxytocin levels are more likely to have secure attachment and higher reflective capacity. While all moms feel upset when their baby is upset, moms with higher oxytocin levels can deal with their baby's distress in a calmer, more empathic way and are thus more effective in soothing their baby.

Attachment, Pain, and Pain Relief

There is an almost universal tendency to use physical pain words to describe the pain of social separation: "My heart aches." "I have a broken heart." "It was a knife to my heart." Pain is pain, no matter the source. The pain of social rejection shares circuitry with physical pain in the *anterior cingulate cortex.* The worse the social rejection feels, the greater the level of anterior cingulate activity (Eisenberger, 2012). Social support, on the other hand, alleviates both social pain and physical pain (Panksepp, 1998). For example, when receiving a small shock, subjects in long-term romantic relationships report less pain and show reduced activity in the pain centers as long as they either hold their partner's hand or view pictures of their partner (Eisenberger et al., 2011).

Oxytocin plays a role in why moms differ in how much emotional pain they experience in the face of their infant's distress. Moms with secure attachment show higher oxytocin levels in their blood when they see their baby sad (Fonagy et al., 2011). Higher oxytocin allows a mom to feel her baby's sad feelings, but not so much that she is so upset that she can't help her baby. By contrast, moms with insecure attachment have lower oxytocin levels and feel more emotional pain when their baby expresses sadness, which makes it especially hard for them to soothe their baby.

The Harm of Drugs of Abuse

All substances of abuse release higher amounts of dopamine and endorphins than real-life experiences do. Therefore, drugs of abuse give a mother more of a "reward hit" than taking care of her baby does. Substance-abusing mothers are less motivated to take care of their babies, are more motivated to seek out drugs, and experience the relationship as less meaningful (Strathearn, 2011). Since the infant's brain is still learning about relationships, babies of these mothers may be prone to expecting a lack of responsiveness or even neglect (Rutherford et al., 2011). Even when moms stop taking drugs, they may remain less emotionally responsive to their babies and experience less pleasure in the mothering role.

On a positive note, mothers who have abused substances can turn things around with their baby. There is evidence that moms in substance abuse programs that focus on enhancing their reflective capacity and sensitivity to the needs of their baby are able to reestablish the relationship bond with their child (Pajulo, et al., 2006). These mothers also show a reduced incidence of relapse. Their increased ability to understand their baby's behavior enables them to feel more connected to their baby as well as experience a greater sense of confidence and reward with her baby. This can reduce their stress level and thereby reduce their craving for drugs (Mayes et al., 2012); (Suchman, Docoste, Rosenberger, & McMahon, 2012).

ATTACHMENT AND REFLECTIVE CAPACITY

The mentalization system is activated as part of the attachment process. Soothing a baby requires a mom to be reflective, because she must be able to see the situation from multiple perspectives, recognize that every problem has many potential solutions, tolerate uncertainty without becoming overly anxious, and calm herself if need be. A mom who starts to lose hope that her baby will *ever* fall asleep can remind herself that it's not really true. She can tell herself that if the first method of soothing doesn't work, there are other ways to try, and that even if this time the baby continues to be fussy, she needn't get too alarmed because she knows that sometimes she just can't fully know what's going on. A mom's reflectiveness gives meaning to her baby's behaviors and expressions and enables her to verbalize those meanings. Studies show that moms with a secure attachment style seem to be more able to grasp the meaning of what their baby does and talk to their babies differently than moms with an insecure attachment.

Within the attachment relationship, what matters is that moms are able to soothe and regulate their baby by being emotionally responsive. However, for the attachment to be secure, the responsiveness must be what is referred to as *marked contingent responsiveness*. *Marked* means the mom is responsive but not too intensely responsive. This requires her to be able to contain her own emotions so they are not too high or too low. *Contingent* means her responses fit the timing of when her baby expresses its needs. This requires her to show empathy *when* the baby indicates a need for empathy. Secure attachment in the baby is fostered only when the mom's emotional response is somewhat reduced from what the baby is feeling but also in sync with when the baby wants it. Secure attachment in moms is associated with their being more reflective, so reflective

SCIENCE SAYS

A Mom's Reflective Ability Is Captured by Her Words

In one study, moms with secure attachment and moms with dismissive attachment were asked to match their preverbal infant's emotional expressions exactly. Both types of moms were good at copying their baby in this way, but the moms differed in their grasp of the meaning of their baby's actions and in the *words* they used to accompany the matching. Securely attached mothers used words expressing a greater understanding of what their baby might be experiencing, whereas moms with *insecure* attachment used words that showed a more superficial understanding of what the child was experiencing. Of course, the preverbal babies didn't understand the words! But the moms' words were a sign of their deeper grasp of what their baby's expressions meant and what their baby might be experiencing.

moms are better at expressing marked contingent responsiveness than insecurely attached moms. One contributing factor is probably that more securely attached moms have higher oxytocin levels than moms with insecure attachment. Oxytocin facilitates marked contingent responsiveness because it helps the mom remain calmer and feel less distress when her baby is distressed.

> Parenting is so much harder when you were not
> parented well.

Many parents suffered trauma, abuse, or neglect in their own childhoods. Fortunately, some of these parents find a way to *resolve* their trauma, meaning that they become aware of the impact the trauma has had on them and on their parenting and find adaptive ways to cope with it. As a result, they are able to be reflective and emotionally responsive. But there are many parents who have not resolved these terrible early experiences, and studies show that this can have negative consequences for their attachment relationship with their own children. Parents with a history of unresolved trauma may misinterpret their baby's expressions or be indifferent to them (S. Kim, Fonagy, Allen, & Strathearn, 2014).

Genes are not destiny!

We are born with all the genes we will ever have. The genes we are born with give us certain built-in tendencies, such as being less or more emotionally reactive or less or more negative (Saphire-Bernsteina, Way, Kim, Sherman, & Taylor, 2011). People born less negative and with less emotional reactivity have more inner resourcefulness. Of course, these people still have problems, because *all* people have problems. But they tend to be more optimistic, have a greater sense of mastery, and have more self-esteem. When they do have problems, they are not knocked down by them as easily and can get back up more readily. If you are like this or your child is like this, you should feel lucky. Other people, however, are born with genes that tend to make them more negative and more likely to be pessimistic and have low self-esteem. It is not their fault. And life tends to be harder for them.

The good news is that genes are not destiny! Being raised in a warm, nurturing environment can counteract the impact of genetic tendencies. Genes are influenced by the environment through a process called *epigenetics*. Epigenetic mechanisms put a chemical tag on the gene, which tends to make the gene less effective without altering the gene's DNA. It's a little like putting a big pin through your nice warm sweater; it will tear the sweater and make it less warm, but it's still the same sweater.

A positive environment of warmth and emotional responsiveness removes epigenetic tags so that the genes involved with oxytocin and cortisol are more effective (Champagne & Curley, 2009; Champagne & Meaney, 2001; Monk, Spicer, & Champagne, 2012). In the opposite

SCIENCE SAYS

Sensitivity Removes Epigenetic Tags

Low levels of maternal sensitivity and nurturance lead to epigenetic tags on the gene involved in shutting off the cortisol response. This has the long-term effect of making these babies highly stress reactive. High sensitivity and nurturance in the mother, by contrast, removes the tags, which in turns improves cortisol shut-off and results in reducing the baby's stress reactivity.

environment, one that lacks warmth and emotional responsiveness, epigenetic tags appear, and oxytocin and cortisol function are impaired.

Your level of sensitivity and nurturance are even more important if your child happens to be on the emotionally sensitive side. Because of epigenetics, being harsh with this type of child can worsen their outcome, and being warmer can improve their outcome. However, epigenetics won't make an already good situation even better. If you are fortunate enough to have good genes and so does your child, you can't improve on that (Monk et al., 2012). Just appreciate it!

Being reflective can improve negative situations.

Moms with insecure attachment are more likely to have babies with insecure attachment. Moms with unresolved trauma are more likely to have disorganized attachment styles, and so are their babies. But parents can change and improve if they are helped to be more reflective. When parents who are distant and not empathic enough work at being more reflective, it improves their ability to recognize their child's need for emotional responsiveness, which in turn will improve their relationship with their child. When parents who are overly anxious or intrusive work at being more reflective, it improves their ability to see their child's need for less emotional intensity and more emotional distance. Studies show that when moms find a way to work on their trauma, it increases the likelihood that their baby will have a better attachment. When moms become able to reflect on their early experiences and the impact those experiences are currently having on their baby, it changes how they interact with the baby and can shift the child's developmental path onto a more positive one (Iyengar, Kim, Martinez, Fonagy, & Strathearn, 2014).

An inborn genetic vulnerability may cause some moms to have more difficulty in the mothering role and some kids to have more difficulty in their "role" as a child. As a parent, you can't do anything about your genes or the genes you pass on to your child. But you can do something about the epigenetic influences on your child. A parent who works to be more reflective can help turn that vulnerability around.

Being reflective means self-examination and figuring out who your child seems to be. Are you or your child or both of you overly reactive to stress? Are you or your child or both of you more reserved and inhibited when it comes to emotions? If such a tendency exists, label it. Give it a name. But don't blame yourself or your child! Feeling guilty or ashamed or blaming someone for a built-in vulnerability doesn't help the situation and can add stress, which will only make matters worse. Keep in mind that even vulnerabilities can have an adaptive function. As mentioned previously, highly emotional people are often more empathic, and less emotional people often demonstrate greater resilience.

Another reflective tool is separating your state of mind from your child's. For example, overly emotional or anxious parents are encouraged to observe their child closely and notice that, often, their child isn't as upset and anxious as they are. These parents need support to hold back and not always swoop in to relieve their child's distress. Parents who are more likely to downplay their child's emotions are encouraged to think about whether they have a child who is more emotionally sensitive and whether their downplaying style is having a negative impact on him or her. If it seems to be having a negative impact, these parents can experiment with being more empathic toward their child and see how that changes the situation. These parents generally will need support because of how awkward they feel in adopting this stance. Fortunately, children are usually happy about these changes and give their parent feedback, perhaps not so much in words but in behavior and other nonverbal cues.

Don't get too carried away by the science of attachment.

The science of attachment causes some parents to incorrectly conclude that separation or emotional distress of any kind is not good for children. They might worry excessively during the first year of their child's life, believing that it's all over by age one. These conclusions fail to put the science into a balanced context. Children need closeness and comfort as well as separateness and some distress. Also, it is not over by age one. The brain remains plastic for years to come.

Attachment is not supposed to protect a child from all distress. Attachment is for coping with and managing the natural distresses and separations that all children will and need to experience. By experiencing mini-separations, such as when a child goes to sleep, or when Mommy and Daddy go out on a date night or go to work, the child builds up a kind of emotional immunity. By having the reassurance that separations can be tolerated, that their distress can be soothed, and that parents do come back, a child builds up a sense of safety and self-confidence that will contribute to their emotional resilience.

Early is better, but it is never too late! While a secure attachment is certainly good to have, too much emphasis on it can cause unnecessary worry for parents and those helping them. A child's brain is plastic and children are adaptable. When it comes to child development, nothing is written in stone in year one or even in year three, not even attachment style! Yes, it may be better to get off on the right foot, but there is time to catch up. There is room for rewiring, and children always remain open for improvements in the relationship. A relationship that was previously rocky or overly emotional can get back on track. It will take a lot of effort and patience on the part of the parent. Fortunately, unlike the *Titanic*, the relation-ship can be turned around.

BE REFLECTIVE

Use all of your reflective tools to build and maintain an optimal attachment with your child as he or she grows.

When your child is upset, much of the time all the situation calls for is nonverbal gestures such as facial expressions, touch, sitting close together, and a soothing tone of voice. Even if you use words, the sound of your voice or the look on your face can capture a bit of how your child is feeling. For example, if your child is expressing anger, there may be some slight tension in your voice and a slight look of anger on your face as you nonverbally match their emotion. The younger the child is, the more it usually comes down to nonverbal cues, even if you use words. As children get older, the actual words become more important, but nonverbal communication always remains important. The effectiveness of words such as "I'm sorry that happened to you. Is there anything I can do to help you feel better?" will depend on the nonverbal elements of how you talk.

Empathize.

Empathy takes many forms; there is no one right form. The point is to express something that signals that you know and care about what your child is going through. You can use sweet words, such as, "I know it's really upsetting," or not-so-sweet ones, such as "It sucks." When something bad happens, some kids are more likely to express emotions of hurt and pain, while others are more likely to express anger or betrayal. Empathize with what they express, but also inquire if they might be feeling one of the other feelings. Empathy is first-aid for their emotions and a way of teaching your child an emotional vocabulary. Since regulating our emotions involves labeling our feelings and putting them into words, each time you go through the process with your child, you are helping them regulate and build up their emotional vocabulary.

Explore the meaning.

Rejection is always painful but not necessarily harmful. What *is* harmful is when a child interprets the rejection in a negative way. Your role is to explore and clarify what it means to your child and to you when your child is rejected. For example, some children *internalize* rejection, interpreting it as meaning that something is wrong with them—that they are defective or unworthy. These kids need help recognizing that rejection doesn't mean that something is bad about them. Some kids *personalize* rejection and interpret it as if they are the only one who gets rejected. These kids need help understanding that rejection happens to everyone! Some kids overgeneralize, as if no one likes them or no one wants to be their friend. These kids need help to *not* generalize by seeing that other people do like them, even if one person does not. Some kids *externalize* rejection and take it to mean that the friend who rejected them is a really terrible person. These kids need help realizing that when someone acts rejecting, they are not always being mean or bad. If your child doesn't understand this, it can make it harder for them to trust other people or to make up with a friend later on.

Be confident that no feeling lasts forever.

Kids tend to think that their bad feelings will last forever. The truth is that bad feelings don't last forever. They go away with time. Reassure your child that no matter how badly they feel now, they will feel better, even if they can't imagine it.

Promote positive attachments with others.

Beyond their attachment with you, it is important to support your child in being able to form positive attachments with others. Often, this involves helping them manage the difficult emotions that arise in other relationships.

Help kids be open-minded.

Some kids feel rejected even when it isn't a rejection. Kids often misunderstand each other's intentions. When kids make plans with other kids, often there are misunderstandings or changes in plans that have nothing to do with anyone intending to leave someone out. While it is always good to be empathic when your child feels rejected, it is helpful to encourage him or her to see the rejection from other perspectives. Here are some other perspectives that might apply, depending on your child and the situation. It might be that the rejection is temporary; it was just this one time on the playground, or just when your child's friend was with this one other friend who doesn't like to share friends. Maybe your child wasn't invited to the party because the parent put limits on how many kids could be invited. No matter the reason, it builds resilience in your child if he or she can see a painful situation from other, less painful perspectives.

Give it time.

If your child is upset, you don't need to help him or her resolve it all at once. Some kids can deal with their feelings only in small doses. Some kids are not ready to talk right away. Sometimes, even if you do nothing, your child will get over it.

Sometimes all you need to do is listen.

When we can tell someone else about our pain and they hear us out, we feel better because we are not as alone with our feelings. Parents tend to forget how valuable *just listening* can be in healing their child's pain. If your child doesn't want to talk, don't push it. Let them know you are always available to listen. And when they do talk, try to just listen! You may discover that is all they want.

STORIES OF PARENTS AND CHILDREN

- **A *socially tentative* child.** Eugene was an emotionally sensitive baby who had a very difficult time with separations and transitions. At age four, he still tended to cling to his mother, Marina, when there were unfamiliar people around. At birthday parties and play dates, he just wanted to sit on his mother's lap. Marina was self-conscious about what other mothers would think of her son, so she tried as forcefully as she dared to get him off her lap, but he refused. Marina had to reflect hard and long to realize that her self-consciousness was making her more anxious, which was adding to Eugene's anxiety. By being so forceful about getting him off her lap, she was not helping him to develop a coping mechanism for dealing with the situation. Marina eventually decided, "To hell with the other mothers. Who cares what they think? Eugene needs to sit on my lap until he is comfortable, and I'm going to help him find a way to do that." She used a balanced approach of reassurance and coping. She told Eugene that he could sit on her lap as long as he needed, but that she was sure that if he did decide to get off her lap, he would discover it wasn't as scary as he thought. She made up funny sounds he could whisper to her when he was ready to get down, making the issue around separation more playful and less dire. In time, Eugene was getting off her lap much more quickly. He was never going to easily jump into social situations, but he got a lot better at it.

- **A *newly clinging* child.** Blair was a confident mom. Her son, four-year-old Carson, had been taking swim lessons for five weeks with no problems. On week six, he refused to go into the pool. Blair felt that her role was to get Carson to take the class because he would enjoy it and she had paid for it. She was baffled as to why he was so determined not to go swimming. She was a no-nonsense, kind but firm parent. She believed kids should do things that are good for them even if they're hesitant about it. Therefore, she told Carson, "You've been here before without any problem. I can't let you not take a lesson when it's already been paid for. Come on, let's not keep the other children waiting." Usually, Blair had good results with her approach, but not on this occasion. Carson wrapped his arms tightly around Blair's leg and cried. Blair was becoming uncertain and anxious about what she should do and didn't like feeling this way. She took Carson home, but she was annoyed at him and rebuffed his efforts to play a game with her. When she saw him hang his head and mope, she became more reflective, saying aloud, "I wonder why Carson didn't want to go into the pool? I wonder if anyone can tell me the answer?" Carson laughed at her silly way of talking and blurted out, "Mommy! The pool is dirty. I could get lice." Blair assumed he'd heard someone say that, so she reassured him that he wouldn't get lice from the pool. With her new perspective, she no longer felt angry with him. She concluded that she must learn to be more flexible and not always force him to do something if he was hesitant. At his next swim lesson, Carson walked right into the pool, no problem.

PUTTING IT INTO WORDS

- *Expressing not knowing.* "I can see you are upset. I can see you want my help. But right now, I'm not really sure what's bothering you."
- *Expressing that you were unpredictable.* "I know it was upsetting that Mommy left so abruptly this morning without saying her usual good-bye. It scared you, and it makes it a little harder for you to calm down now, even though I'm back."
- *Expressing that you overreacted.* "I know you were really upset, and Mommy was upset and got angry. That scared you. I'm calmer now, so let's try again."
- *Expressing that you misunderstood.* "I think that before when you were scared, I didn't realize it. So I didn't come to help you and you had to deal with it by yourself. I'm sorry. I apologize. I will try to do better next time."

TAKE-HOME LESSONS

- For a few days, pay close attention to the *sensations* you have in your body when your child is upset about separation. Is there pressure in your chest? In your abdomen? Is your heart rate increased? Are your shoulder muscles tense? Touch the spot or spots where you are sensing something and describe the sensation.

- For a few days, pay close attention to the *emotions* you have when your child is upset about separation. You might feel angry, scared, helpless, rejected, confused, irritated, or hopeless. You may have more than one emotion at a time. Acknowledge the emotion. Label it. Go one step further and tell someone you trust, someone who will understand and not judge you, what you really feel. Now pay attention to how that feels.

- For a few days, pay close attention to what comes up from your childhood when your child is upset about separation or anything else. What your child is going through is bound to stir up memories and feelings from your past about similarly upsetting situations. Acknowledge them.

- If something painful from your past gets stirred up, *mother the mother*. Validate and empathize with what happened to you. If that's not enough, reach out to someone who can provide empathy. Another method is to think about how you would have liked your parent to react. It might be hard to imagine your harsh parent ever being warm, or your overly anxious parent ever being calm. But this is an imaginary, make-believe exercise. You can make up an imaginary parent if you need to. The point is to have an image of a benevolent parent. It's like talking to yourself in the way you wish your parent had talked to you. This technique has been referred to as creating an "angel in the nursery" (A. F. Lieberman, Padrón, Van Horn, & Harris, 2005).

- For a few days, notice whether you tend to expect too much of yourself. For example, do you always feel you have to handle everything? Is it hard for you to ask for help? If so, practice admitting that a situation is just too much for you and asking for help. For instance, if you and your co-parent are trying to sleep-train your baby but you simply get too upset and overwhelmed when the baby cries, have your partner do the training instead of you. Your baby doesn't need you to always be the hero; you're not superman or superwoman. Actually, your child does best if you can admit to yourself that you are vulnerable and need help some of the time.

- For a few days, notice whether you don't believe enough in yourself. Do you tend to get hopeless quickly about being able to comfort your child? Do you tend to assume that other parents are parenting better than you are? If so, practice some self-talk. Keep reminding yourself that no matter how upset your child is, he or she will eventually feel better. Tell yourself that even if your baby doesn't calm down, you are still helping him or her by just being there and trying. Tell your-self not to buy into the myth that there is a perfect kind of parent. It is not true! All parenting is messy and inexact. Remind yourself that other mothers don't tend to show when they are having a problem because they feel the same way you do—that is, they feel insecure about their parenting and worry that others will judge them.

- Practice helping your child deal with social rejection. Whether it involves not being invited to a friend's party or being excluded from a group of friends playing together, rejection feels painful! You can't prevent rejection or the pain that rejection brings, because these are normal parts of life. But there are things you can try to help reduce the pain—things we all need when we are rejected, no matter what age we are. Help your child to see that sometimes a rejection is not really a rejection, to take rejections less personally, to accept that not everyone needs to like them, to realize that even close friends may sometimes hurt their feelings, and to understand that just because someone rejects them, it doesn't mean something is wrong with them.

SEVEN

Parenting and Stress

Calming and Coping

BRAIN BASICS

The brain operates best in the middle range. Too much or even too little stress can be harmful and impair resiliency. Calming and coping maintain the brain's state of equilibrium.

YOUR CHILD'S MAIN STRESS REGULATOR: YOU!

Stress has a bad rap. The truth is that for healthy living, we absolutely need some degree of stress! However, that stress must be well-regulated, meaning that we can calm down and recover from the stress. Helping your child regulate stress is so important that it is given its own chapter. The attachment bond you form with your child identifies you as your child's main *stress regulator*—the trusted person your child turns to for help in times of stress. At first, you do most of the regulating. As your child gets older, you turn more of it over to them so that they can *self-regulate*.

Nature knows life is not stress free! Our brains and bodies are designed to expect, handle, and even require some stress in order to function in a healthy fashion, as long as we can "destress" relatively quickly. Built into the brain systems for dealing with stress are mechanisms to turn to others for help when we can't manage stress on our own. Your reflective capacity is required to figure out whether your child can handle a particular stress by themselves or if they need you to provide comfort, soothing, support, and possibly some coping strategies to help them recover and bring their stress level back down (Grienenberger, Denham, & Reynolds, 2015; Shonkoff et al., 2012). Remember to put your own oxygen mask on first. You have to reduce your own stress level before you can help your child.

STRESS, THE STRESS RESPONSE, AND STRESS RECOVERY

Stress is what happens when we face a challenge that requires more resources than we usually have. The *stress response* is the brain's way of providing those extra resources. As good as those extra resources can be, if they hang around too long, they can end up causing damage to the brain, body, and mind. Therefore, people also need *stress recovery* to stop the stress response and return them to a state of equilibrium. As your child's stress regulator, you help with the stress recovery phase by comforting, validating, and empathizing with your child and eventually by teaching her or him effective coping skills.

Stress is subjective! What is stressful to one person may not be to another person. What is stressful to you may not be stressful to your child; what is stressful to your child may not be stressful to you. No matter the source of the stress, we each have our own level of stress that we can manage. People who are more *resilient* get stressed less often and recover more quickly. People who are more vulnerable, or *stress reactive*, get stressed more often and have a harder time recovering. The degree of resiliency we have will vary according to our genes and biology; our age, temperament, and psychological perspective on life; and our personal experiences.

HEALTH IS COPING WITH STRESS

Health is not the absence of stress. Health is adaptively recovering and coping with whatever stresses come our way. Scientists use the term *good stress* for challenges that build resilience by making us feel more alive, competent, and in charge of our lives. Good stress is what your young child experiences when they are excited about going down the slide for the first time, when they are called on to speak in front of the class, when they are about to go for a sleepover for the first time, when they are studying for an important test, or when they are trying out for a part in a play or having a job interview. Good stress is like doing a hard workout. It is challenging, even exhausting, but when we cope with it, it usually leaves us feeling positive, accomplished, and content.

The term *bad stress* is used for stress that so overwhelms us that we can't cope or recover. It leaves us feeling fuzzy-headed, unable to concentrate, physically uncomfortable, distractible, depleted, defeated, and maybe even depressed. For a child, bad stress can be turned around as long as there is a stress-regulating parent to help out.

The Goldilocks Rule applies to stress, too.

In the story of "Goldilocks and the Three Bears," there is a bowl of porridge that is too hot, one that is too cold, and one that is *just right*. There is also a "just-right" amount of stress that sustains our optimal functioning. This "just-right" amount of stress is referred to as a person's optimal range. As long as we remain within that range, our performance will not suffer, whether we are at work, at school, doing after-school activities, or at play. If we go outside that range, our performance levels drop off (see Figure 7.1). Therefore, one of your roles as a reflective parent is to recognize when you or your child is functioning outside your optimal range and to take steps to get back there.

Everyone also has a "just-right" *threshold* for stress, beyond which the person can't recover on their own and needs to turn to another person for help. When stress goes beyond a person's threshold and there is no one to

151

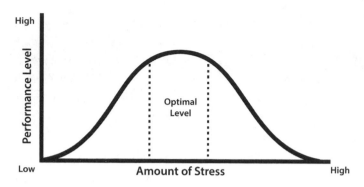

Figure 7.1. Performance levels drop outside the optimum stress level.

help, functioning can be seriously impaired. Infants and young children have a much lower threshold than older children and adults. Your role is to sense when your child is near their threshold and needs you to fill in and provide them comfort, support, scaffolding, and even coping skills so that they can recover. Like it or not, we each have a threshold, and when we pass it, we usually do better if we ask for help. This is an essential lesson to teach your child and to teach yourself. If your child is past their threshold, they can't learn. You will have to help them calm down before you can do any instructing or guiding as a parent. Similarly, as a reflective parent, you must recognize and accept your own threshold. If you are past your threshold, you can't be of help to anyone.

When your child can't recover from stress on their own, this is when they cry out or signal their need and expect someone to come and help. Being reflective allows you to sense not only when they need help, but also when they do not need help. How much they need you to step in will change as they develop. The reflective motto is "Step in when they need it. Stay back when they can manage on their own."

Not talking about stress has negative effects.

When parents don't recognize or talk about their child's stress experience, the child doesn't recognize it either (Borelli et al., 2010). This can make kids unable to identify and communicate their emotional distress. Though the child's mind may be unaware of the stress and they may appear calm on the outside, measures of their body physiology indicate a high stress state. Unfortunately, because they can't help themselves and don't know how to reach out to others, they may end up with chronic levels of unregulated stress (Borelli, Crowley, Snavely, & Mayes, 2013).

Stress regulation improves peer relationships in children.

An important lesson for kids to learn is that parents accept you no matter how you behave, but peers do not. One contributing factor to poor peer relationships in children and teens is an inability to regulate negative emotion and stress (Morris, Silk, Steinberg, Myers, & Robinson, 2007). Social competence requires that when children are upset in social situations, they express their distress in a socially appropriate way. Peers don't mind if the child gets upset as long as she or he is not too emotional, hostile, or withdrawn. A child who cannot tolerate negative emotions is more likely to behave inappropriately, such as by crying or yelling, socially withdrawing, or impulsively lashing out. Children whose parents remain empathic, supportive, and encouraging while avoiding being dismissive, punitive, or harsh in the face of their child's emotional distress are more likely to foster better social outcomes because they are better at helping children tolerate their bad feelings (Morris et al., 2007). Kids who are more emotionally reactive and less able to tolerate negative emotions need a reflective parent even more than the average child.

Secure attachment fosters stress regulation.

Secure attachment in babies and parents is associated with lower levels of cortisol—a sign of less reactivity to stress (Borelli et al., 2010). On the other hand, infants and parents with insecure attachment tend to be more reactive to stress and have higher cortisol levels during novel or frightening circumstances.

Reflective capacity goes out the window during
times of stress.

Stress impairs reflective capacity, which returns to normal when the stress
is relieved (see Figure 7.2). Even mild stress can reduce reflective capacity
to some degree and impair the performance of tasks that require complex,
flexible thinking (Arnsten, 2009). When reflective capacity is impaired by
stress, parents begin to react in a more knee-jerk fashion and their thinking becomes more "black-and-white." They lose the ability for perspective
taking, which causes them to feel hopeless and helpless and to be more
likely to misinterpret the meaning of their child's behavior. Under stress,
the amygdala can activate a fight, flight, or freeze mode of responding, in
which people either go into attack mode, remove themselves altogether
from whatever is causing the stress, or become immobilized. While each of
these mechanisms can be adaptive in real danger, they are maladaptive
within the parent–child relationship and can harm the connection.

Under high stress, even a parent with good reflective capacity may
lose some of their reflective ability, which can lead to misattunement,
relationship rupture, and added stress for their child. It isn't your fault if
your reflective thinking narrows under stress. That's just how the brain
operates. This is why the principles of reflective parenting aim to keep a
parent's stress level down as much as possible.

You are human. Even though there will be times when you are overwhelmed by stress, it helps to be honest about it. You can let your child
know that you are stressed and that it's your problem, not theirs. If you
are so stressed that you end up being insensitive or unkind to your child,

Figure 7.2. When stress goes up, reflective capacity goes down.

all is not lost. You can go back and repair the situation. "Daddy was stressed at the dinner table because of something that happened at work. That's why I overreacted when you interrupted me. Listen, we all get stressed at times. I made too big a deal of things. And I'm sorry if I hurt your feelings." Your child does *not* need a big mea culpa or for you to feel deeply guilty. Your child *does* need acknowledgment of their feelings and to know that you feel sorry to have hurt them. Children can accept that, from time to time, their parent will be stressed and will not always be warm and kind. They just can't handle it when it occurs too much, especially if the parent doesn't repair the rupture.

Some antidotes when you are under stress include being present in the moment as much as possible and staying focused on what needs to be done now, not on worse things that might possibly happen in the future.

THE NEUROBIOLOGY OF STRESS AND STRESS RECOVERY

You are overwhelmed with work deadlines and childcare responsibilities, and somehow you still need to take your car in for repairs and get the leaky faucet fixed. In other words, you are stressed. Stress is what causes you to feel pressure in your chest, your heart to race, and your muscles to tense. It makes your face look strained, your emotions to be anxious and irritable, your mind to be fuzzy, and your thoughts to race. From a biological perspective, each of these elements can have an adaptive function. Even the difficulty concentrating should serve as a sign that you should not make any important decisions until you are not so stressed.

Adrenaline and Cortisol

The stress response first produces *adrenaline*, which increases alertness, awareness, and preparedness in the short run, and afterward produces *cortisol*, which increases glucose levels and initiates other body changes for greater endurance.

Adrenaline helps you deal with an immediate, short-term stressful situation. If the stress quickly clears up, the amygdala stops adrenaline production. This is what happens when your child falls down but is not hurt. People who are highly stress reactive turn on their adrenaline alert to even seemingly minor ripples in life, such as when someone arrives a few minutes late. Cortisol is produced when the stressful situation is more prolonged. Cortisol creates a slow burn of amped-up resources to provide endurance, perseverance, and fortitude. Cortisol increases arousal; stimulates glucose release, high blood pressure, a high heart rate, and a high respiratory rate; and stops inflammation. Cortisol gives us the strength and energy to cope with the stress and helps us regulate our immune response. Then the cortisol itself actually *shuts off* all aspects of the stress response to initiate recovery. Recovery is like the cool-down and rest you take after a hard workout. It's good to flex your muscles and get hot, sweaty, and tired, but you need a recovery process afterward. Without stress recovery, a person is vulnerable to developing physical diseases, mental conditions such as depression, and depletion of their ability to manage stress in the future.

Stress and the Immune System

When stress occurs, it also turns on the immune system to activate *cytokines*, which produce inflammation and fatigue. Remember that our brains and bodies evolved hundreds of thousands of years ago, when nomadic hunter-gatherers lived under more primitive conditions and the stresses they faced more often involved injury and infection. Despite our better living conditions, stress still activates inflammation so that we're ready to fight infection or respond to injury, even when there is none (Powell et al., 2013). Unfortunately, prolonged levels of inflammation can damage body tissues such as the blood vessels in the heart, increase allergies, and even contribute to autoimmune conditions (Powell et al., 2013). If you have *chronic stress*, it plays a role in programming cells to have an overly aggressive inflammatory response and to become less sensitive to the anti-inflammatory effects of cortisol.

The Negative Effects of Stress on the Brain

Stress is good for dealing with threats but not good for social relationships (Arnsten, 2009). Adrenaline weakens the prefrontal cortex, which is the seat of social perspective-taking and self-control, but enhances the amygdala, which is the seat of detecting, responding to, and remembering threats. If your prefrontal control is weakened, you will *overfocus* on danger or other aversive stimuli. In the grip of amygdala control, a stressed person can quickly become even more stressed because of an increased focus on threat. For example, if your child is unhappy, stress can cause you to read too much danger into what they are feeling. A stressed parent's weakened prefrontal cortex makes them more likely to misread their child's intention, to react more on impulse than to act rationally, and to be less able to assess when they are off the mark in regard to their child. A child's prefrontal cortex is less mature than an adult's, which explains why kids who are stressed find it harder to concentrate at school and do their homework, are more impulsive, and have greater difficulty reading social cues.

RESPONDING TO CHILDREN'S STRESS IN A REFLECTIVE WAY

Being reflective enables you to sense what your child is experiencing during stress and to tailor your efforts at regulating their stress to your particular child and their particular situation. Reflective capacity is especially useful in dealing with stress derived from a stress-inducing mindset. Even the wish to protect children from all stress and the belief that we can and should do so can add to a parent's stress and their child's. It is an impossible expectation and only causes parents to worry excessively about stress. And when parents try too hard to protect their child from stress or jump in too quickly to fix the stressful situation, it tends to breed in the child insecurity, low self-confidence, and unrealistic expectations of how life is supposed to be.

A belief that stress is a normal part of life and that it can be managed reduces stress and builds resilience. The attuned, reflective parent is able to step in and help regulate their child's stress response *when* the child needs it, *only as much* as they need it, and knows when to offer strategies for coping with stress. This approach fosters development of inner strength in the child, teaching them to handle stress more and more on their own and giving them the tools to manage the bigger stresses that come later in life.

Just Be There!

Parents tend to underestimate how important their physical presence is to their child when she or he is in a stressful situation. The physical presence of a loved one has been shown to reduce pain, lower cortisol levels, slow the heart rate, and reduce the need for anesthetic medications (Coan, Schaefer, & Davidson, 2006; Krahé, 2013; Lynch, 1994). Even adolescents report feeling better knowing that their parent is there with them.

The Power of Touch

Human touch has health benefits. For example, premature babies who are given skin-to-skin contact have more release of growth hormone and leave the hospital sooner than those who aren't (Field, Diego, & Hernandez-Reif, 2010). Being stroked, held, or hugged or just having one's hand held during a stressful time can calm the nervous system (Coan et al., 2006). Sometimes just a wordless pat on the head or a gentle brush of the skin can be enough to calm a child down.

Containing Your Child's Stress

Containing and holding your child's stress is like giving them a larger pail to put their sand into so that it doesn't spill over, or like helping them to carry their heavy backpack. It makes the stress more manageable and lightens its weight. Using your reflective capacity to understand what is going on inside your child's mind enables you to better contain their stress as you employ *emotional attunement*, *validation*, and *empathy*. Containment also reassures children they are not alone, allowing them to experience the good inner feeling of having a safe harbor, which is so necessary to emotional and physical well-being.

Attunement uses soothing sounds, gestures, and words that resonate with the child's emotion, such as "Hmmm, yeah, I know, I know. It's hard, isn't it?" Validation says, "I can understand why you're feeling so stressed." Empathy says, "I can feel what you are feeling." Even intense or "big" feelings can be stressful because they can overwhelm a child's resources. Parents intent on helping their child contain her or his stress can say something like, "I know you're feeling scared and overwhelmed right now. I understand. I'm here, and I will help you. Together we will figure it out." Big feelings are not as big when someone helps you hold them.

What if you've tried to contain your child's stress, but she or he remains upset? Keep trying. Even your efforts at containment become wired into a child's stress recovery circuits. They still add to the inner recovery mechanisms your child falls back on when you aren't around.

Being a good listener is a terrific container. Often all a child wants and needs is for you to listen to what is upsetting them. They aren't looking for advice or opinions or suggestions or even for understanding. They are just looking to be heard. So just listen! Don't be surprised, however, if after you do all this good listening, your child feels fine but you are left holding your child's stress and bad feelings. That was the point. Your child was performing a *stress transfer*, so the stress burden is now on your shoulders and off theirs. At the brain level, when children turn to others for help with stress, it gives their coping system a rest in order to replenish its reserves.

Regulating Doesn't Mean Giving In

Regulating your child's stress does *not* mean giving in to your child's demands, allowing them to express their distress in any way they want,

159

or having to always be sweet and speak calmly. A big part of regulating a child's stress involves setting limits on how they can act and establishing boundaries beyond which they cannot go—but doing it in a firm, confident, and relatively calm way. Limits help your child feel safer. It is stressful for a child to not know what the rules are or what is expected of them. A child with no limits has the same degree of anxiety you would feel driving at night in an unfamiliar place and not having any idea where the side of the road was or where the lane divider between you and oncoming traffic was.

If it annoys you when your child misbehaves and you don't set a limit, your child senses that you are angry, and it makes them anxious and stressed. It even induces them to test the limit just to find out where you really stand on the subject. For example, one mother felt so guilty about being a single working mom that she wasn't able to properly set limits on her 15-year-old daughter's snide complaints about her being a single mom. She kept trying to be empathic with her daughter and reason with her about it, ignoring how intolerable it was to have her daughter be so nasty. Eventually, she had to learn not to let her guilt interfere with setting a clear limit. She told her daughter what she was willing to put up with and learned to pull back and not engage with her when she was being cruel. This greatly reduced the daughter's unkind behavior.

It is not good to set limits when you feel out of control. Nor is it good to act too 'sanitized' when you set a limit. While the ideal might be to be calm, sometimes calm comes across to the child as too detached or impersonal, and therefore the child does not know the parent really means it. For this reason there are times when the parent must express some emotion of anger so that the parent seems more real, and the child takes them more seriously. The critical point is to express the anger without becoming punitive or mean.

Some parents are reluctant to validate and empathize with a child's stress when they are acting up because they fear it means they have to go along with what the child wants or demands. But empathy and validation only mean that you are being reflective and can understand and see your child's perspective—not that you agree or are caving in to their perspective. For example, suppose a child says, "I don't want to move and go to a new school" when a job promotion requires the family to move to a new town. The parent might say, "I know it's scary not to know anyone. I know it's going to be hard." Or suppose a child refuses to get dressed, saying, "I don't want to go to school today because my teacher scolded me in front of the class when all I did was take my cell phone out." The parent might say, "It sucks when a teacher gets angry at you in front of everyone. I can understand being worried about having to see that teacher again." These parents are not telling the child they are right or wrong for how they feel or telling the child they don't have to move or go to school. They are just letting the child know they "get it." They are not giving in to the child's demands or going along with their child's way of handling the stress. The reflective parent realizes that in so many life decisions, it is ultimately up to the parent to decide what a child must do or how the child should handle the situation, but that even as the "decider," the parent can still offer empathy, validation, and support for what the child is going through. As a reflective parent, you might say, "I know it's hard to not have a choice in the matter, and many kids would probably feel the same way you do. But I have faith in you that you will be able to handle the situation."

Stressful Attitudes and Beliefs

Your mindset can be a source of stress and can make it more difficult to regulate your own or your child's stress. "All-or-none" beliefs, such as that one small mistake means the whole thing is ruined, or that unless you are perfect you are inadequate, can leave a child susceptible to feeling highly stressed in so many situations. A reflective parent recognizes the maladaptive belief and helps their child develop an alternative, more moderate one. It may be the parent who has a maladaptive mindset, such as the tendency to jump to the worst-case scenario. If a child doesn't do their homework in fourth grade, a parent may panic because they believe it means the child will never graduate high school. If their 10th-grader still needs help with organization and structure, the parent may get overly anxious because they believe it means the child will never be able to make it in college. Reflective parenting emphasizes the adaptive mindset that stress is not inevitably harmful to children and that it can be dealt with. Use your reflective capacity to identify whether you have a maladaptive mindset and to make the effort to change if necessary.

What Is Your Child's Behavior Really Saying?

The behavior of a really stressed child can look a lot like "misbehavior" that needs limits or consequences. It is hard to resist the immediate reaction of telling them to stop their bad behavior or trying to teach them a moral lesson, but too often that only exacerbates their negative behavior. Reflective parenting emphasizes that when children are stressed, they tend to act inappropriately and misbehave as a form of communication of how overwhelmed they are. A child who was teased at school earlier in the day may tease their brother at the dinner table more than usual or lie about not having homework. You will do better if you can "listen" to what they are communicating. Limit-setting and teaching kids appropriate behavior are important, but sometimes you have to put the stressful "fire" out first. There is no point in trying to teach a child a lesson or to get them to do their homework if they are so overwhelmed that their mind isn't going to be open to learning or problem-solving.

Children often communicate stress only by complaining that they don't feel well. For example, they might have a stomachache before school, or get a headache when they have to do homework, or get thirsty just when they have to go to bed. Of course, make sure they don't have a fever and aren't vomiting! And there is nothing wrong with getting the water. But also try to help kids connect their physical sensations with their feelings. If your child responds, "Mom, I really do have a tummy ache," it's a sign that your child is still learning how to connect their body with their emotions and their words.

We tell kids to "use your words," but a child who is stressed may be too overwhelmed to put what they're feeling into words. We need to teach kids to talk instead of hitting and grabbing. But when they are stressed, it's good to remember that at the moment they may not have the resources to talk. Haven't you ever gotten too frazzled or overwhelmed to think, let alone tell someone what's bothering you? Also remember that kids typically assume that you can read their mind so that they don't need to *tell* you how overwhelmed they are. You are supposed to know it already. Some of their difficult behavior when they are stressed results from their frustration that you are not reading their mind as they expect you to. This is probably the essence of many temper tantrums—your child's new discovery that you are not the miracle worker who can always read their mind and fix things. In teaching them that people can't always read their minds, be patient and empathic. It is a lesson many are still learning even as adults.

Who Is Having More Difficulty: Your Child or You?

The mother of a 15-year-old girl was really stressed because her daughter was going on a weekend field trip with her class. The daughter was upset because she had been having a conflict with her friends and was afraid they wouldn't want to room with her. The mom envisioned her daughter being rejected and alone on the trip. She was so worried that she said, "You know, you don't *have* to go." The girl got more upset. The mom pushed her internal pause button, self-reflected, and recalled that as a teen, a similar thing happened to her but she had no one to talk with. It remained a painful memory. This helped her realize that she was more stressed than her daughter. She saw that her daughter was upset but really wanted to go on the trip. She asked her daughter if she wanted to talk about it, but her daughter said, "No, Mom. Just stop worrying. I will figure it out." She went on the trip and successfully handled it.

Parents, Use Your Words!

When we are able to put our emotional distress into words, it is inherently calming. When we use our verbal brain centers, our emotional experiencing centers are less dominant. For example, suppose your child cries after getting a shot. You say, "That hurt, didn't it?" and they say, "It hurt too much!" Verbalizing the experience reduces the pain a little. If a child can't put their feelings into words, they may be calmed and contained when their parent is able to label their feelings and narrate what they may be experiencing. Even if you don't get it absolutely right, the very fact that you're listening and trying to put what they feel into your own words gives them the connection they need to feel less worried. It serves as a demonstration that feelings can be expressed in words and is the beginning of your child being able to do so.

All Distressing Feelings Get Better over Time

Imagine that you are upset and you think you will never feel better. That's pretty stressful. Now imagine being upset but knowing you will feel better in time. That's much more comforting. Distress, hurt, and disappointment can be frightening to a child because they assume it's going to go on forever. But, as a reflective parent, you know better. Reflective capacity includes the awareness that all feelings inevitably get better over time, even really bad feelings. The child doesn't realize this, but the grown-up should. In fact, having this knowledge under your belt usually helps you as a parent to feel less panicked or hopeless in the face of your child's difficulty. This isn't the first thing you should say to your child, however, because the first thing to do is to empathize and let your child know you understand what they are feeling. At some point, however, it's good to share your reflective wisdom that all bad feelings do get better in time, no matter what. Your child may not believe it at the time, but if you say it often, they will internalize your message and use it later on.

Stress Is in the Eye of the Beholder

You may think that a particular situation should *not* be stressful for your child and that their behavior is inappropriate, silly, unnecessary, or rude or that they're being weak or spoiled. Remember that stress is subjective. It is a state of biologic disequilibrium in the person under stress. The point is that when your stressed child is crying, hitting, or complaining, *from their perspective* they are in a state of disequilibrium, whether you think they should be or not. There is no point in telling them that they shouldn't be so stressed, any more than there would be in telling a child with a fever not to feel so hot. It is much better to accept their perspective and then help them with the stress they are experiencing.

The Distress Is in Your Child, Not You

It is helpful to emotionally resonate with your child's emotional distress by nonverbally and verbally communicating that you know what they're feeling. But you don't need to actually feel exactly what they're feeling. This is when you should use marked empathy—feeling their stress but less so, so that you can express your empathy in a way that helps them move out of their distress level. When parents' empathy makes them feel as distressed as their child, it can elevate the child's stress level by causing them to worry that—on top of everything else—they are harming their parent by making the parent feel terrible. For example, suppose your son tells you he's scared that he failed the test and that he won't ever get into a good college. It's not helpful to say, "Oh, that's awful! It would be terrible if you failed." That only makes things worse for your child's stress.

It's Wise to Normalize!

Probably the most calming words a stressed parent can hear are, "What you are going through is really common. It happens in every family!" Parents can't see through walls to know that other families experience the same kinds of stressful situations with their children. If adults need this, kids need it even more. If people feel that a difficulty they have is something that all people go through, it lessens the sense of stress they feel. Whenever you can, *normalize* your child's stressful experiences. Often, it's also *you* who needs to remind yourself that the situation is one that all children go through so that you are in a better position to help your child realize that the stresses of disappointments, hurts, and failures are normal parts of life.

You Are the Adult

Being reflective helps you keep perspective on who is the child and who is the adult. Sure, there are stressful times when kids are moody and stubborn and don't want to do anything you ask. That's when you have to remember that they are the kids and you are the adult. You have to fight the urge to get into a stubborn grudge match with them.

It is natural and common for parents to wish that their children were sympathetic about how difficult and stressful it is to be a parent. And kids, in an age-appropriate way, are able to care about their parents' stress and to try to relieve it somewhat. But children are the ones who need parenting. They are *not* supposed to have to parent their parent. Kids should not be made to feel responsible for empathizing with their parent's stress or for reducing it. You can let your child know you are feeling stressed or expect them to stay out of your way a little for the time being, or maybe you can ask them to help a little extra around the house. This is different than expecting your child to take on the role of calming you down or worrying about what you are going through. It's a fine line sometimes, because kids do empathize with parents, but it's an issue parents need to be aware of so that their child's empathy doesn't lead to their feeling responsible for what their parent is going through. One mother put it to her child this way: "Mommy is going through a rough patch. I appreciate that you're trying to make me feel better. But I also want you to know that I'm going through a grown-up problem, not one that kids are able to or supposed to fix. I will be able to handle it."

Be Humble

When kids act up because they are stressed, it's hard to keep in mind that the child's annoying behavior is their way of letting you know they need assistance of some sort. It's natural to get frustrated with a grumpy, short-tempered child. Reflective note to self: Be humble. Not every one of *your* stress behaviors is so adaptive! You also tend to get grumpy and short-tempered with everyone because you have too many deadlines to meet. Remember that even you, as an adult, sometimes wish or expect others to read your mind and know exactly what you need when you're under stress. It's childish, perhaps, but all adults get like this from time to time.

The fact is that your child *is* childish and expects you to read their mind quite a lot. Therefore, you will be clarifying and teaching an important lesson to your child in an ongoing way: that, for the most part, people can't read their mind, and that they have to actually let others know what they want and need. It will help you to be less frustrated with your child if you remember that during childhood, it takes a long time to learn this lesson. And even you as an adult will sometimes fall prey to believing that your child or your spouse should read your mind.

Be Positive

Good stresses are the age-appropriate bumps in the road that every child goes through at one time or another. By seeing the positive life lesson of stress—that it is beneficial to learn how to cope with it—you help promote a child's competence and resilience. Perhaps your daughter is working on a school project and worried that she won't get a good grade. You encourage her to remember that she has what it takes and not to worry about the grade, but just to focus on the present and do what she can. Or suppose your son is not one of the teacher's "favorites" and feels rejected. You validate and emphasize with him, saying you know that it's tough to be in that kind of situation, but also tell him that you have faith in his ability to learn how to manage. You reassure him that we all need to learn how to tolerate things we don't like, such as not being someone's favorite.

Experiences like this in childhood also help your child to be better at bringing up what bothers them with their boss, co-worker, or romantic partner in the future. Like exercise that strengthens your muscles and increases your endurance, good stress increases your reserves. The chemicals released during times of *good* and *regulated* stress contribute to brain growth and learning in your child. Only when the stress is bad do unregulated stress hormones damage brain growth and learning.

Telling good stress from bad stress isn't easy, and how to alleviate a given stress is not always obvious. Remember this reflective idea and teach it to your child: "Life is messy, and it's not always completely clear what the best way to manage a stressful situation is."

Give Your Child a Chance

Through repetition, children gain mastery. When they learn a new skill, such as going down the slide at the playground or building a tall tower of blocks or learning a new trick on their scooter, children like to repeat it over and over. This is how they learn to master their new skills and gain confidence in their abilities. It's the same with developing mastery over stressful experiences. If you jump in too quickly to fix things, you rob your child of the pleasure of mastery and competence. By reflecting, you will become more able to communicate that you understand what they are feeling but also to communicate that their stress experience is something that can be managed and mastered (Fonagy et al., 2004).

No Blame or Labels

No parent likes being on the receiving end of their child's negative stress behaviors, especially if the child is being blaming, rejecting, or hurtful toward the parent. It can be terribly painful. It is even natural for parents to sometimes have the urge to retaliate by criticizing their kids back, but this is never helpful and can impair their children's coping ability. What is needed is support, not criticism. For example, suppose that Curtis, age 11, is a highly stress-reactive child. He frequently badgers his parents about all the attention his younger brother gets, is angry and bangs the table when he is frustrated, and stamps his feet and protests loudly if he has to wait to get help with his science homework when his father is busy. Certainly, Curtis needs help managing his reaction to stress in a more adaptive way so that he doesn't bother other people so much with it. However, Curtis is not trying to be a bad or disrespectful child. He is wired to be more stressed and react more poorly to stress than some other kids. Unfortunately, his father takes it personally and calls him a "drama queen," which riles Curtis up even further. The point to keep in mind is that stress in all people, and especially in children because their prefrontal cortex is less mature, reduces their ability to see the world from the perspective of other people. When children are caught up in their own negative emotions, they typically are less able to be cooperative or socially appropriate.

Here are some things to consider as a parent to help you remain more empathic and less judgmental of how your child behaves when they are stressed. Try to take their self-centeredness in stride as a developmental issue and not a problem of character. Recognize and accept that they are having a hard time coping, even if you think they shouldn't. Of course, it is important to be clear and teach them about self-control. Just don't attack their character as you do it. Avoid shaming, blaming, or naming, such as calling your child a baby or a brat. That only makes things worse. If your child is acting up when they are stressed, it is more productive to accept them and empathize with their difficulty even as you explain that they need to find a way to behave differently. Sometimes all a parent can do is survive the storm of their child's stressful time while being careful not to take it personally so that they don't add any extra thunder by belittling or blowing up at their child. Hopefully, you are lucky enough to have supportive friends and relatives. If you don't, you may benefit from a reflective parenting group that can provide support and also build a stronger reflective capacity in you so that you are better at regulating your stress level in the first place.

Reframe and Reinterpret

As humans, we all crave a reason for what is happening to us, and our brain and our mind are happy to oblige. The brain-mind will grasp whatever interpretation is readily available and then build its case to prove that its conclusion is correct. Because the brain constructs our experiences, and because the mind underlies our behavior, what we feel and how we behave results more from our perspective or interpretation of events than the events themselves. And as shocking as it may be to your sense of reality, the brain-mind goes looking for any detail that supports the perspective or interpretation it already holds and prematurely jumps to conclusions about how to make sense of what is happening. This is why, when a person feels that no one loves them, they are really good at seeing when people reject them but blind to seeing all the times that people are quite loving. Once we have our conclusion, it is hard to see the situation in any other way. No wonder relationships can be so hard to work on and they require so much work! Reflective parenting is designed to help parents resist the urge to be convinced that they are absolutely right about their perspective by helping them to reframe their observations and remain open-minded to other possibilities.

Reframing is especially useful for helping kids with stress. Kids who are very self-conscious or anxious in social situations or kids with perfectionism often misinterpret criticism as a sign that someone doesn't like them or that something is wrong with them. Here are some reframing possibilities: "Just because your teacher criticized you doesn't mean she doesn't like you." "When someone criticizes you, it doesn't mean you are bad. It doesn't mean they are right. It's just their opinion. It is not the truth about you." "Maybe some kids are critical and judging, but most are not. They are more worried about themselves than they are about noticing what you're wearing or doing." "Everyone makes mistakes. It doesn't mean you are a failure. It's not a disaster. It's just human!" Yes, of course we want our child to take criticism constructively and we want them to try to avoid making mistakes. But to do this, they first need to learn not to put such negative meanings on being criticized or on making mistakes.

Reframing rejection is also frequently important. Take the situation where a child feels rejected by peers. The more a child interprets malevolent intent on the part of their peers, the more upset and aggressive they are likely to be, the more likely they will be to deduce that they have little control over improving the situation, and the less they will get along with their peers. Kids who are less likely to assume malevolent intent tend to feel they have more control over the situation, are less upset and less aggressive, and get along better with peers. Here are some reframing possibilities: "I know there are bullies and mean kids who really want others to feel bad, but most kids aren't that way, even if they act rejecting. Usually, if kids seem to be acting mean or rejecting, they are just caught up in their own issues and were not trying to be mean to you." "I know it feels like Melissa hurt your feelings on purpose, but maybe she didn't mean to or didn't even realize she was upsetting you."

There Is No Right Perspective

Suppose your child is stressed and you aren't able to help reduce their distress. Now what? Is it better to make your child do something they say they don't want to do, or can't do, or are scared of? Or is it better to let them *not* do it? Reflective parenting says, *there is no right answer* and *be flexible!* The neuroscience indicates that children will do well with either approach as long as the insistence or the lenience is not too extreme. It also indicates that for some kids, your firm belief that they can handle it and that the situation will turn out fine will be calming enough, while others may need extra help or time to pull back and refuel.

The Stress of Disadvantage and Misfortune

Many children in our communities are poor and disadvantaged and are growing up in highly stressful circumstances such as poverty, a broken family, mental illness in a parent, substance abuse in a parent, witnessing violence, or being abused or neglected. If a child experiences a number of these stresses without the comfort, support, understanding, and safety of a parent, the stress can become toxic and have long-term negative effects on the child's brain and body as well as on their social, emotional, and cognitive development. Although this may never happen in your family directly, in the long run, the damage that happens for these underprivileged children eventually negatively impacts our whole community. Economists have shown that the cost of the social services to help kids who are growing up in adverse circumstances is less than the cost of what will be required when these kids grow up and have higher rates of school dropout, crime, substance abuse, unemployment, and dependency on the social welfare system. The good news is that enhancing the reflective capacity of the children's parents or other primary caretakers is protective and helps prevent the negative impact of these kinds of stresses (Grienenberger et al., 2015).

STORIES OF PARENTS AND CHILDREN

- *Stress can be coped with.* Valerie is a single widowed mother raising her young son, Gregory, who was only three years old when his father was killed in an accident. Valerie is overwhelmed with grief, fear, and anger over the loss of her husband. Gregory, who used to be cheerful and exuberant until his father died, is now sad, afraid, and angry. It tugs at Valerie's heartstrings that her son has no father. She is overwhelmed doing it alone and worries that she will not be able to give Gregory all that he needs. She is frightened that he will feel an empty hole all his life and that she will not be able to help him heal this wound. Valerie, despite all her grief and fear, is nevertheless a very reflective mom. She does her best to listen, soothe, comfort, and reassure Gregory. She is able to empathize with and validate all of Gregory's feelings about the loss of his dad. In an age-appropriate way, she sensitively answers his questions, even though they stir up a lot of pain in her. She slips up from time to time, as any normal parent would, but basically she hangs in there with him. As he gets older, she also helps teach him ways to cope with situations that are especially difficult, such as when people ask him about his father or when other kids have their fathers along at sports or school events. It takes time for him return to his cheerful exuberant self, but with Valerie's help, he gets there.

- *Don't take it personally and try not to panic.* Belinda, age eight, is crying because her older brother is teasing her. She feels rejected by a friend at school and is hurt that the teacher doesn't call on her much. She blows up when her mom says she can't watch more TV. Kevin, age 12, is ashamed that his skin is breaking out and embarrassed because a girl at school found out that he likes her. He starts teasing his younger sister and is grumpy and annoying at the dinner table. Monique, age 14, is worried about an upcoming test, irritated that she has to do her chores, and angry that she has to miss soccer practice because of a family gathering and ends up being sullen all day. The kids' stresses are stressful for the parents. Tracy, their mom, is almost in tears, feeling hurt and questioning whether she is doing a good job. Michael, their dad, feels irritated and disrespected by their bad behavior. The mom and dad do their best to be reflective. They normalize the situation and recognize that their kids are experiencing the usual and necessary stresses of growing up. They try to not take their kids' behavior personally so that they can remain empathic. They reduce their own helpless and irritated feelings by remembering that they can't and shouldn't fix it all.

- *Set limits to contain stress.* Even in second grade, Megan's son Joey complains every morning about going to school and is really slow about getting ready. Megan realizes it is separation anxiety, because once he is busy at school, he is fine. She does her best to understand and talk with him about his feelings and gives him tips and techniques for how to handle the situation. But nothing improves. When Megan self-reflects, she remembers how her father, a policeman, did not discuss feelings. One morning she had to get on the school bus alone because her sister was sick. She cried and pleaded with her dad to drive her to school. He said, "No way! Get on the bus and stop blubbering." She remembers his words as harsh and hurtful. But she also remembers, "As soon as we picked up more kids, I knew I was fine, and I learned I could cope." It becomes apparent to her that her experience of feeling hurt by her dad's harshness has been making her try too hard to be empathic so as not to be hard-nosed and insensitive like her father, and this has been preventing her from being clear with her son about what she expects. She realizes she has to be direct, clear, and confident with Joey. "Joey, everyone in a family has their own responsibilities, and one of yours is to get yourself ready for school on time. Dad and I believe we would be neglectful parents if we did not teach you how to be responsible. So we expect you to get yourself ready, no matter what. We are sure you can handle it." The exact words aren't as important as Megan's sense of clarity and conviction.

- *Change your perspective.* Chase is having a lot of stress with her 11-year-old daughter, Olivia. Olivia procrastinates on her homework until nighttime and then wants Chase to sit with her the whole time and help. Chase is resentful and thinks Olivia is being lazy and inconsiderate about her mother's time, so she constantly nags and pressures her to get her work done earlier. When Chase reflects, however, she gets in touch with how helpless she feels because she has been trying for a long time to teach her daughter to do her homework assignments in a more timely fashion. Chase believes she *should* have been able to get her daughter on a better homework schedule by now. She feels guilty and thinks she is not a good mother, because a good mother would be happy to talk or help with homework as much as the daughter wanted. Chase works to reframe the situation. She realizes her daughter procrastinates because she is anxious and gets easily overwhelmed when doing her work, so she avoids it. This helps Chase not be so angry with Olivia and makes her realize that she needs to focus on calming her daughter down about her schoolwork rather than fighting with her. She also sees she is a good mother because she knows how important it is to help her daughter have better work habits. This positive reframing helps Chase be more effective with her daughter.

PUTTING IT INTO WORDS

- *Marked empathy.* Words or sounds like "O-o-o-h. Oh, my-y-y-y. Ho-o-ne-e-e-y. There, there. I-I-I'm sorry" expressed in a tone of voice that comes near the level of the child's stress but does not match it exactly.

- **Comfort by connecting.** Any words that express that the child is not alone with what they are going through, such as "I'm right here. I'm with you in this. Remember you are not alone; we will help you. I'd like to help if you want me to, but if not, just remember I'm always available."

- **Comfort by listening.** "I really want to just hear what happened. I promise I will just listen; I won't interrupt or give suggestions."

- **Building resilience by reframing.** "I know it seems right now that because you didn't get picked for the [fill in the blank], everything is terrible and you will never succeed. But just because you didn't get picked doesn't mean you won't succeed. All the people you think are successful have all not been picked for something. There are so many different paths to success."

- **Building resilience by having faith in your child.** "I know you're having a hard time with all this, but I believe in you, and you will find a way to overcome this situation. I am willing to help, but I have confidence that you can also come up with good ideas."

- **Building resilience by giving encouragement to overcome a challenge.** "It is really hard right now. And I know it makes you want to give up. I can totally understand that. I have certainly felt that way myself at times. But I can tell you from everything I know that giving up will probably make you feel worse. If you face it and give it your best try, you will feel better about yourself and stronger in the end."

TAKE-HOME LESSONS

- Notice how your child tends to deal with challenge. Pay attention to things like whether (a) your child seems able to deal with or is even excited about dealing with the challenge on their own; (b) your child looks hesitant or anxious, but if you wait just a bit, they take care of things on their own; (c) your child looks upset and distressed, but if you provide some reassurance, they calm down and handle the situation well; (d) your child looks distressed and needs you to spend time reassuring and comforting them and offering alternative perspectives; or (e) your child seems to need you to jump in and fix the situation. The younger your child is, the more you will be doing c, d, or e. With older kids, there will be more a, b, and c.

- Parents are so good at offering help that they too often neglect to ask if their child even needs or wants help. You can practice using "wondering" or "just in case" ways of asking: "I'm wondering if you want help" or "You may not need any help, but I have some ideas in case you're interested."

- Make a stress list. What causes stress for you? For your child? Describe how you and your child tend to express your stress. Think about ways in which you and your child are similar or different from each other with regard to what makes you stressed and how you express it. Think about whether your child's reactivity to stress is more on the inborn, genetic side or more on the learned, experiential side.

- Learn more about yourself. Think about whether you are someone who is relatively calm and resilient in the face of stress or someone who is more stress-reactive and has difficulty rebounding after a stressful situation. Are you more matter-of-fact when your child is stressed or more likely to express emotional empathy with your child? Are you the type to encourage your child to "push through the difficulty," or are you more likely to encourage your child to take a break if they feel stressed? You are to be commended for doing this take-home lesson, since self-reflecting in this way is hard! It takes bravery, especially if you think you will find areas that may "need improvement," so to speak.

- Focus on your child and her or his strengths. Collect examples of when you and your child handle a stressful situation well. There are always some stressful areas that a person handles well. For example, you may be especially good at the stress of juggling a lot of responsibilities. You may be good under the stress of someone being sick or good at the stress of losing your keys, even though there are stressful situations that you don't handle well—for example, perhaps you get completely overwhelmed when your kids are bickering. Do the same with the types of stress your child is more resilient about.

EIGHT

Parenting from Infancy through Childhood

BRAIN BASICS

The largest spurts of brain growth occur during gestation, infancy, and adolescence. Experiences stimulate the growth of new brain connections. Repeated and important experiences stimulate stronger connections. Healthy brain development requires an emotionally responsive relationship with a parent or other primary caretaker.

WHAT DOES IT TAKE TO CREATE A BRAIN?

Your efforts at understanding, comforting, soothing, empathizing, validating, being patient, scaffolding, perspective-taking, limit-setting, and teaching coping skills are literally building the pathways of your child's brain (Shonkoff & Phillips, 2000). Activities provide stimulation, challenges, and social experiences with other people. But what really counts in terms of brain development is what your relationship is like with your child on a daily basis—how you interact and communicate about whatever is going on in your child's life. Not even reflective parenting can guarantee that your child will have no problems. Nothing can guarantee that. What reflective parenting *can* do is increase the chances for healthy development in your child and enable your child to cope well with the problems they do have.

You don't have control over the "givens" your child is born with, such as their temperament, talents, strengths, and weaknesses. What you *have* some control over is how well your child manages with the givens they are born with. How you emotionally respond to your child and how you help your child learn to calm down, inhibit their behaviors, cope, and bounce back from problems all contribute to creating the necessary brain wiring your child needs to succeed and get along with others. Your relationship together lays down the right brain pathways for your child to be able to manage life in the most adaptive way.

Fortunately, nature is forgiving. Nature leaves lots of room for *inaccurate* responsiveness as well as accurate responsiveness. Children do not need or even benefit from responsiveness that is perfectly accurate. All scientific measures of healthy outcomes indicate that parents and their children are emotionally in sync about a third of the time, out of sync a third of the time, and getting back in sync about a third of the time. As long as your child can count on you to be emotionally responsive to whatever is going on inside them as well as to repair moments when your responsiveness is incorrect, your child's brain will develop in a healthy way. It is this *reliability* of your emotional responsiveness that is more important than the specific stimulation or activities you provide your child.

BRAIN DEVELOPMENT: THE MAIN THEMES AND BIG PICTURE

Being reflective allows you to get inside your child's mind. Now, the technology of neuroscience allows you to get inside your child's brain. A child's brain development is experience-dependent, meaning it is wired by the experiences your child actually has, especially parent–child relationship experiences. Genes provide a basic sketch of where neurons and their connections should go; experience tailors those neurons and connections and individualizes a child's brain. The reason that the wiring of the human brain is experience-dependent is because the generic blueprint embedded in the genes cannot meet the specifications of all the particular details of the environment in which the child is raised. Experience-dependent development enables each child to get the brain they need for adapting to the circumstances they live in. Here is a thought experiment to illustrate experience-dependent development: Imagine that an architect constructs plans for building a house. But instead of building the house exactly as the plans show, the contractor invites the family whose house it will be to move in during construction. As the builder builds, adjustments to the plans are made in coordination with the family's actual needs and desires. Maybe a room is enlarged, a door is widened, and even a few walls and windows are removed along the way, none of which was in the original plan.

The abilities that really count for long-term success are self-control, social perspective-taking, and resilience. The brain areas for these abilities are where you as a parent will have the most impact. Don't worry about doing it right all the time. There is a great deal of plasticity in the developing brain.

The Raw Materials, Processes, and Patterns of Brain Development

Your relationship shapes brain growth and impacts the speed, effectiveness, and reliability of how the brain operates. A child's brain starts growing before they are born and continues to grow until they reach young adulthood (Gazzaniga, Ivry, & Mangun, 2002; Tau & Peterson, 2010). The raw materials of brain development include *neurons* and their axon and dendrite connections to other neurons; *synapses*, the little points at which neurons communicate with one another; and *myelin*, the fatty substance that forms an insulating sheath around the axons. There are 3 basic processes involved: overgrowth and pruning; synapse remodeling; and myelinization.

There is a distinctive pattern to the growth, with three waves of exuberant overgrowth each followed by a period of pruning back the excess. The first wave occurs during gestation, the second wave from birth to age three, and the third during adolescence. During each wave, there is an overgrowth of neurons and synapses. This allows for enormous potential in terms of what a child is able to learn. As children acquire new skills and knowledge, the neurons and synapses that are used remain, while those not used are pruned back. Overgrowth and pruning is a bit like what happens when actors audition for a part in a movie. The movie director has a script for a film that requires 30 actors. At auditions, 1,000 people initially try out for the parts. Over a period of time, some of the actors that don't do so well are culled away and others, that do better, are given a few more scenes to try out for. Eventually, the original pool of 1,000 narrows down to the most talented 30 actors who will be in the movie.

The effect of pruning in the case of culling out unused neurons is to refine the precision of brain circuits. The circuits that remain after pruning become wrapped in myelin and have their synapses remodeled. Myelin is a lot like how an electrical wire gets wrapped in a plastic insulator. The effect of myelin is to speed the transmission of the electrical signal, which enables the brain to process information more rapidly. To imagine how this works think about a single-lane highway where traffic tends to go slowly. To speed things up, eventually engineers add passing lanes so that savvy drivers can scoot ahead of the slower cars and get to their destinations sooner. In myelinated neurons, electricity literally can jump ahead at certain spots to move the signal along more quickly.

Synaptic remodeling is dependent on how frequently electrical signals are transmitted across particular synapses. When synapses receive more signals, they release more neurotransmitter, which strengthens the synapses and makes it easier for the signal to cross the next time. When they receive less signal, the opposite occurs; they are weakened, releasing less neurotransmitter, and the signal does not cross as easily the next time. Remodeling is why, once we repeat a skill many times, it becomes easier to do. Synaptic remodeling is a bit like how traffic engineers alter the timing of traffic lights to regulate the traffic flow. Imagine a grid of city roads built in a new community. Traffic lights are placed at various intersections, with the timing of the red and green lights being equal in either direction. Over time it becomes clear that some roads are used

SCIENCE SAYS

Fun Facts about the Brain

At birth, the brain is only 25% of the size of an adult brain. By 12 months of life, it is about 60% of the size of an adult's, and by five years old, it is almost the size of an adult's (Kolb et al., 2012).

Brain development occurs "backward," meaning that brain regions begin to come "online" from back to front. The sensory regions mature first, followed by the motor regions and then the prefrontal cortex, where executive functions reside. It is as if the brain hires the employees first and then the managers before it hires the CEO.

more often than others, and that there are lots of places where intersections have a busy road with lots of cars, crossing a less busy road with fewer cars. The engineers eventually adjust the timing of the green lights so that the busier road at the intersection is actually easier to travel on than the less busy one.

The growth of neurons and synapses is associated with a child learning something, such as a new behavioral skill or cognitive ability. The pruning, myelinating, and synaptic remodeling are associated with the child mastering and becoming more precise about what he or she has learned. This is why the processes of pruning, myelinating, and remodeling are referred to as indicators of brain circuit maturation.

YOUR CHILD'S MILESTONES

Every new skill or ability your child is capable of is the result of your child's brain circuitry wiring up (Kagan & Baird, 2004). Developmental milestones can be thought of as the outward manifestation of an unfolding timeline of developments going on inside your child's brain. Your relationship will have an impact on those brain developments.

Whether it be the manner of soothing you use, the way you encourage your child to slow down when they read or think about how it makes someone else feel when they hit or grab a toy, or the way you teach your child to follow routines or set limits on their behavior, your guidance activates specific brain pathways in your child's brain. The more often you repeat these learning experiences, the stronger and more effective those brain circuits in your child's brain will be. This is the legacy you leave inside your child's brain, because it is these same circuits your child will use when they are independent and you are not around.

The arc of development from the womb to the end of childhood

During pregnancy you can feel and also see on a sonogram that the baby in your womb is already developing skills such as kicking, swallowing, and sucking their thumb, as the underlying brain circuits in motor and sensory areas become wired. The first wave of rapid and exuberant overgrowth of neurons and synapses occurs before a baby is born. Toward the latter half of pregnancy, the fetal brain can grow approximately 250,000 new neurons per minute, reaching a total of about 100 billion neurons at birth (Eliot, 2000). The peak number of neurons in the human brain occurs during week 28 of gestation. Yes, that's right! Your child's brain has as many neurons as it will ever have by the time you are seven months pregnant. At week 34 of gestation, almost 40,000 new synapses are being formed every second. The brain develops enough by the time your baby is born that he or she can see, hear, taste, smell, touch, feel emotion, feel pain, move, nurse, be interested in your face, and even copy some of your mouth movements. All the abilities your baby needs to learn how to relate to you and the immediate physical world are in place.

Beginning at birth and continuing during the first three years of life, there is a second wave of rapid overgrowth of neurons and synapses. Maturation begins as well, by way of pruning, myelinating, and remodeling. However unlike the overgrowth, which is rapid and ends by 3yrs of age, maturation occurs slowly over the ensuing years, until about age 11. The excess neurons and connections that form during overgrowth cause your child to initially be awkward and all over the place when first learning a behavior. Maturation is what enables your child to become more accurate and coordinated in their behavior.

Too many connections explains why your infant moves his or her arm in all directions in attempting to reach for a toy. It's as if your child initially has too many possible ways to move. In time, they figure out which movements they will use, and this brings about the pruning of unused connections so that your baby is able to reach more precisely for the toy. It's the same when your child learns to read. At first, they use their hands and ears along with their eyes, pointing at the words and sounding out the letters or saying the words out loud. Eventually, as unused connections are winnowed away and the remaining ones are strengthened, your child is able to read silently just with their eyes.

A clear example of abundant overgrowth followed by pruning involves the recognition of speech sounds. Overgrowth in speech areas allows young infants to recognize and reproduce sounds from any language. By six months of age, pruning causes them to start to recognize and copy only sounds from the language they are born into. An example of maturation is seen in motor regions when your child switches from holding a crayon with their whole hand to holding it between their thumb and forefinger. Maturation in prefrontal circuits is what enables your child to develop behavior and impulse control so that they can continue sitting in the circle in kindergarten despite being distracted by something interesting in the back of the room.

Whenever you are frustrated by how uncoordinated or confused your child is, imagine yourself plugging an address into your GPS and having it spit out thousands of possible routes you could take. That's your child's brain before pruning. You would be pretty confused too! The importance of timely pruning cannot be overemphasized. Certain conditions of delayed development, such as autism, are considered to be the result of too rapid an acceleration of brain growth without sufficient pruning.

At around four to seven years of age the pruning gets fierce as the brain begins to significantly cut back excess connections. The rate of pruning slows down after that but continues until about age 11. This rapid pruning from four to seven is *the dawning of self-control* as circuits connecting sensory, motor, emotion, speech, and memory regions with prefrontal cortex "control" centers are pruned. Pruning makes your child *school ready* as the inhibitory ability of the prefrontal cortex becomes more able to help your child sit still, hold a pencil, write their name, wait their turn, and cooperate in a group—all of which require quite a lot of self-control.

The Birth of the Social Child: 2 to 4 Months:

Around two to three months of age, there is reduced crying, increased social smiling, and increased ability to pay attention to *all* objects, faces, and sounds. At four months of age, babies start to pay *extra* attention to novel, unfamiliar stimuli. At this same age, babies need and seek out lots of facial engagement and are most interested in the emotionally responsive faces of their caretakers. They also begin to form expectations of how their mothers will respond and how the physical world works.

The expectancy of the infant is a first step in their developing an attachment. Expectancy only gets stronger as children develop. Keep the importance of expectancy in mind the next time your child complains that they want the hotdog you promised them for dinner (but that you couldn't give them because you forgot to buy the hotdogs). Your child may get upset and complain, "But you promised!" As frustrating as it might be, the capacity to expect the hotdog you promised is what enables your three-year-old child to know that they can expect you to come and pick them up after preschool and thus stay calm during school time.

The Birth of Self-Control: 7–12 Months

An extra spurt of prefrontal cortex development at 7 to 12 months of age is responsible for the first appearance of working memory and behavioral control (Gilmore & Johnson, 1995). Working memory can retain a few bits of information for a short period of time and manipulate it so that it can be used for a particular task. The classic example of working memory is hearing a 10-digit phone number and remembering it for more than a few seconds so that you can write it down. Infants younger than seven and a half months don't have working memory. They fail to retrieve a hidden object if there is any delay between hiding and retrieval. Infants older than seven and a half months show the onset of working memory because they will remember the object and retrieve it after delays of two to three seconds, and by 12 months they will succeed in retrieving the object after up to 10 seconds.

An example illustrating behavioral control is when a five-month-old baby will use both hands to reach for any object, small or large, whereas an eight-month-old reaches with one hand for small objects and with two hands for larger ones.

Working memory is highly correlated with cognitive achievement. It is what your child uses when they read a paragraph and then need to quickly answer some questions about the paragraph without being able to look back at it. Working memory is crucial for problem-solving because it allows your child to hold in mind a number of possible solutions to a problem, and even to try them on for size, before deciding on which one to use. Working memory is vulnerable and easily disrupted by distractions, which is what happens when your child answers the phone after you asked them to clean their room and doesn't remember to go back to finish cleaning. The point here is not to justify forgetfulness. The point is that holding more than a few bits of information in mind all at the same time is hard for anyone and is especially difficult for children, because their prefrontal cortex is still in the process of maturing.

The Birth of the Self: 12–24 Months

The capacity for inference emerges as a result of increased connections between sensory brain areas and the social-emotional brain areas involved in creating meanings. These enable two-year-olds to draw inferences about what is going on in someone else's mind. By their second birthday, infants can draw inferences from their mother's eye gaze, meaning that they will know just by her glance where a toy is hidden or where to look at an object of interest. Inference-making is also why babies show empathic behaviors when they see someone in distress—for example, helping to pick up someone's pen when it drops.

By two years of age, children can mentally represent prohibited behaviors. For example, they will hesitate when asked to perform a behavior that doesn't fit with family norms. This ability corresponds to an underlying increase in neural connectivity between the left and right hemispheres, the most likely explanation being that emotion associated with the parent's criticisms and punishments are held more on the right side of the brain, while the meanings of the words the parent uses are held more on the left side of the brain.

Signs of self-awareness appear in children this age, including the ability to recognize themselves when looking in a mirror, the ability to direct a parent to perform certain actions, distress if they can't imitate the actions of another and pride when they can, and the ability to describe in speech what they are doing as they are doing it. The onset of self-awareness is also associated with the increased connectivity between the two hemispheres. Since the right side is dominant for emotion and sensory experience and the left side is dominant for speech, thought, and meaning, the increased connections link the child's awareness of what they feel with what their intentions are.

The Birth of Competence: 2–8 Years

Over this period, a child acquires greater self-control, better language skills, enhanced memory, and recognition of causality. By the time a child is somewhere between five and eight, these abilities transform him or her into someone who is "teachable" and capable of some degree of responsibility, which is why children this age are often referred to as being *kindergarten ready*. Around seven, children become more aware of their impact on the world and start to *wonder why* things happen the way they do. They can see, for example, how their clumsy behavior caused damage to another child's toy and are capable of feeling remorse. They become able to recognize that if they made a mistake in solving a problem, the error was connected to their not having carefully considered alternative solutions.

The distinctive brain changes associated with these abilities include a very high growth rate in the cortex, which is responsible for all higher cognitive abilities, and a spurt of myelinization in the circuits linking the left and right hemispheres and increasing connectivity within each hemisphere, speeding up communication between brain areas. The continual pruning that occurs until a child is 11 further refines and strengthens all their newly acquired abilities.

SUPPORT HOW CHILDREN LEARN BEST

Children learn better through self-discovery and trial-and-error experimentation. After they explore, they come back to demonstrate to their parents what they have discovered, and they want to repeat the discovery again and again until they have mastered what needs to be learned. As a reflective parent, your role is to support and be responsive to this kind of learning. As you observe their actions, as they show or tell you what they have learned, and as you talk about it together over and over, it is strengthening all parts of the circuit involved in that learning, including your child's executive control centers. If sometimes you feel bored or even irritated as your child wants to do something over and over, try to remember that it's the *repetition* that makes the learning permanent.

It's not just learning skills and facts that results in a child doing well. It's the development of their mind that informs them what to *believe* and how to *think about* these skills and facts so that they can be used in a socially appropriate way and in keeping with their personal goals and their family's values and expectations. You develop your child's mind by exercising their mind. You do this when you talk about how people's feelings, intentions, and beliefs help explain their behavior and engage your child in a conversation about these ideas. Encourage your child to make their own links between behaviors, feelings, beliefs, and intentions and to share them with you. You don't have to agree with how your child puts it all together, but you do need to express your interest and curiosity. For example, suppose your nine-year-old son's friend invites him for a sleepover. Your son likes his friend and doesn't want to hurt his feelings, but he doesn't really want to sleep over because he has other things he wants to do. You could just make the decision for him, but if you do, you'll lose an opportunity to build up his reflective capacity. If you have a conversation about ways to think about the situation and ask him about the ways *he* thinks would be a good way to handle it, you exercise his mind. He will have *child age* ideas, but he will be building connections from the thinking part of his brain to the doing and feeling parts. And, in the end, you can still make the decision if you feel that is best.

The timing of development of your child's reflective capacity parallels the development of their executive functions, because both involve prefrontal cortex circuits. By the time a child is in school, they have some reflective capacity, so they are able to inhibit—for instance—their hitting, not just because it is prohibited, but also because they now can apply their understanding that hitting hurts people's feelings. Reflective capacity, with its awareness of mind, enables your child to use techniques such as self-talk, "playing it out" beforehand, or developing positive imagery that they can draw upon to control themselves at a later time. Positive imagery means imagining a scene that helps the child feel better. For example, a child afraid of talking in class might imagine themselves successfully raising their hand and answering a question correctly. It is similar to how a basketball player might imagine the ball going into the hoop before shooting a free throw. These kinds of techniques can be employed by parents when they help a child think through and anticipate exactly what is going to happen when they go to the doctor or what they might feel on the first day of kindergarten or on a field trip. This is similar to what parents are doing when they help a shy child who is worried about an upcoming social event by having them recall that they usually feel better rather quickly or having them think about who they will know so they can go up to someone familiar.

Reflect to reframe the terrible twos.

Anytime a parent is able to reframe a negative experience with their child into a more positive one, it helps calm the parent, and they engage with their child in a more adaptive way. One stage of development when this can be especially useful is during what is often referred to in a negative way as the "terrible twos." One way to reframe is to see the negative behavior as a positive sign that the child's brain has achieved a new level of development in memory circuits and in self-awareness circuits. The frustration, lack of cooperation, and even tantrums your toddler expresses indicate that their memory storage has increased enough to hold on to what they want and explain why they want it for a longer period than they ever have before. Their prefrontal cortex has created a sense of "me" that they never had before! That is what a temper tantrum is about. The child can't handle the situation, but their greater sense of "me" promotes a surge in independence, so they won't let their parent help. A younger infant is fine about being soothed or redirected. But by around age two, when you tell your child no, they can hold on to what they want tenaciously, and even though they may clearly need soothing, they push it away. An additional explanation for their stubbornness and tantrums is that they have improved memory and a sense of self that allow them to desire things strongly, but they don't yet have enough prefrontal cortex control to handle the disappointment of not being able to always get it. As a reflective parent, you can reframe the terrible twos as the *terrific twos*. It is a positive step in brain development and represents the acquisition of new, independent abilities. You should feel good because it means you provided them with the right input for their brain to grow.

Remember, your child is born almost 100% ignorant of the ways of the world. Everything, and that means *everything*, must be learned. The toddler's brain is actually designed to work together with you so that you can teach them the ropes for how to be a person, how to live within your family, and how to act within the community and culture you are a part of. But you have to be sensitive to their surge of "me" and increased need for independence. Another way to reframe is to remember that your 2-year-old's abilities to assert what they want, to be really motivated to try to get what they want, and to say "no," and not let anyone push them around, are actually positive traits you want your child to have when they are grown up. Reframing won't prevent you from having to rein in your 2-year-old or prevent you from having to endure a temper tantrum, but it will allow you to handle their demands and outbursts with more tact and less hostility.

Reflect to slow down; development takes time.

A child's age determines their level of brain development and puts limits on what they can and cannot do. This issue comes up a lot around decisions about discipline. One parent of a 15-month-old said, "My son is hitting and biting. How do I discipline him not to do this?" She didn't realize that a 15-month-old can't be disciplined. They understand that you don't want them to do something, but their brain is not developed enough to control their impulses. Upon hearing this, the mother heaved a sigh of relief. "You mean it's normal? I was afraid that if I didn't discipline him now, he would grow up to be a spoiled brat."

This issue also comes up a lot around academic achievement. We have a one-size-fits-all school system, but children come in all sizes. Kids' brains each develop on their own time course. If your child is not yet able to organize their homework in fourth grade or even middle school, don't panic; there is still so much time for brain development to kick in. Don't get hung up on the idea that your child should be in lockstep with every other child, following a single path to success. Appreciate the beauty of your child's individual brain, and you will better appreciate your child for who he or she is. You will thus form a stronger bond with your child and help them do better in life. There are many children who get left behind in first grade only to forge ahead in college. There are many kids who are totally disorganized in middle school but shape up when they get a job. There are kids who are shy and have few friends when they're young but blossom later on when more prefrontal cortex kicks in. There are kids who don't fit in that well with their local peer group but finally find their social niche when they go to college where there are more people like them. Be patient with the slowness of brain development.

The rate of brain development also presents dilemmas around such issues as appreciation and gratitude. Parents commonly resent that their child doesn't fully appreciate all that they do for them. It may help to think about your own tendencies. Do you appreciate oxygen? Do you appreciate gravity? No, you don't even think about them. You take them for granted. Oxygen and gravity are so ubiquitous in the environment that your brain doesn't pick them out as distinct entities to pay attention to. In many respects, the experiences your child has are the assumed givens of their world. If you give your child a big birthday present every year, they assume big birthday presents are a given. If you drive them halfway across town so they can go to a better public school or send them to a fancy private school, they assume that is the given. If you knock yourself out to leave work early so you can watch their soccer practice, they assume it's a given that you will be there. They are grateful and appreciative of these things, but generally not in the active way many parents wish they would. They love their parents. They are happy about what their parents do for them and with them. But typically they can't quite appreciate those things the way an adult would. They are not being thoughtless or ungrateful if they don't actively appreciate it. They simply have no experience, and therefore no brain circuitry, to really understand what it means to *not* have these things. They are not able to fully "get" what it means to be responsible for working and making enough money to raise a family or having to negotiate to leave work in order to be with that family. They only know what they know. In some sense, they trust that you will be there for them in the way you always have, and it's kind of beautiful to think about it that way. It's why your three-year-old will jump off the side of the pool into your arms: They trust you will be there to catch them. You don't expect the baby to be "grateful" that you caught them. Children trust that you want to give them all the things you give them.

Eventually, children do have to learn good manners and good values. You can teach your child to show appreciation by saying thank you when something is done for them, such as when you throw them a birthday party or take them to their friend's house. But if you insist that they *feel* grateful for all your efforts and how hard you had to work to give them all that you do, you are asking them to do something that they don't yet have the depth of understanding to do. Most kids are happy and thankful to have the parent they have, but they can't really put themselves in your shoes until they are older.

Reflect to raise the child you have.

Being reflective helps you better understand your child's temperament and teach your child how to best manage the temperament they have. Temperament is neither good nor bad; it just *is* the child's tendency. Yet parents tend to worry a great deal about what a child's temperament bodes for their child's future success. A reflective motto would be, "Stop worrying so much about the future and just help your child with what is going on now!" You can do so much more to benefit your child's future by sticking with the *now* of what is happening than you can if you are focused on *later on down the road*. In fact, there is evidence that many temperament traits are modified when the child is older and that only the extremes of temperament are likely to remain over the life span. (Hornbuckle, 2010; Kagan & Baird, 2004). Traits such as shyness and gregariousness typically remain stable throughout life, but not always (Kagan, 2003).

For children to optimally manage whatever tendency they have and to be as resilient as possible despite their vulnerability, your role is to figure out what they need and what works best for meeting that need. A highly gregarious child, for example, may be much more distraught when they are not invited to a birthday party than a child who is more intro-

SCIENCE SAYS

About 40% of babies are born with an easy temperament, readily adjusting to new situations, easily establishing routines, and generally staying cheerful and calm. That means that 60% of babies have a more *difficult* temperament that causes them to be more vulnerable in one way or another.

verted. They may need you to be a lot more empathic, understanding, and comforting of their feelings of rejection in this case. The introverted child, on the other hand, may need more help when it comes to the discomfort they experience in groups or any new situation. These children will need their parents to be more empathic, understanding, and comforting about their social distress and anxiety. How you go about setting limits for each of these different children will also be different. One may need to be reined in from going to too many parties, while the other may need to be pushed to at least attend the party of a close friend.

It is understandable that many parents worry about the fact that their child is shy and more inhibited or fearful than other children. A shy child will not necessarily always be shy or more likely to have problems later on if they receive the kind of emotionally sensitive parenting they need (Kagan, 2003). You don't help your child if you try to turn your shy, inhibited child into someone more "outgoing" or your anxious child into someone more "brave." The most important factor in helping shy, inhibited, or anxious children to do as well as possible is to be warm and nonjudgmental about how they feel. These children will be more likely to handle their emotions *adaptively* if they feel that their parent gives them a safe place to have these feelings. It is this quality in the relationship that enables a child to better tolerate their painful emotions and maximizes what they are able to deal with. The child who is made to feel like there is something wrong with them because they are shy, inhibited, or anxious is more likely to suffer negative attitudes about themselves and feel more of a need to escape with substances of abuse.

Although the understandable urge to protect these types of children causes parents to steer them away from upsetting situations, research indicates that parents would do better to resist this urge. Avoiding the situation deprives the child of developing a sense of control over their environment, and this only adds to their fearfulness and reticence. Only by your gentle and kind support of their efforts to master situations will your child build the self-confidence that they can handle them. Science indicates that these kids require a lot more warmth and support than other kids.

Reflect to promote play.

Play is not just for fun. Play is a child's work, coordinating his or her body to interact with the physical and social world. Play stimulates the emotion of joy and triggers laughter to indicate to others that the child is in a carefree mood and has a feeling of social camaraderie. Play wires the brain, strengthening brain circuits the child will use in adult life.

Play with other kids starts around two years old, peaks during childhood, and diminishes during puberty. Children learn a lot through play. They learn about other people's limits. They learn to cooperate and solve problems. What stimulates the most brain growth is unstructured play where there is plenty of room for trial-and-error self-learning. Kids even use rough-and-tumble or chasing play for establishing a dominance hierarchy and learning each other's limits. Engaging in rough-and-tumble play, as long as it does not become too aggressive, improves a child's social competence (Flanders, Leo, Paquette, Pihl, & Séguin, 2009; Ginsburg, 2007).

Unfortunately, these days kids don't have enough opportunity for unstructured play. It's hard for parents not to get caught up in the pressure for kids to achieve and be on that elite path toward success. But we know that kids are becoming overly anxious on this treadmill and also are losing their ability to solve problems and think things through on their own. You can make a difference in your child's life by being an advocate for more playtime.

Reflect to tolerate conflict.

Only with the maturation of the prefrontal cortex, and the self-reflective consciousness it makes possible, does a child become self-aware and aware of others. It is especially hard for children to be aware of others if their own needs and interests conflict with those of others. They will prioritize their own needs in such cases. For example, suppose you arrive home with your preschooler and he doesn't say hello to Grandma as he quickly rushes to his room. Is your son being rude? Perhaps. But another possibility is that he is in autopilot mode. He always goes right to his room after preschool to continue playing with his Lego set. He may not have noticed his grandmother, or he may not have been able to inhibit his habit to stop himself long enough to say hello. Yes, he needs to learn, but labeling his behavior as rude is name-calling, not teaching. Too much harshness activates stress and diminishes learning.

Or suppose your daughter sees you and automatically starts asking you questions, even if you are on the phone or visiting with a friend. From your child's perspective, you are right in front of their eyes, and you usually are perfectly happy to answer their questions. What is it your child has to learn in this situation? They have to learn to wait their turn, to ask if it is OK to interrupt, and to see the situation from Mommy's perspective of being busy and unavailable for the moment. This kind of learning takes time and repetition as prefrontal circuits are building up. This is why you must draw their attention to it over and over again so they can practice and make it part of their habitual way of being.

Much parent–child conflict occurs when a parent has one goal and the child another. For example, suppose that, after picking up your daughter at school, your goal is to stop at the shoemaker's to get the shoes you need for work tomorrow before driving across town to coach your daughter's basketball team. Your daughter's goal is to get ice cream before the game, but that doesn't leave you time for getting the shoes you need. You both are in a rush to make it to the game on time, but each fixed on a different goal along the way. "Dad, I'm starving. I need something to eat. You can wear different shoes!" "Honey, no I can't, and after the game the store will be closed." Clash, anger, stalemate as each of you operates in a fixed and rigid way. Someone has to step back and reflect. It's usually you, the parent, because you're better at it—at least in theory. "Honey, let's figure it out. You need to eat, and I need to get my shoes before the game. Otherwise I have to drive all the way back near your school to get my shoes and be late to coaching." By engaging in conversation rather than battle, your child is more likely to be cooperative and say, "Okay, Dad! I have an old stale granola bar in my backpack. Next time do your errand before you pick me up." Being reflective takes time, but so does shouting and conflict. All the repeated reflective efforts and discussion and teaching pay out in the end, especially if they have been delivered with the empathic awareness of your child's normal brain limitations.

Reflect to hold the feelings and hold the line.

The attitude you have when you set limits and boundaries becomes incorporated into the wiring of your child's brain circuits for self-control. Being reflective helps you remember that you can put limits on your child's behavior, but not on their inner emotions. For example, you might say, "I totally understand you are in a bad mood, but even if you feel badly, you can't curse at me."

Being reflective reminds you to balance *emotional responsiveness* with *limit-setting*. In fact, too much emphasis on understanding and validating can get in the way of effective limit-setting. Children learn limits in three stages: exploration, testing to find out from others what is acceptable and what is not, and internalizing previously unknown boundaries (Brazelton, 1983). Imagine being blindfolded and walking around until you hit a wall. That doesn't feel good. But you might check it out again, maybe a few times, to make sure the wall is still there. Then you know for certain not to keep going in that direction.

Many parents find it difficult to set limits because they don't realize that limits and boundaries are subjective. They are the limits and boundaries *of the parents*. Parents have to figure out what their limits and boundaries are before they can be effective in setting them. *You* have to be clear about what really matters to *you* so that you can set limits more clearly, confidently, and firmly. That way, your child is more likely to know you really mean it. They may still test, but probably less so.

On the other hand, it is common for parents to worry that validating a child's distressed feelings or letting a child fully express what they are upset about will only make things worse. The problem for these parents is that they often confuse validation and room for expression with giving in or having the same perspective as the child. True validation means only that the parent sees why the child is distressed *from the child's perspective*. When parents validate a child's feelings, make room for the child to express their distress, and are able to listen without judgment, it usually has a calming effect. Don't you like it when someone sees your perspective, even if they don't agree with you? Don't you like it when someone gives you the space to vent and is willing to just listen? That's how kids are, too, but even more so!

THE BENEFITS OF BOTH A WOMAN'S AND A MAN'S APPROACH

Children are born with a drive to seek out and connect with their fathers just as much as they are born with the instinct to seek out and connect with their mothers (Pruett, 2000). By the time they are 6-8 weeks of age, infants recognize and can anticipate the differences in style of care between moms and dads. It is clear from the chapters on maternal care and attachment just how important it is for mothers to be nurturing, comforting, and emotionally responsive toward their child. In fact it is emphasized that a mother's brain actually gets wired to be this way as she cares for her young infant.

For too long, however, research has focused primarily on moms, to the exclusion of dads. Fortunately a shift is occurring. It is increasingly clear that fathers play an extremely beneficial role in the lives of children in all domains of life, whether the father lives in the home with the mother or lives outside the home (Pruett, 2000). In today's more gender-diverse atmosphere, even though we try not to dichotomize female and male characteristics into such distinct boxes, studies do show dads tend to parent differently than moms and that having two parents with different styles is good for kids. The research strongly indicates that moms tend to be more on the protective side and dads are more likely to encourage independence. Dads tend to be more comfortable with a child's frustration in working on a task and see more of the problem-solving value of their efforts. Moms tend to try to make it a little easier for the child. Kids know their parents are different; and the difference is good for kids especially when parents respect each other's approach (Pruett & Pruett, 2009). The differences provide children with greater flexibility and resiliency because they can internalize multiple possible approaches to life. What this indicates is that it does not always have to be "a united front," as long as both parents recognize the value of each other's style. The relationship between Mom's style and Dad's style is the like relationship between our need for oxygen and our need for water. We need both to do well.

Verbal Skills and Academic Achievement

Children with involved, caring fathers when they are young have better verbal skills and educational outcomes that extend all the way through adolescence and young adulthood; which may be due to the fact that fathers are more likely to emphasize achievement and mothers to emphasize nurturance (Rosenberg & Wilcox, 2006; Flouri, & Buchanan, 2004; Coley & Hernandez, 2006; Fagan & Palm, 2004; McWayne et al., 2013; Allen & Daly 2007). For example, they are more likely to be ready for kindergarten, are better at handling the stresses and frustrations of school, show more curiosity and problem solving skills, have better reading and math skills, get better grades in school, and have higher educational achievement and occupational mobility relative to their parents.

Social Competence and Emotional Wellbeing

Children with involved fathers tend to do better socially with peers and are more likely to have healthy emotional development (Rosenberg & Wilcox, 2006; Pruett, 2000; Pruett & Pruett, 2009; Fagan & Palm, 2004; Allen & Daly, 2007). It is proposed that this is because of the differences between men and women with respect to how they play with their kids, and their differences with respect to issues such as coping, independence and mastery.

Fathers (even stay-at-home dads) spend more 1:1 time in stimulating, playful, and rough housing activity with young children than do mothers. This enables children to learn how to deal with aggressive impulses and physical contact without losing control of their emotions. By having to speak up to tell their dads when the play is getting 'too rough' for them, children learn from their fathers how to be more assertive and set boundaries.

Mothers tend to step in to nurture, comfort, reassure, and assist more quickly when children are upset, frustrated, fearful, or stressed. By contrast, fathers tend to encourage their children to tolerate negative emotions for a longer period of time, foster coping with difficulties, support exploration, and promote mastery of skills. The fact that fathers focus more on tolerating and managing the slings and arrows of life does not mean that fathers make kids "tough." In fact, have a caring and involved father is often associated with a greater capacity for empathy in children and the ability to cooperate, be helpful, and get along well with others. Fathers are more likely to promote independence, self-sufficiency, and an orientation to the outside world, which enables children with involved fathers to be more comfortable exploring the world around them, and more able to control themselves in school and other social situations.

It is not that moms or dads are better at dealing with a child's emotions. It's just that they are different. Here are some other differences. Moms and dads tend to differ in how well they can tolerate challenging behaviors in their children. Dads tend to be less upset by temper tantrums, hitting, and biting than moms, but they tend to get more upset by sleeping and eating problems than moms. Moms and dads also tend to approach discipline differently. Dads emphasize the real-world hazards of misbehavior ("Since you tore your friend's jacket, you're going to have to pay to replace it."), whereas moms emphasize the interpersonal consequences of misbehavior ("People aren't going to like you if you mistreat their things."). Another example is that Dad's communication style is different than Mom's, with fathers' language tending to be more complicated and fathers tending to be less responsive and less likely to understand what their child says and less likely to ask for clarification than moms. It is as if mothers prepare their child to communicate well with people they are close to or intimate with, whereas fathers prepare their child for communicating more with the outside world, with people they are less close to and less familiar with.

STORIES OF PARENTS AND CHILDREN

- **Children are different.** Shawna, the mother of 15-month-old Emmanuel, revealed her deep worry. "My son has always had difficulty sleeping. I know they say not to let a child sleep with you in bed, but we had to. As a tiny baby, the only place he would sleep was on my chest. What was I to do? It was the only way he would calm down enough to sleep. Even now, at 15 months, he has trouble settling down at night. It worries me that we might be doing something wrong. I hear about all these other parents whose kids just calmly go to sleep at night. Ours doesn't. We are so afraid we are causing him problems." What this mother needs is support for raising a child with a more difficult temperament. She needs to know that just because her child is having difficulty with sleeping doesn't mean she is doing something wrong. In fact, she appears to be doing an amazing job, trying valiantly to help him get to sleep. The thing for a parent in this kind of situation to know is that we all come into the world with our own set of strengths and vulnerabilities. This baby has lots of strengths, but getting to sleep is not one of them. He needs extra soothing and scaffolding to help him get to sleep. What matters even more than trying to get your child to overcome their vulnerability is to show your child how much you are *there* for them and how much you care about helping them with their vulnerability, no matter how well or how poorly they do.

- *Executive functions improve self-control.* Risa has a 10-year-old daughter, Madison, who is an extremely sensitive girl and still has occassional meltdowns when she is anxious. Madison has to take medication for a skin condition, which adds to her anxiety because she thinks other kids are laughing at her, and she worries that it will never get better. Any attention to the condition activates her anxiety, and all of this causes her to get upset, argue, yell, and refuse to take her medication. When Risa pushes Madison to take it, Madison starts screaming. Risa feels frightened and helpless when Madison refuses her medications, which leads Risa to make threats to punish her unless she cooperates. When Risa steps back to reflect, she realizes how the outbursts make her (Risa) feel helpless, scared, and compelled to make Madison stop screaming. She also realizes that Madison's screaming is her way of communicating that she is anxious. Reflecting relaxes Risa, and her thinking becomes more flexible. Instead of trying to make Madison stop screamng, Risa decides to use a little humor and engage Madison's attention and curiosity, which are associated with the prefrontal cortex executive functions. "Do you know the story of my friend who had a skin condition when she was a kid? She grew up to be a fashion designer just like you want to be. She had to take medication and her skin improved. Things find a way of getting worked out. Let's try and think more about how skin conditions can improve." The screaming is left behind as Madison shifts her attention and says, "Mom, do you still know your friend? Tell me more about her."

- *Children's brains are immature and need scaffolding.* Tom is the father of nine-year-old Seth. Tom is a great tennis player and has been looking forward to being able to play with Seth. Tom wants to teach Seth how to play well, so he hits to his forehand, then to his backhand. Seth can't hit the balls back that well and gets discouraged easily. Seth wants his dad to hit the ball directly at him so he can always hit it back. Tom agrees to just rally but can't contain his disappointment and is irritated by his son's lack of "motivation to succeed." Seth picks up Tom's attitude and soon starts to lose interest in playing tennis, which only makes Tom more disappointed and annoyed. Fortunately, Tom has a sympathetic but insightful wife. She tells Tom that while it is important for Seth to learn how to play better at tennis and to also learn how to deal with his feelings without just giving up, what matters more is the relationship—Seth needs Tom's help in building up his confidence and coping. She adds that Tom isn't coping well himself, so how is he going to be able to help his son? Tom reframes the situation as a time to just be together, which makes his attitude more positive. When they rally and Seth misses the ball, Tom kindly says that missing is just as important as hitting. Seth starts enjoying playing with his dad. The happy ending is that after about six months, Seth actually asks his dad to start hitting more challenging balls to him. Seth will never be the tennis player Tom had hoped he'd be, but Tom vastly increases Seth's proficiency by his more reflective approach to relating to his son. As a bonus, Tom feels better about himself as a father.

PUTTING IT INTO WORDS

- When you verbally link sensations, feelings, actions, impulses, and mind, both in the here and now and over time, you help build the interconnections between brain regions and build tolerance for negative emotions.
  - *With a six-month-old:* "You rolled over from your back to your tummy. You tried hard and you did it! That was fun!"
  - *With a two-year old:* "You were upset that I wouldn't let you have another piece of bread. You kicked your feet to let me know you

were mad. Then you had a hard time calming. So we hugged, and now you feel better."

- *With a five-year-old:* "I know you like it when Daddy walks you into your classroom, but now it's time for you to learn how to do that yourself. It's going to feel a little scary and maybe a little icky with butterflies in your stomach. Let's think of some way to make it easier for you. Maybe you could be in charge and say, 'Dad, go home now!' in a loud voice."

- **All learning requires time for the brain circuits to wire.**
  - "Don't get upset with yourself when [fill in the blank] is hard to do at first. Most people aren't good at it right way. I know I wasn't. I promise you will get better with time."
  - "I know you wish you were better at [fill in the blank] because other kids are better than you. But it takes time and practice to learn any skill. Try not to compare yourself to others. Just focus on you and give yourself the time to improve."
- Repetition increases the strength of brain circuits, making it easier for the brain to perform a repeated routine.
  - *Reminding your three-year-old of the bedtime routine.* "I know you don't want to go to bed, but remember our routine. First you go into your bath. Then you get into your pajamas and get into bed. Then we read three books and it's time to go to sleep. So let's get started with your bath."
  - *Reminding your seven-year-old of the teeth-brushing routine.* "Remember, first you get your 30 minutes of TV, and then it's time to brush your teeth."

- Children internalize your intense feelings. That's why it's important to own your feelings. For example: "I think I got too disappointed when you didn't want to go to the baseball game with me and wanted to go to your friend's birthday instead. So I acted kind of annoyed with you and made you feel bad. That wasn't fair. I'm sorry for how I dealt with my feelings. It's OK for me to feel disappointed but not OK for me to get angry with *you* about it."

TAKE-HOME LESSONS

- Think of two areas where your child is uncooperative. See if you can create a routine for these situations. If you already have a routine, check in with yourself and make sure it really matters to you that your child cooperates in this area and that you are expressing your expectations clearly and confidently. Routines are not magic, but they do provide a familiar expectation that is calming for children. You don't have to follow routines rigidly, but use them to form a basis of what's expected.

- Make sure your child has enough time to play freely without an adult structuring their time. When children play unsupervised instead of listening to what adults are expecting them to do, they are engaging in meaningful social learning. You might not like the idea, but when children play freely, they naturally get into conflict. Be more accepting of the conflict, because it contributes to how children learn each other's limits and how to deal with them.

- Allow enough *downtime*, even time to be bored and do nothing. This allows children to go inward and be creative and to feel more of a sense of connection with their own mind. Resist the urge to tell your child what to do when they are bored. Instead, encourage them to figure it out by thinking about what they are in the mood to do or might be interested in. If they can't, this is the time to teach them that we all have to learn how to deal with being bored. Learning how to be OK with being bored is a skill like anything else.

NINE

Parenting from Adolescence through Adulthood

BRAIN BASICS

Adolescent brain development uses the same mechanisms as childhood brain development, but with a different emphasis. Adolescence provides a second chance for brain development so that teenagers can adapt to their changing circumstances and take on the responsibilities of adult life.

THE ADOLESCENT JOURNEY

Aristotle was referring to adolescents when he said, "The young are heated by Nature as drunken men by wine." Adolescence is that time between childhood and adulthood when a child must acquire the knowledge and skills they need to separate from and function independently of the protective environment of the family. What seem like troublesome traits to parents are considered adaptive survival mechanisms by developmental scientists (Somerville, 2013). For this reason, the adolescent brain goes through a third wave of exuberant overgrowth of neurons and synapses in the specific brain areas responsible for the unique kinds of learning experiences that teens must undergo (National Institute of Mental Health, 2011). As a side benefit, the new period of brain growth provides a developmental second chance—an opportunity for the teen to developmentally catch up and for the parent to make up for previous weaknesses in the parenting relationship.

If you are like many parents, you wish you had more control over your teenager—that instead of taking risks, they would listen to you! But nature thinks differently. Nature knows that it makes a child an *even more competent* adult if they have navigated *themselves* through their emotionality and risk-taking. Your role in the process is really important, but it is more that of a wise, supportive guide than that of a director.

WHY ADOLESCENCE OCCURS: A POSITIVE, ADAPTIVE PERSPECTIVE

An adolescent's emotional reactivity, impulsivity, novelty-seeking, sensation-seeking, and risk-taking are the brain's way of ensuring that they learn all the new information they will need to function as an adult. Although it is adaptive for teens to be this way, it can be hard on the parent–child relationship. It is natural for concerned and loving parents to feel anxious about their child's safety and to feel a sense of loss and rejection when kids pull away. One of the aims of this chapter is to reduce some of the conflict and turmoil.

Focus on the relationship: Your teen still wants you in their life.

Despite the fact that your teenager may seem dismissive and critical of you, it should comfort you to know that three-quarters of young people between ages 13 and 24 say that their relationship with their parents is what makes them happy (Noveck & Tompson, 2007). It is *not* electronics, pop music, money, or even sex or drugs that makes them happy. And that's teenagers and young adults we're talking about, the ones who are supposedly breaking away from the nest and rejecting their parents.

Teens have a lot to learn.

Your teen must learn to separate from the cushiness of home life with parents and move into the much more stressful and complicated world beyond the home, where they will form new intimate and romantic connections with other people, start to think for themselves, and function on their own as an independent adult. Essentially, your teenager is traveling to the foreign country we call *adulthood*. Their companions in this new country will be their peers, not you. Since they are going without you, they must be open to learning things on their own. This perspective explains why their peer relationships take on a heightened importance, why they care so deeply about whether they are accepted or rejected by peers, and why they are more adventuresome and risk-taking than before. Neuroscience emphasizes that the very traits that drive parents crazy are the ones that evolution has selected so that teenagers can survive the process of growing up and becoming full-fledged adults in their own right.

When your teen judges and criticizes you, when they only want to be with their friends, and when they do things despite your prohibitions, do you feel hurt, rejected, and disrespected? When they are impulsive and risk-taking, are you critical and judgmental of them? This is when you must see the situation from their perspective, which is that they are doing what they need to do. And from the point of view of biology, they are right. They are acquiring the tools they need for the job of becoming an adult.

Puberty and adolescence are not synonymous.

Puberty and adolescence are separate processes. (Sisk & Zehr, 2005). Scientists say *puberty is for making eggs and sperm; adolescence is for learning how to bring egg and sperm together in a responsible way.* Puberty typically begins before adolescence with the release of the steroid sex hormones that result in body changes such as breast development and ovulation (females) and facial hair and sperm production (males). Adolescence is heralded by new behaviors and thinking patterns caused by a remodeling of the brain.

TEEN BRAIN DEVELOPMENT

The teen brain has two separate paths of brain development, which explains why teens are both more mature and more difficult than younger kids (Casey, Jones, & Hare, 2008). They have more self-control, are more goal-directed, and are better able to delay gratification than younger kids. One path, referred to as the *linear path*, leads to increased memory and self-control and is a straight-line continuation of the pruning, remodeling, and myelination that started in infancy (Blakemore & Choudhury, 2006). An example of the linear path is the increase in myelin in the *corpus callosum*, which connects the left and right brain hemispheres. This allows for better communication between the two halves of the brain. Another example is that stronger links develop between the memory region of the hippocampus and the prefrontal cortex that establishes goals and priorities.

A second path, called the *nonlinear path* of brain development, leads to the novelty-seeking, emotionality, and risk-taking so characteristic of the more challenging teenage behaviors (Blakemore & Choudhury, 2006; Crone & Dahl, 2012). The nonlinear path is totally unique to the period of adolescence. It constitutes the brain's third wave of abundant overgrowth of neurons and synapses followed by a third wave of pruning back (Casey et al., 2008). It is the nonlinear path that revamps the brain in such a way as to enable teens to acquire the pioneer spirit, nerves of steel, and flexibility that will enable them to succeed in the new world of adulthood. Whenever you get too frightened by your teenager's escapades, think of Christopher Columbus or Lewis and Clark. Think of successful modern entrepreneurs like Bill Gates, Steve Jobs, and Richard Branson—pioneers, novelty-seekers, and risk-takers all.

Teens are preoccupied with peer relationships.

As a result of the nonlinear path of brain development, teens engage in more frequent contact with peers. Relationships with peers become less about having friends as "activity partners" and more about having intimate, even romantic relations. Adolescent relationships are more likely to wax and wane, and therefore peer rejection becomes more common. Teens exhibit an increased self-consciousness and a heightened sensitivity to the social judgments of peers. What makes all this so intense for them is that the social-emotional brain matures earlier than the prefrontal control centers, so they have difficulty containing their social-emotional impulses and feelings.

Teens are highly sensitive to being evaluated by others.

If it seems to you that your teenager is thinking only about themselves, think again! People actually think more about others as teens than they do at any other time of life. Studies show that teenagers, when in a social evaluation situation, have heightened activity in their social-emotional brain circuits, especially their mentalizing system, compared to both children and adults.

The mentalizing system interprets the thoughts and feelings going on in the minds of others and links this information to its personal relevance to the self (Abraham, 2013). It's as if the part of the brain that pays attention to, thinks about, and interprets the minds of others is on overdrive. Their mentalizing system overvalues social judgment. Therefore, teens interpret what peers say as more highly important and significant to them personally than they did when they were kids and than they will when they become adults.

This is why when teens receive negative social feedback from peers, they feel more down and more anxious than do adults or younger children. This is why teenagers tend to be more self-conscious and emotionally reactive in social situations and tend to be on high alert for people

SCIENCE SAYS

Teens Are Very Sensitive to Social Judgments and Rejection

- When teens know someone is looking at a photograph of them, it activates their nucleus accumbens and anterior cingulate (areas that determine the value of social information) to a greater extent than adults.
- Teens engaged in games where they might be socially excluded activate their mentalizing system (which processes social judgments) more strongly than adults but engage the *lateral* prefrontal cortex (which regulates emotions) less strongly than adults.

judging them. Teens are so prone to angst and turmoil because they engage their social-emotional brain circuits *more* robustly than either children or adults but engage their prefrontal cortex regulatory circuits *less* than children or adults (Somerville, 2013). Although teens are highly aware of and motivated to understand the mental experiences of other people, maybe even more so than adults, they may not always behave or contain their impulses as an adult might.

Adolescent brain development is uneven.

The research shows that teenage brain development occurs in a slow and uneven arc (Marek, Hwang, Foran, Haliquist, & Luna, 2015). This is why teens show such inconsistent behavior. They can be sweet in the morning and irritating by noon, competent one day and seemingly incompetent the next. Remembering this can help you be more patient, rather than assuming your child's inconsistency is sign of them being flakey, or willfully difficult.

For teens, faces are the hottest ticket in town.

Humans of all ages are drawn to faces because they express so much. But teens place more emphasis on faces and facial expressions than either children or adults. Facial expressions carry the important social information about who other people are, how they're feeling, and what they're thinking that is critical for determining how to interact with them in an adaptive fashion. Therefore, it should come as no surprise that teens are more drawn than either children or adults to emotional cues in faces (Blakemore, 2008; Lawrence, Campbell, & Skuse, 2015) as well as to cues related to the attractiveness, trustworthiness, competence, and social status of faces, especially peer-aged faces (Sherf, Behrmann, & Dahl, 2012). Teens are better able than children to recognize the subtleties of expressions and the ways that facial expressions fluidly shift from one emotion to another. Even in tasks that have nothing to do with identifying emotion, such as determining which way a person is looking, teens pay more attention to the emotional cues in a person's face than either children or adults. Their increased drive to be accepted by peers and their increased sensitivity to peer evaluation, however, causes teens to extract more judgment-related information from facial expressions and to consider emotional facial features as having more relevance to them. This is why your teen is so likely to "read" judgment in your face even if you're not feeling that way.

THE ADOLESCENT REWARD SYSTEM

As a result of their nonlinear path of brain development, teenagers consistently perceive all reward situations as more rewarding than adults do. This is partly why they engage in more sensation- and risk-seeking behavior than adults. The cause is a major remodeling of the *reward circuitry* in the adolescent brain. A reflective parent can try to reduce their fears about their teenager's safety and lessen the conflict with their teen by keeping in mind that evolution designed them this way to make them more proficient adults.

The engine has extra power before the brakes are strong.

Teenagers get more bang for their buck with novelty and excitement because they release more dopamine in these situations than either children or adults. Therefore, they are more motivated to seek out and engage in novel, highly stimulating, emotionally intense, and risk-taking behaviors than either children or adults. All these behaviors feel so much more pleasurable to them than they feel to you. That's why they do them and you don't.

The wave of overproduction of dopamine neurons and synapses makes teens more sensitive to all aspects of reward, whether social or nonsocial ones, actual or anticipated. This increased growth of dopamine connections occurs first in the nucleus accumbens and amygdala and only later in the prefrontal cortex (Casey et al., 2008). Thus, reward-seeking increases in teens before they are capable of fully regulating their behavior and before they can fully grasp the long-term effects of this behavior (Galvan, 2010).

There appears to be a gender difference in terms of overproduction, with teenage boys producing more dopamine receptors than teenage girls. This may account for the fact that boys tend to be more risk-taking than girls on average.

Teens process rewards differently.

Teens seek different kinds of rewards than children and adults. For children, rewards are typically sweets, and for adults, they typically involve money. For teens, rewards are more social, such as being considered desirable by peers. Teens also consider risk-taking to be more fun and rewarding than adults do. There is even a difference in teens regarding whether a reward is rewarding *enough* (Galvan et al., 2006). Teens, as compared with adults and children, show increased activation in their dopamine-rich nucleus accumbens in response to *high* rewards but a diminished response to low rewards. In other words, unless something is *really* exciting, not just sort of exciting, a teenager may not be interested. This is why your teenager's younger sibling may be delighted to go out to dinner with you while your teenager says, "Meh!"

Teens are quite able to reason through and understand the risks of the behaviors in which they engage, just as adults do (Reyna and Farley, 2006). However, because reward systems mature before the prefrontal cortex, teens *assess risks as being of greater value to them* than adults, but can't control their emotions and impulses as well as adults can.

Why do adolescents make "poor" decisions?

A teen's increased sense of reward and pleasure can override their decision-making ability and behavioral inhibition, even if they know better. A teenage brain's heightened dopamine release to all rewards, coupled with their less active prefrontal cortex, makes them more prone to—for example—experimenting with drugs and alcohol.

When a teenager makes a poor decision, it's not because they don't comprehend the risks involved in their behavior. They *do* intellectually comprehend them. However, teens assess rewards as being more *valuable* than do adults. Therefore, teens will put in more effort and take more risks to obtain rewards and be more impulsive about doing so.

Teen decision-making is biased toward the *immediate* rather than the long run. This is because of higher activity in the subcortical social-emotional-reward centers and relatively lower activity in the prefrontal cortex. The subcortex is more about immediate gratification and the prefrontal cortex is more about delay of gratification. The greater strength of subcortex over cortex biases teens to make decisions based on short-term gains rather than long-term outcomes.

Why are teens psychologically vulnerable?

The same imbalance between the stronger social-emotional-reward centers in the brain and the less effective top-down modulation of these centers by the prefrontal cortex, although adaptive for the kinds of learning experiences that teens must go through, makes teenagers more vulnerable to developing psychological problems (Casey et al., 2008; Nelson, Leibenluft, McClure, & Pine, 2005). Adolescents' heightened sensitivity to the facial expressions, actions, and emotions of others, along with their decreased ability to fully contain the feelings and impulses that result from their heightened sensitivity, renders them more prone to taking things personally, feeling hurt and rejected, and feeling worried. This can make teens more susceptible to developing depression and anxiety.

Certain childhood traits are predictive of greater difficulties in adolescence. Kids who tend to be more impulsive will also tend to be more on the impulsive side as teens, whereas children who have better self-control tend to have more self-control over their impulses later on as teens (Eigsti et al., 2006). When the normal rise in amygdala activity fails to subside normally as it does in most teens, a teenager will be more prone to being anxious (Casey et al., 2008).

SCIENCE SAYS

When subjects are told, "Do not look at the flickering light! Look instead in the opposite direction," their normal instinct is to *immediately look* at the flickering light. Teens are a lot better than children at resisting this urge, and almost as good as adults, but not quite. They can resist the temptation to look at the light about 70 to 80 percent of the time, just like adults, but only if they are highly motivated to do so!

THE BOSS OF THE BRAIN IS LAST
TO MATURE

A teenager's executive skills are almost but not completely in place (Marek et al., 2015). However teenage brains are less likely to activate the prefrontal executive region than adult brains. This is why adults are better than teens at using their brain's monitoring, planning, oversight, and temptation-resisting resources.

What's so adaptive about all this?

You might think that it is not adaptive for the prefrontal cortex, so important for complex problem-solving, decision-making, and self-control, to be the last brain area to mature and operate quickly and efficiently. However, nature, as always, has an adaptive reason. Speed and efficiency reduce the flexibility of the brain. The adolescent brain needs heightened flexibility to meet the rapidly changing demands of the adolescent stage of development. If teenagers were wiser and smarter sooner, they would have less ability to adapt and learn from the new experiences of adolescence and young adulthood. Adolescence is a time for gathering and responding to new and wider spheres of life. You don't want them to close up possibilities at this stage of life; otherwise, their later adult life will be more limited.

You can motivate your teen.

Adolescents can resist temptation if they have the motivation to do so. That doesn't mean you should give them motivations such as promising to buy them a new outfit or a car. Believe it or not, your child is actually motivated to have a good relationship with you. They want your positive regard. In order to keep it, your child will be somewhat more motivated to put in the effort to control their impulses. This is why it is so important to express what you really expect and want from your teenager and what you believe they are capable of. Don't do it in a demeaning or controlling way. Just tell them, simply and in as few words as possible. Then trust that your message has gotten inside and that they will use it to the best of their ability. Keep in mind that their brains are not fully mature and that, as much as they care about you and what you expect, they are going to mess up from time to time.

BEING REFLECTIVE WITH TEENS: SAME TOOLS, CHANGED EMPHASIS

As a reflective parent of a teenager, you will use all the same thinking skills and principles as you did with your younger child, but with an extra *emphasis* on separation, independence, and relinquishing control. Remember, your connection with your teenager still matters a lot to them. Your input helps them rein in some of their emotional volatility, peer obsession, novelty-seeking, and risk-taking, warding off some of the worst hazards and nudging them toward more appropriate responses. The point is that you can't rein them in fully. You can't entirely change their course. Trying to will typically backfire. Studies show that adolescents want to learn primarily, but not entirely, from their friends (DeVore & Ginsberg, 2005). At some level, teens want those kernels of wisdom you have. There will be times when your teen wants to know what you struggled with at their age and what you learned about how the world works. But use your advice sparingly.

How you respond to your child's actions depends more on how you interpret the meaning of those actions than on the actions themselves. Fortunately, the science supports a positive and optimistic way of framing your teenager's social, emotional, and reward-seeking behaviors (Giedd et al., 1999). When you are overly focused on the negative, try to reframe the situation from a more positive perspective. It will aid you in the supportive kind of letting go that is necessary. When you treat your teen in a more positive, less controlling way, they don't have to shut you out as forcefully. By being more positive about them, you get them to take in more of what you have to say.

There is an upside to novelty-seeking.

Teens' increased dopamine activates an increase in *novelty-seeking*, which is the source of their motivation to widen their social circle and to be open to new opportunities and new sources of support, safety, education, and even financial security in the form of employment. Without it, your teen would choose to live at home for the rest of her or his life.

Don't take rejection or criticism so personally.

One of the most painful aspects of having a teenager is how rejected you can feel when they separate. No matter how loudly they criticize your clothes, the way you talk, or the music you like; no matter how much they protest your limits; and no matter how convinced they are that you are not that smart or competent, remember that it's not about you personally. It's about their need to pull away so that they can learn how to function on their own. They don't want you to take it personally or to feel awful about yourself. They just want you to be less *tempting* so that they can give you up more easily.

A parent's impulsive risk is a teenager's well-planned reward.

We all like a little jolt of excitement or some adventure on occasion. As we have discovered, however, teenagers *value* it way more than adults do. When adolescents are out for a thrill, it doesn't necessarily mean they are behaving impulsively. In fact, impulsive behavior diminishes starting at around age 10. Teens often plan their thrill-seeking activities well ahead of time, weighing the risks and dangers as adults do and even overestimating the risks as adults do (Steinberg, 2008). They see the same risks as adults, but if the reward is high, they don't let the risk get in their way as it would for an adult. It may take all your reflective capacity to accept, but teenagers are not being silly, stupid, or even that particularly risk-taking *from their perspective*.

SCIENCE SAYS

Under *emotionally cool* conditions when no friends or acquaintances are along, teens take risks at the same rate as adults. Under more *emotionally hot* conditions, when there are potential rewards that teens care about, such as appearing tough or impressing a friend, teens take twice as many risks as adults would. For example, when teenagers drive with friends in the car, they are much more likely to push on the gas and try to make it through a light. Adults, by contrast, drive no differently when friends are along.

Not even reflective parenting can reduce your worry about your teen entirely. It wouldn't even be good. Your teen needs you to worry and watch out for them to some extent. But balance your worry with *optimism* by remembering that valuing the reward in spite of the risks is what moves your teenager off the couch and into the real world of adult life.

> The drama of peer relationships is about finding
> compatriots for life.

Adolescence once again mobilizes the attachment system and causes intense, dramatic relationships with peers, where separations and rejections can lead to powerfully negative moods. Teens prefer the company of people their own age more and more, because other teenagers provide them more novelty and reward (dopamine) and more sense of connection (oxytocin) than you and your family do. This is why they are more likely to talk about their troubles with their friends than with you.

As hard as it is for you, the parent, this is what your teen needs. It's not as if you lose importance entirely. You are just not front and center anymore. Reframe your loss as their gain, and maybe even take it one step further by also reframing your loss as *your* gain! Their intense peer relationships are building your teen's skills in social situations. When your teen reacts to a romantic breakup or the betrayal of a friend as if it is life and death, biologically speaking it is true, because it is their peer network upon which their future survival depends. Their brains are wired for drama *now* so that they can work it out and be secure and successful with people *later on*.

All people feel pain from social exclusion. It's just that your teenager is feeling the pain more acutely as a result of their adolescent brain wiring. It will aid their resiliency if you validate and feel some of the pain along with them, but also remind yourself and them that what feels so painful now will get better and that life will in fact go on.

Reframe your goals as a parent.

Many families these days place too much pressure on children to succeed. They try to control what their child does in order to guarantee success. Unfortunately, this creates a lot of anxiety around the issue of failure. Children can become so anxious about academic success and making money that they are afraid to explore the environment of creative ideas and interests that might not produce the necessary credentials for an Ivy League college or a high-paying job. Individual parents are not to blame. The pressure is in the whole of society. As a reflective parent, you are encouraged to think more for yourself. You might do your child a better service by shifting away from so much pressure, even if you are the only parent on the block doing it. Educational leaders would support you in this.

Our modern fixation on elite colleges is creating a generation of children who are anxious and not fully satisfied with their lives (Deresiewicz, 2014). Many kids who end up in elite colleges have always experienced success. When they don't succeed, they feel terrified, depressed, or unglued. There is no margin for error. Some of these kids become totally risk averse. This goes against all that we know about what adolescents need. Adolescents need to learn how to become their own individual by exploring and journeying beyond what's comfortable, familiar, and guaranteed. They need to try things out for their own sake to see what suits them, what they like and don't like, agree with and don't agree with. This is how a *self* is created. Your teen will do better if they feel secure enough to take risks, to fail, and to go down alleys that don't turn up anything of value except the fact that it was interesting to explore. The safety to fail builds resilience and serves as a kind of insurance policy for your child's future (Duhigg, 2016).

Often, in their wish for control, parents too quickly tell children what to do and how to think about difficult situations. Parents would do better to resist that urge and opt instead for *being curious*. Wonder and inquire about your teen's ideas on the situation. Ask them questions such as "What do you think you should do?" When kids are given more freedom to decide on their own, it helps build their motivation to handle difficult situations (Duhigg, 2016). This is not to say that you should go along with every idea your child comes up with. That is not realistic, nor does your child expect it. The important idea is that even if you don't follow their input, you should still make sure your child feels you have heard them and taken them seriously. It's a risk for your teenager to really share what they think. Make sure this is one risk they feel safe to take.

Make limit-setting a negotiation.

The principle of *focusing on the relationship* implies that you can't impose limits on your adolescent. Limits will work better if they are incorporated into your newly evolving relationship together. Setting limits with a teenager is a lot like the win-win or "getting to yes" negotiation strategies used in the workplace. Each side gives their input. Each side feels heard. Each side gets some of what they need. Let's say you want your teenager to call you anytime they have a change of plans when they're out with friends. You could insist on it, perhaps even taking their phone away as a consequence if they don't comply. This is not necessarily a bad way to go about things, but there is a more relationship- and development-enhancing way. Adolescents need to learn to develop their own decision-making skills, and authoritarian parenting methods are not as good for that as relationship-based parenting methods.

Here is just one example of the kind of conversation you might have. You say what you want: "While you are out today with your friends, I want you to call me whenever you change plans." They say, "What for?" You share that *you* are worried about their safety, and they say, "Just chill! We will be fine and totally safe!" Then you add that *you* worry, even though you also respect that *they* are convinced they are safe, because that is *how parents are.* You might add that you believe kids do better when they know their parents are involved. Your words convey that it isn't personal to them—that your feelings and your actions are yours and that you respect them as a separate individual. Then you turn the conversation over to them. You find out how they feel about your request and see if they can think of any strategy that will deal with your concern and feelings in a way that works better for them. They may say, "It's embarrassing to have to call and tell you all the details. You're treating me like a baby. How about this? I will text 'Change of plans.'" You say, "OK, I'm open to trying that, but I would prefer it if at least you would text where your new plans are." They make a face and groan, saying, "Don't press your luck!" When you say good-bye, if you need to say anything (you don't actually need to, but if you feel you must), you might say, "I'm glad we talked about it, and I trust that you understand and will use good judgment." Remember that in turning over the baton in a relay race, one runner still holds on to it—but not too firmly—as they pass it into the next runner's hand.

There are no right answers about what rules to follow, how much leeway to give, or how much to inhibit your child. The best guide is to check in with yourself about what limits you want your child to abide by and figure out why those limits are important to you before any limits are actually set. Make sure you communicate your interest in seeing their perspective and getting their input as well. When parents leave out either side—self-introspection or understanding their child's perspective—they are more likely to waffle on limit-setting or to be too dogmatic about it, which isn't good for either the child or the parent.

Hang in there through thick and thin.

It can be emotionally hard on a parent to try to maintain that strong relationship bond with a teenager who is developmentally pushing away. It is easy to get discouraged when so often it feels that they don't want your opinion and don't care what you think and that what you say goes in one ear and out the other. But the truth is, some of what you say does remain inside their heads. If you talk to them and listen to them in a reflective way, you are helping your adolescent hone their reflective thinking skills. Have conversations about people's feelings and motives, about how there is always more than one way to think about a situation, or about how conflict and uncertainty are normal and must be accepted. Even if your adolescent isn't specifically talking with you about their problems, they do carry the reflective thinking skills they are receiving at home with them into their peer relationships. They may not give you credit for this or even tell you about it, but we know that teens internalize their parents' reasoning, prohibitions, and values even if they never "fess up." When your child messes up, *their* best chance for cleaning up the mess happens when you "hang in" with being reflective, repair any ruptures in the relationship that may have occurred, and continue to provide a relationship of emotional support, guidance, and confidence in their ability to change.

STORIES OF PARENTS AND CHILDREN

- Two mothers, Ann and Emily, are encouraged in a reflective parenting group to self-reflect and figure out for themselves what limits to set for their teenage daughters:

    Ann: What do I do about my daughter having an attitude?
    Leader: Can you tell us a little more about this attitude situation?

Ann: So many times when I'm talking with her, her attitude is bad. Like, she will ignore me as if she hasn't even heard what I've said, or she will give one-word answers or make a face.

Leader: How do you feel when she does this?

Ann: I feel I need to stop her and teach her that it's wrong. I mean, isn't that what we're supposed to do as parents, teach them how to behave properly?

Leader: Yes, we do play a role in teaching our kids how to behave. I guess I'm also wondering what emotion you might be feeling when she gives you an attitude.

Ann: I feel awful. I feel rejected and disrespected. That's why I want to teach her that she can't behave that way.

Leader: What do you think she's feeling?

Ann: Well, I think she's trying to break away from me. And actually I'm glad about that because she's mostly such a good girl. I think it's good for her to begin to separate.

Leader: So I guess you have mixed feelings: rejected on the one hand, but pleased on the other. And that makes it hard to know how to respond.

Ann: Exactly! That's why I asked you what to do, because I don't know if I should just ignore it or teach her she can't do it.

Leader: It's so hard for us as parents to sit with the uncertainty. And there is no right answer on this. But now that you realize you feel both bad and good, is there any way you can think of how to handle it?

Ann: Well, now that you ask, I guess I can ignore it mostly, if it's not too much of an attitude, but if it gets to be a lot, then I can tell her it hurts my feelings and see how she reacts to that.

Emily: I won't put up with attitude. I just tell my daughter she can't talk like that to me. I tell her there is a consequence, like I will take her phone away.

Leader: In your case, it is really important to you that your daughter does *not* express an attitude. So you handle it differently than

Ann. Perhaps you can share with us how it makes you feel when your daughter shows an attitude.

Emily: It drives me wild. I treated my own mother terribly. I was mean, I had a terrible attitude, and I always wanted her to tell me to quit it. But she had a laissez-faire approach. And when I got older, I felt so terribly guilty about how I treated her when I was young. I don't want my daughter to feel that way. So I tell her in no uncertain terms that she can't talk to me disrespectfully . . . I don't want her to regret later on how she treated me.

Leader: I can certainly understand that. I wonder, what is your sense of how your daughter feels about it?

Emily: Now that I listen to Ann talk, I realize I have no idea about how it affects my daughter. It makes me think about whether I'm overreacting with my daughter because of what happened with my mom and me. My mother never spoke up about how I affected her. I can probably tell my daughter how it makes me feel and not be quite so intense and personal about it as I am now. I don't always have to bring it back to my personal feelings. I can be more neutral sometimes and maybe say something like, "People don't like it when they are on the receiving end of too much attitude." I can ask her if she ever thinks about this.

- The parents of one teenager learned to do less to get more. Lynne and Gregg talked about how their daughter Felicity was doing poorly in school. They explained that she was not engaged at all in her academics and that her grades were terrible. They decided that it was best to be positive, and so they used financial rewards and gifts as a way of motivating her. But it didn't work. It only led to more tension and arguments about things like whether she should get a reward for a C and not just for A's and B's. There was no improvement in her study habits, grades, or interest in doing well. Stymied, the parents were getting angrier and angrier about the situation and started giving Felicity more consequences and punishments for poor grades. That didn't work either, and it felt awful to them to be in such a negative space in their relationship with their daughter. They tried one more avenue, mostly out of despair, but fortuitously it led to an amazing discovery. They decided to pull back—not angrily, not uncaringly, not in a detached manner—just back. They explained that they could see that all their pushing and prodding wasn't helping and that they had decided to step back and see what happened. What happened is that Felicity stepped up to the plate. She started taking more initiative and spending more time on her schoolwork. Her grades came up and she was pleased with herself. Her parents, of course, were pleased too. But what they chose to say was not so much how good they felt about her improved academic performance but that they realized they had probably been choking off her motivation. Now that they had given her the space to shine, she showed how wonderfully competent she was and how much she could be trusted to know how to do things.

- One father, Doug, learned to trust that his teenage daughter could make up her own mind. Doug and his ex-wife had divorced when their daughter, Joelle, was just a baby. Now, at 14 years of age, Joelle was protective of her mother. Doug felt that his ex was telling untrue stories about him and the reasons for their divorce. He was respectful of his daughter's need to think well of her mother, but he wanted to know when he could tell her the true reasons for the divorce. Another father in the group asked Doug if he wanted the truth told because he felt his daughter really needed the information or whether it was more about setting the record straight and correcting his own bad reputation. Doug responded, "Doesn't the truth matter?" A mother in the group inquired if the fact that his wife was badmouthing him had caused problems in his relationship with his daughter, and he explained that they had a terrific relationship and loved going to movies together and playing tennis. Doug finally drew his own conclusion, saying, "She can think for herself. She knows who her father really is and has a good opinion of him. The truth is not going to improve things. It will only make her upset by painting her mom in a bad light and make her jump to defend her mom."

PUTTING IT INTO WORDS

- **What to say after your teenager pours out to you all their anger and disappointment with a friend:** One option is to say nothing except possibly make some sympathetic noises. Keep in mind that your teen uses you as a sack for holding their bad feelings so they can move on.

- **What to say when your teenager is leaving the house to drive to a party with friends:** "I know I can trust you to use good judgment about not drinking and driving. I am available at any time to come and pick you up if need be. No questions asked."

- **What to say to your teenager who just got dumped and can't imagine the world without their lost boyfriend or girlfriend:** Whatever you say, you don't have to say it all at once. Not all teens want to talk, and teens don't give their parents a lot of time for input. Your lovesick teenager will need time to heal, and you will have a number of chances to talk. Dole out your empathy and your wisdom in small "sound bites." "I am so sorry this happened to you. I know how much these things hurt." At another time, you might say, "I know it feels like you will never recover, but everyone does eventually. It is hard to believe now, but you will feel better in time." Maybe, on yet another occasion, you can share an experience from when you were a teenager and you were dumped. "This kind of thing happens to everyone. I was dumped and I felt crummy just like you do."

TAKE-HOME LESSONS

- **Practice teaching by having a conversation rather than by instruction.** Traits such as perseverance, self-control, and optimism are associated with children doing better as adults. Traits such as understanding what makes people tick and feelings of gratitude help a person relate better to other people. Traits such as curiosity, open-mindedness, and zest for learning promote independent thinking. As a parent, if you want to teach these traits to your teenager, practice doing so as part of having a conversation with your child. As particular situations arise, such as when your teen is having difficulty and feels like giving up or when they get down on themselves for making a mistake, it's a good time to try to have a conversation about it. Remember that true conversations are open-ended and two-way. You might open up by sharing why you think it's good to pursue a goal despite setbacks, or why there is value in making mistakes, or why it's worthwhile to put in strong effort even if the outcome isn't so great. Then be curious about out what your teen thinks and be a good listener. Practice having discussions about people in the news or elsewhere in which you include trying to understand people's inner feelings and motives or discuss the importance of gratitude toward others. Be sure not to make negative comments about the people's character, such as that they're lazy or have a bad attitude. Don't dictate what values you think your teenager should have. Don't even worry if they don't want to talk much. Your values seep in even when your teen is grumpy with you. But remember that when you talk with your teen, it should be a discussion, not a monologue. Remember to keep it a conversation and not to make it a lecture.

- *Practice being an even better listener than you are a talker.* Your teenager will have interests that differ from yours. If you want to encourage their curiosity and zest for learning, you must be really open-minded and allow them to freely express their interests, ideas, values, theories, and beliefs. Spend more time learning about their opinion than you do sharing yours.

- *Practice bouncing back from conflict and hurt.* Teens and parents can get into some pretty gnarly arguments, and your teen is apt to say some pretty hurtful and even nasty things about you. They are apt to make unreasonable demands of you and then lack the gratitude for all the efforts you make in helping them. They can reject your invitation to do activities together and put you down for your ideas or the things you like. They can dump all their problems on you and sometimes even blame you for them. It's not easy to be on the receiving end of all of this. It's no wonder that parents can feel sorry for themselves or even feel like a victim and have the urge to take revenge. However, when your teenager bounces back and wants to talk to you again, you have to bounce back too. Teens can be in a really bad mood and rejecting one minute and cheerful and wanting to engage the next. They do this on their own time frame, not yours. Perhaps you have just set a limit by refusing to drive them across town to a party and they have thrown a fit, told you they hate you and that you have ruined their life, mumbled some obscenities under their breath, and gone to their room and slammed the door. You may be in your room licking your wounds or perhaps savoring how angry and hurt you are. Then, lo and behold, 10 minutes later they flop on your bed and want to chat. Try your absolute best to shift from *hurt and anger* mode into *cheerful chat* mode. Don't ask why all of a sudden they are in a good mood. Try not to tell them you are still too hurt and angry to talk. Mostly just be grateful inside that they are in a better mood. Parenting a teen is a lot like hopping from stone to stone as you cross a raging river. Be grateful for the moments of rest, and don't pay as much attention to the turbulence in between.

Epilogue

Every story has an ending, and the story of how to raise your child in a reflective way is no different. The end of the story is that your child grows up and becomes an adult and you will need to use reflective parenting as much as you ever did. I know I do. In fact, when I started to write this book, I was writing it because it was the book I needed when my kids were little. However, now that my kids are in their thirties and I'm a grandparent, I realize that everything I said in this book applies equally well to how I must parent even today. It's not easy pulling back and forging a new kind of relationship with a fully-fledged adult. I have to keep my reflective skills honed to make sure I don't step on their toes too much and impair our relationship. The fact that I still have to be so reflective should come as no surprise. Being reflective is the key to having a strong relationship with anyone: with kids, romantic partners, spouses, friends, acquaintances, teachers, students, co-workers, employees, employers. It's an across-the-board relationship builder.

You will need to use your reflective capacity no matter how old your child is, even when your child becomes a parent. This is because *once a parent, always a parent!* Although your child will grow up and become an adult, you will always be their parent and they will always be your child—but differently. They will still want you to be proud of them and to think positively about them. They will still be hypersensitive to the possibility of your negative judgment. You will still have the urge to protect and counsel them. It goes with the territory. The main point to keep in mind is that more than ever, reflective parenting requires you to see your child as independent, competent, and able to decide for themselves how to run their lives. If you can do this, you are much more likely to retain a good relationship with them. If you can hold your tongue, not give advice unless asked (and then only very cautiously), and not talk much about how hurt you feel that they didn't call, you will keep your relationship healthy and mature. In the end, being reflective with your adult child will help ensure that they still want to visit and enjoy being with you. That is your gift for being reflective. They may not want to visit or talk as much as you would like, but being reflective is your greatest chance at having the best relationship possible. And that should be reward enough.

References

Abraham, A. (2013). The world according to me: Personal relevance and the medial prefrontal cortex. *Frontiers in Human Neuroscience, 7,* 1–4.

Ainsworth, M. S., Blehar, M. C., Waters, E., & Wall, S. (1978). Patterns of attachment: A psychological *Theories study of the strange situation.* Hillsdale, NJ: Erlbaum.

Allen, S. & Daly, K. (2007). *The effects of father involvement: An updated research summary of the evidence inventory.* Guelph, Ontario, Canada: Centre for Families, Work & Well-Being.

Arnsten, A. F. T. (2009). Stress signalling pathways that impair prefrontal cortex structure and function. *Nature Reviews Neuroscience, 10,* 410–422.

Baron-Cohen, S., Tager-Flusberg, H., & Cohen, D. (2007). *Understanding other minds: Perspectives from developmental cognitive neuroscience* (2nd ed.). New York, NY: Oxford University Press.

Beebe, B. (2006). Co-constructing mother–infant distress in face-to-face interactions: Contributions of microanalysis. *Infant Observation, 9,* 151–164.

Beebe, B., Jaffe, J., Markese, S., Buck, K., Chen, H., Cohen, P., . . . Feldstein, S. (2010). The origins of 12-month attachment: A microanalysis of 4-month mother–infant interaction. *Attachment and Human Development, 12,* 3–141.

Blakemore, S. J. (2008). The social brain in adolescence. *Nature Reviews Neuroscience, 9,* 267–277.

Blakemore, S.-J., & Choudhury, S. (2006). Development of the adolescent brain: Implications for executive function and social cognition. *Journal of Child Psychology and Psychiatry, 47,* 296–312.

Borelli, J. L., Crowley, M. J., David, D. H., Sbarra, D. A., Anderson, G.

M., & Mayes, L. C. (2010). Attachment and emotion in school-aged children. *Emotion, 10*(4), 475–485.

Borelli, J. L., Crowley, M. J., Snavely, J. E., & Mayes, L. C. (2013). Dismissing children's perceptions of their emotional experience and parental care: Preliminary evidence of positive bias. *Child Psychiatry and Human Development, 44,* 70–88.

Brazelton, T. (1983). *Infants and mothers: Differences in development.* New York, NY: Delacorte.

Brothers, L. (1990). The social brain: A project for integrating primate behavior and neurophysiology in a new domain. *Concepts in Neuroscience, 1,* 27–51.

Brown, D. J. (2014). *Boys in the boat: Nine Americans and their epic quest for gold at the 1936 Berlin Olympics.* New York, NY: Penguin.

Bruner, J. S. (1972). Nature and uses of immaturity. *American Psychologist, 27,* 1–23.

Buckner, R. L., Andrews-Hanna, J. R., & Schacter, D. L. (2008). The brain's default network: Anatomy, function and relevance to diseaase. *Annals of the New York Academy of Sciences, 1124,* 1–38.

Casey, B. J., Jones, R. M., & Hare, T. A. (2008). The adolescent brain. *Annals of the New York Academy of Sciences, 1124,* 111–126.

Cattaneo, L., & Rizzolatti, G. (2009). The mirror neuron system. *Archives of Neurology, 66,* 557–560.

Champagne, F., & Curley, J. (2009). Epigenetic mechanisms mediating the long-term effects of maternal care on development. *Neuroscience and Biobehavioral Reviews, 33,* 593–600.

Champagne, F., & Meaney, M. (2001). Like mother, like daughter: Evidence for non-genomic transmission of parental behavior and stress responsivity. *Progress in Brain Research, 133,* 287–302.

Chartrand, T. L., & Bargh, J. A. (1999). The chameleon effect: The perception–behavior link and social interaction. *Journal of Personality and Social Psychology, 76,* 893–910.

Coan, J. A., Schaefer, H. S., & Davidson, R. J. (2006). Lending a hand: Social regulation of the neural response to threat. *Psychological Science, 17,* 1032–1039.

Coley, R. L. & Hernandez, D. C. (2006). Predictors of paternal involvement for resident and nonresident low-income fathers. *Developmental Psychology, 42*, 1041-1056.

Crone, E. A., & Dahl, R. E. (2012). Understanding adolescence as a period of social-affective engagement and goal flexibility. *Nature Reviews Neuroscience, 13*, 636–650.

Decety, J., & Ickes, W. (2011). *The social neuroscience of empathy.* Cambridge, MA: First MIT Press.

Decety, J., & Jackson, P. (2006). A social-neuroscience perspective on empathy. *Current Directions in Psychological Science, 15*, 54–58.

Deresiewicz, W. (2014). *Excellent sheep: The miseducation of the American elite.* New York, NY: Free Press.

DeVore, E. R., & Ginsberg, K. R. (2005). The protective effects of good parenting on adolescents. *Current Opinion in Pediatrics, 17*, 460–465.

Diamond, A. (2013). Want to optimize executive functions and outcomes? Simple, just nourish the human spirit. In P. D. Zelazo & M. D. Sera (Eds.), *Minnesota Symposia on Child Psychology: Developing Cognitive Control Processes: Mechanisms, Implications, and Interventions* (Vol. 37). Hoboken, NJ: Wiley.

Dias-Ferreira, E., Sousa, J., Melo, I., Morgado, P., Mesquita, A. R., Cerqueira, J. J., . . . Sousa, N. (2009). Chronic stress causes frontostriatal reorganization and affects decision-making. *Science, 325*, 621–625.

Domes, G., Heinrichs, M., Glascher, J., Buchel, C., Braus, D., & Herpertz, S. (2007). Oxytocin attenuates amygdala responses to emotional faces regardless of valence. *Biological Psychiatry, 62*, 1187–1190.

Domes, G., Heinrichs, M., Michel, A., Berger, C., & Herpertz, S. C. (2007). Oxytocin improves "mind-reading" in humans. *Biological Psychiatry, 61*, 731–733.

Drake, N. (2014) Why do people see faces in the moon? *National Geographic.* Retrieved from http://news.nationalgeographic.com/news/2014/04/140412-moon-faces-brain-culture-space-neurology/.

Duhigg, C. (2016). *Smarter faster better: The secrets of being productive in life and business.* New York, NY: Random House.

Dunbar, R. I., & Shultz, S. (2007). Evolution in the social brain. *Science, 317*, 1344–1347.

Ebstein, R., Salomon, I., Lerer, E., Uzefovsky, F., Shalev, I., Gritsenko, I., . . . Riebold, M. (2009). Arginine vasopressin and oxytocin modulate human social behavior. *Annals of the New York Academy of Sciences, 1167*, 87–102.

Eigsti, I.-M., Zayas, V., Mischel, W., Shoda, Y., Ayduk, O., Dadlani, M. B., . . . Casey, B. J. (2006). Predicting cognitive control from preschool to late adolescence and young adulthood. *Psychological Science, 17*, 478–484.

Eisenberger, N. I. (2012). Broken hearts and broken bones: A neural perspective on the similarities between social and physical pain. *Current Directions in Psychological Science, 21*, 42–47.

Eisenberger, N. I., Jarcho, J. M., Lieberman, M. D., & Naliboff, B. D. (2006). An experimental study of shared sensitivity to physical pain and social rejection. *Pain, 126*, 132–138.

Eisenberger, N. I., Master, S. L, Inagaki, T. K., Taylor, S. E., Shirinyan, D., Lieberman, M. D., & Naliboff, B. D. (2011). Attachment figures activate a safety signal-related neural region and reduce pain experience. *Proceedings of the National Academy of Sciences*, 11721–11726.

Eliot, L. (2000). *What's going on in there? How the brain and mind develop in the first five years of life.* New York, NY: Bantam Books.

Epley, N., Waytz, A., & Cacioppo, J. T. (2007). On seeing human: A three-factor theory of anthropomorphism. *Psychological Review, 114*, 864–886.

Fagan, J. & Palm, G. (2004). *Fathers and early childhood programs.* Clifton Park, NY: Delmar Learning.

Faulkner, W. (1951). *Requiem for a nun.* New York, NY: Random House.

Field, T., Diego, M., & Hernandez-Reif, M. (2010). Preterm Infant Massage Therapy Research: A Review. *Infant Behavior & Development, 33*(2), 115–124. http://doi.org/10.1016/j.infbeh.2009.12.004.

Flanders, J. L., Leo, V., Paquette, D., Pihl, R. O., & Séguin, J. R. (2009). Rough-and-tumble play and the regulation of aggression: An observational study of father–child play dyads. *Aggressive Behavior, 35,* 285–295.

Flouri, E., & Buchanan, A. (2004). Early father's and mother's involvement and child's later educational outcomes. *British Journal of Educational Psychology, 74,* 141-153.

Fonagy, P., Bateman, A., & Bateman, A. (2011). The widening scope of mentalizing: A discussion. *Psychology and Psychotherapy: Theory, Research and Practice, 84,* 98–110.

Fonagy, P., Gergely, G., Jurist, E., & Target, M. (2004). *Affect regulation, mentalization, and the development of the self.* New York, NY: Other Press.

Fonagy, P., & Target, M. (2006). The mentalization-based approach to self pathology. *Journal of Personality Disorders, 20,* 544–576.

Fonagy, P., & Target, M. (2007). The rooting of the mind in the body: New links between attachment theory and psychoanalytic thought. *Journal of the American Psychoanalytic Association, 55,* 411–456.

Frank, M. C., Vul, E., & Johnson, S. P. (2000). Development of infants' attention to faces during the first year. *Cognition, 110,* 160–170.

Fuster, J. (1998). *The prefrontal cortex: Anatomy, physiology, and neuropsychology of the frontal lobe* (3rd ed.). New York, NY: Raven.

Galvan, A. (2010). Adolescent development of the reward system. *Frontiers in Human Neuroscience, 4,* 1–9.

Galvan, A., Hare, T. A., Parra, C. E., Penn, J., Voss, H., Glover, G., & Casey, B. J. (2006). Earlier development of the accumbens relative to orbitofrontal cortex might underlie risk-taking behavior in adolescents. *Journal of Neuroscience, 26,* 6885–6892.

Gander, M., & Buchheim, A. (2015). Attachment classification, psychophysiology and frontal EEG asymmetry across the lifespan: A review. *Frontiers in Human Neuroscience, 9,* 1–39.

Gazzaniga, M. S., Ivry, R. B., & Mangun, G. R. (2002). *Cognitive neuroscience.* New York, NY: W. W. Norton.

Giedd, J. N., Blumenthal, J., Jeffries, N. O., Castellanos, F. X., Liu, H., Zijdenbos, A., . . . Rapoport, J. L. (1999). Brain development during childhood and adolescence: A longitudinal MRI study. *Nature Neuroscience, 2,* 861–863.

Gilmore, R.O. & Johnson, M. H. (1995). Working memory in infancy: Six-month-olds' performance on two versions of the oculomotor delayed response task. *Journal of Experimental Child Psychology, 59,* 397-418.

Ginsburg, K. R. (2007). The importance of play in promoting healthy child development and maintaining strong parent–child bonds. *Pediatrics, 119.* Retrieved from http://pediatrics.aappublications.org/content/119/1/182.full

Goldsmith, M., with Reiter, M. (2007). *What got you here won't get you there: How successful people become even more successful.* New York, NY: Hyperion

Grienenberger, J., Denham, W., & Reynolds, D. (2015). Reflective and mindful parenting: A new relational model of assessment, prevention, and early intervention. In P. Luyten, L. C. Mayes, P. Fonagy, M. Target, & S. J. Blatt (Eds.), *Handbook of psychodynamic approaches to psychopathology.* New York, NY: Guilford Press.

Grienenberger, J., Kelly, K., & Slade, A. (2005). Maternal reflective functioning, mother–infant affective communication and infant attachment: Exploring the link between mental states and observed caregiving behavior in the intergenerational transmission of attachment. *Attachment and Human Development, 7,* 299–311.

Grossman, P., Niemann, L., Schmidt, S., & Walach, H. (2004). Mindfulness-based stress reduction and health benefits: A meta-analysis. *Journal of Psychosomatic Research, 57,* 35–43.

Gusnard, D. A., Akbudak, E., Shulman, G. L., & Raichle, M. E. (2001). Medial prefrontal cortex and self-referential mental activity: Relation to a default mode of brain function. *Proceedings of the National Academy of Sciences, 98,* 4259–4264.

Hauser, M. D., Chomsky, N., & Fitch, T. W. (2002). The faculty of language: What is it, who has it, and how did it evolve? *Science, 298,* 1569–1579.

Herbet, G., Lafargue, G., Bonnetblanc, F., Moritz-Gasser, S., Menjot de Champfleur, N., & Duffau, H. (2014). Inferring a dual-stream model of mentalizing from associative white matter fibres disconnection. *Brain, 137,* 944–959.

Hornbuckle, S. R. (2010). Factors impacting the child with behavioral inhibition. *Forum on Public Policy Online* (Vol. 2010, No. 5).

Hove, M. J., & Risen, J. (2009). It's all in the timing: Interpersonal synchrony increases affiliation. *Social Cognition, 27,* 949–961.

Iacoboni, M. (2008). *Mirroring people: The new science of how we connect with others.* New York, NY: Farrar, Straus and Giroux.

Iacoboni, M., & Dapretto, M. (2006). The mirror neuron system and the consequences of its dysfunction. *Nature Reviews Neuroscience, 7,* 942–951.

Iacoboni, M., Molnar-Szakacs, I., Gallese, V., Buccino, G., Mazziotta, J. C., & Rizzolatti, G. (2005). Grasping the intentions of others with one's own mirror neuron system. *PLOS Biology, 3*(3). doi: 10.1371/journal.pbio.0030079.

Iyengar, U., Kim, S., Martinez, S., Fonagy, P., & Strathearn, L. (2014). Unresolved trauma in mothers: Intergenerational effects and the role of reorganization. *Frontiers in Psychology.* Retrieved July 6, 2016, from http://journal.frontiersin.org/article/10.3389/fpsyg.2014.00966/full.

Jacobsen, T., & Hofmann, V. (1997). Children's attachment representations: Longitudinal relations to school behavior and academic competency in middle childhood and adolescence. *Developmental Psychology, 33*(4), 703–710.

Lundström, J. N., Mathe, A., Schaal, B., Frasnelli, J., Nitzsche, K., Gerber, J., & Hummel, T. (2013). Maternal status regulates cortical responses to the body odor of newborns. *Fronteirs in Psychology.* Retrieved July 6, 2016, from http://journal.frontiersin.org/article/10.3389/fpsyg.2013.00597/full.

Kabat-Zinn, J. (1994). *Wherever you go, there you are.* New York, NY: Hyperion.

Kagan, J. (2003). Biology, context, and developmental inquiry. *Annual Review of Psychology, 54,* 1–23.

Kagan, J., & Baird, A. (2004). Brain and behavioral development during childhood. In M. S. Gazzaniga (Ed.), *The cognitive neurosciences III* (pp. 93–103). Cambridge, MA: MIT Press.

Keysers, C. (2011). *The empathic brain.* Netherlands: Frontiers.

Keysers, C., Wicker, B., Gazzola, V., Anton, J.-L., Fogassi, L., & Gallese, V. (2004). A touching sight: SII/PV activation during the observation and experience of touch. *Neuron, 42,* 335–346.

Kim, P., Leckman, J. F., Mayes, L. C., Feldman, R., Wang, X., & Swain, J. E. (2010). The plasticity of human maternal brain: Longitudinal changes in brain anatomy during the early postpartum period. *Behavioral Neuroscience, 124,* 695–700.

Kim, S., Fonagy, P., Allen, J., & Strathearn, L. (2014). Mothers' unresolved trauma blunts amygdala response to infant distress. *Social Neuroscience, 9,* 352–363.

Klein, R. (2002). *The dawn of human culture.* New York, NY: Wiley.

Kobak, R. R.-G. (1993). Attachment and emotion regulation during mother-teen problem solving: A control theory analysis. *Child Development, 64,* 231–245.

Kolb, B., Mychasiuk, R., Muhammad, A., Li, Y., Frost, D. O., & Gibb, R. (2012). Experience and the developing prefrontal cortex. *Proceedings of the National Academy of Sciences, 109,* 17186–17193.

Korb, A. (2015). *The upward spiral: Using neuroscience to reverse the course of depression, one small change at a time.* Oakland, CA: New Harbinger.

Kovács, Á. M., Téglás, E., & Endress, A. D. (2010). The social sense: Susceptibility to others' beliefs in human infants and adults. *Science, 330,* 1830–1834.

Krahé, C., Springer, A., Weinman, J. A., & Fotopoulou, A. (2013). The social modulation of pain: Others as predictive signals of salience – a systematic review. *Frontiers in Human Neuroscience, 7,* 386. http://doi.org/10.3389/fnhum.2013.00386.

Larose, S., & Bernier, A. (2001). Social support processes: Mediators of attachment state of mind and adjustment in late adolescence. *Attachment and Human Development, 3*(1), 96–120.

Lawrence, K., Campbell, R., & Skuse, D. (2015). Age, gender, and puberty influence the development of facial emotion recognition. *Frontiers in Psychology*, 6, article 761.

Leckman, J. F., Feldman, R., Swain, J. E., Eicher, V., Thompson, N., & Mayes, L. C. (2004). Primary parental preoccupation: Circuits, genes, and the crucial role of the environment. *Journal of Neural Transmission*, 111, 753–771.

Lieberman, A. F., Padrón, E., Van Horn, P., & Harris, W. W. (2005). Angels in the nursery: The intergenerational transmission of benevolent parental influences. *Infant Mental Health Journal*, 26, 504–520.

Lieberman, M. D. (2003). Reflexive and reflective judgment processes: A social cognitive neuroscience approach. In J. Forgas, K. Williams, & W. von Hippel (Eds.), *Social judgments: Implicit and explicit processes* (pp. 44–67). Cambridge, UK: Cambridge University Press.

Lieberman, M. D. (2007). Social cognitive neuroscience: A review of core processes. *Annual Review of Psychology*, 58, 259–289.

Lieberman, M. D. (2013). *Social: Why our brains are wired to connect*. New York, NY: Crown.

Llinas, R. (2001). *I of the vortex: From neurons to self*. Cambridge, MA: MIT Press.

Lynch, M. (1994). Preparing children for day surgery. *Children's Health Care*, 23(2) 75–85.

Lyons Ruth, K., & Jacobvitz, D. (1999). Attachment disorganization: Unresolved loss, relational violence, and lapses in behavioral and attentional strategies. In J. Cassidy & P. E. Shaver, *Handbook of attachment: Theory, research, and clinical implications* (pp. 520–554). New York, NY: Guilford Press.

Lyons-Ruth, K., & Spielman, E. (2004). Disorganized infant attachment strategies and helpless-fearful profiles of parenting: Integrating attachment research with clinical Intervention. *Infant Mental Health Journal*, 25(4), 318–335.

Macdonald, K., & Macdonald, T. M. (2010). The peptide that binds: A systematic review of oxytocin and its prosocial effects in humans. *Harvard Review Psychiatry*, 18, 1–21.

MacLean, P. C., Rynes, K. N., Aragón, C., Caprihan, A., Phillips, J. P., &

Lowe, J. R. (2014). Mother–infant mutual eye gaze supports emotion regulation in infancy during the Still-Face paradigm. *Infant Behavior and Development, 37,* 512–522.

Marek, S., Hwang, K., Foran, W., Haliquist, M., & Luna, B. (2015). The contribution of network organization and integration to the development of cognitive control. *PLOS Biology, 13,* 1–25.

Mars, R. B., Neubert, F. X., Noonan, M. A., Sallet, J., Toni, I., & Rushworth, M. S. (2012). On the relationship between the "default mode network" and the "social brain." *Frontiers in Human Neuroscience.* Retrieved July 6, 2016, from http://journal.frontiersin.org/article/10.3389/fnhum.2012.00189/full

Mayes, L., Rutherford, H., Suchman, N., & Close, N. (2012). The Neural and Psychological Dynamics of Adults' Transition to Parenthood. *Zero to Three,33*(2), 83–84.

McWayne , C., Downer, J., Campos, R., & Harris, R. (2013). Father involvement during early childhood and its association with children's early learning: A meta-analysis, early education and development, 24:6, 898-922.

Meltzoff, A. N. (1999). Born to learn: What infants learn from watching us. In N. A. Fox, L. A. Leavitt, & J. G. Worhol (Eds.), *The role of early experience in early development* (pp. 145–164). Johnson & Johnson Pediatric Institute Pediatric Round Table Series.

Meltzoff, A. N., & Decety, J. (2003). What imitation tells us about social cognition: A rapprochement between development psychology and cognitive neuroscience. *Philosophical Transactions of the Royal Society B, 358,* 491–500.

Monk, C., Spicer, J., & Champagne, F. A. (2012). Linking prenatal maternal adversity to developmental outcomes in infants: The role of epigenetic pathways. *Development and Psychopathology, 24,* 1361–1376.

Morris, A. S., Silk, J. S., Steinberg, L., Myers, S. S., & Robinson, E. (2007). The role of the family context in the development of emotion regulation. *Social Development, 16,* 361–388.

Moutsiana, C., Johnstone, T., Fearon, P., Cooper, P. J., Pliatsikas, C.,

Goodyer, I., & Halligan, S. L. (2015). Insecure attachment during infancy predicts greater amygdala volumes in early adulthood. *Journal of Child Psychology and Psychiatry, 56,* 540–548.

National Institute of Mental Health. (2011). The teen brain: Still under construction [Web article]. Retrieved July 6, 2016, from http://www.nimh.nih.gov/health/publications/the-teen-brain-still-under-construction/index.shtml

National Scientific Council on the Developing Child. (2004). *Young children develop in an environment of relationships* (Working Paper 1). Center on the Developing Child, Harvard University.

Nelson, E. E., Leibenluft, E., McClure, E. B., & Pine, D. S. (2005, February). The social re-orientation of adolescence: A neuroscience perspective on the process and its relation to psychopathology. *Psychological Medicine,* 163–174.

Noveck, J., & Tompson, T. (2007). Family ties key to youth happiness [Survey]. *Associated Press.* Retrieved July 4, 2016, from http://www.washingtonpost.com/wp-dyn/content/article/2007/08/20/AR2007082000451.html.

Ochsner, K. N., Knierim, K., Ludlow, D. H., Hanelin, J., Ramachandran, T., Glover, G., & Mackey, S. C. (2004). Reflecting upon feelings: An fMRI study of neural systems supporting the attribution of emotion to self and other. *Journal of Cognitive Neuroscience, 16,* 1746–1772.

O'Connor, M., Sanson, A., Hawkins, M. T., Letcher, P., Toumbourou, J. W., Smart, D., . . . Olsson, C. A. (2011). Predictors of positive development in emerging adulthood. *Journal of Youth and Adolescence, 40,* 860–874.

Olson, S. (2012). *From neurons to neighborhoods: An update: Workshop summary.* Washington, DC: National Academies Press.

Pally, R. (2001). *The mind-brain relationship.* New York, NY: Other Press.

Pally, R. (2007). The predicting brain: Unconscious repetition, conscious reflection and therapeutic change. *International Journal of Psychoanalysis, 88,* 861–881.

Pally, R. (2010). The brain's shared circuits of interpersonal understanding: Implications for psychoanalysis and psychodynamic psychotherapy. *Journal of the American Acadamy of Psychoanalysis and Dynamic Psychiatry, 38,* 381–411.

Panksepp, J. (1998). *Affective neuroscience: The foundations of human and animal emotions.* New York, NY: Oxford University Press.

Pajulo, M., Suchman, N. E., Kalland, M., & Mayes, L. C. (2006). Enhancing the effectiveness of residential treatment for substance abusing pregnant and parenting women: focus on maternal reflective functioning and mother-child relationship, *Infant Mental Health Journal, 27,* 448-465.

Powell, N. D., Sloan, E. K., Bailey, M. T., Arevalo, J. M. G., Miller, G. E., Chen, E., . . . Cole, S. W. (2013). Social stress up-regulates inflammatory gene expression in the leukocyte transcriptome via ß-adrenergic induction of myelopoiesis. *Proceedings of the National Academy of Sciences, 110,* 16574–16579 .

Pruett, K. (2000). *Fatherneed: Why father care is as essential as mother care for your child.* New York, NY: Broadway Books.

Pruett, K. & Pruett, M.K. (2009). *Partnership parenting: How men and women parent differently--why it helps your kids and can strengthen your marriage.* Cambridge, MA: Da Capo Press,

Quinn, N. (2005). Universals of child rearing. *Anthropologic Theory, 5,* 477-516.

Reyna, V., & Farley, F. (2006). Risk and rationality in adolescent decision-making: Implications for theory, practice, and public policy. *Psychological Science in the Public Interest, 7,* 1–44.

Rosenberg, J. & Wilcox, W.B. (2006). The impact of fathers on cognitive ability and educational achievement. *U.S. Department of Health and Human Services Administration for Children and Families Administration on Children, Youth and Families Children's Bureau Office on Child Abuse and Neglect.*

Rutherford, H. J., Williams, S. K., Moy, S., Mayes, L. C., & Johns, J. J. (2011). Disruption of maternal parenting circuitry by addictive process: Rewiring of reward and stress systems. *Frontiers in Psychiatry.* Retrieved July 7, 2016, from http://journal.frontiersin.org/article/10.3389/fpsyt.2011.00037/full

Saphire-Bernsteina, S., Way, B. M., Kim, H. S., Sherman, D. K., & Taylor, S. E. (2011). Oxytocin receptor gene (OXTR) is related to psychological resources. *Proceedings of the National Academy of Sciences, 108*, 15118–15122.

Sherf, K. S., Behrmann, M., & Dahl, R. E. (2012). Facing changes and changing faces in adolescence: A new model for investigating adolescent-specific interactions between pubertal, brain and behavioral development. *Developmental Cognitive Neuroscience, 2*, 199–219.

Shonkoff, J. P., Garner, A. S., Siegel, B. S., Dobbins, M. I., Earls, M. F., McGuinn, L., . . . Wood, D. L. (2012). The lifelong effects of early childhood adversity and toxic stress. *Pediatrics, 129*(1), e232–e246.

Shonkoff, J. P., & Phillips, D. A. (Eds.). (2000). *From neurons to neighborhoods: The science of early childhood development.* Washington, DC: National Academies Press.

Sisk, C. L., & Zehr, J. L. (2005). Pubertal hormones organize the adolescent brain and behavior. *Frontiers in Neuroendocrinology, 26*, 163–174.

Slade, A. (2006). Reflective parenting programs: Theory and development. *Psychoanalytic Inquiry, 26*, 640–657.

Slade, A., Grienenberger, G., Bernbach, E., Levy, D., & Locker, A. (2005). Maternal reflective functioning, attachment, and the transmission gap: A preliminary study. *Attachment and Human Development, 7*, 283–298.

Somerville, L. H. (2013). Special issue on the teenage brain: Sensitivity to social evaluation. *Current Directions in Psychological Science, 22*, 121–127.

Sperduti, G. S., Guionnet, S., Fossati, P., & Nadel, J. (2014). Mirror neuron system and mentalizing system connect during online social interaction. *Cognitive Processing, 15*, 307–316.

Spunt, R. P., Meyer, M. L., & Lieberman, M. D. (2015). *Journal of Cognitive Neuroscience, 27*, 1116–1124.

Steinberg, L. (2008). A social neuroscience perspective on adolescent risk-taking. *Developmental Review, 28*, 78–106.

Strathearn, L. (2011). Maternal neglect: Oxytocin, dopamine and the neurobiology of attachment. *Journal of Neuroendocrinology, 23,* 1054–1065.

Strathearn, L., Fonagy, P., & Montague, P. (2008). What's in a smile? Maternal brain responses to infant facial cues. *Pediatrics, 122,* 40–51.

Suchman, N. E., Docoste, C., Rosenberger, P., & McMahon, T. J. (2012). Attachment-based intervention for substance-using mothers: A preliminary test of the proposed mechanisms of change. *Infant Mental Health Journal, 33,* 360–371.

Swain, J. E. (2011a). Becoming a parent: Biobehavioral and brain science perspectives. *Current Problems in Pediatric and Adolescent Health Care, 41,* 192–196.

Swain, J. E. (2011b). The human parental brain: In vivo neuroimaging. *Progress in Neuro-psychopharmacology and Biological Psychiatry, 35,* 1242–1254.

Swain, J. E., Lorberbaum, J. P., Kose, S., & Strathearn, L. (2007). Brain basis of early parent–infant interactions: Psychology, physiology, and in vivo functional neuroimaging studies. *Jouranl of Child Psychology and Psychiatry, 48,* 262–287.

Takahashi, H. K., Kitada, R., Sasaki, A. T., Kawamichi, H., Okazaki, S., Kochiyama, T., & Sadato, N. (2015). Brain networks of affective mentalizing revealed by the tear effect: The integrative role of the medial prefrontal cortex and precuneus. *Neuroscience Research, 101,* 32–43.

Tau, G. Z., & Peterson, B. S. (2010). Normal development of brain circuits. *Neuropsychopharmacology Reviews, 35,* 147–168.

Tomasello, M. (1999). *The cultural origins of human cognition.* Cambridge, MA: Harvard University Press.

Tomasello, M., Carpenter, M., & Liszkowski. (2007). A new look at infant pointing. *Child Development, 78,* 705–722.

Tononi, G., & Edelman, G. M. (1998). Consciousness and complexity. *Science, 282,* 1845–1851.

Tronick, E. (2007). *The neurobehavioral and social-emotional development of infants and children.* New York, NY: W. W. Norton.

Wager, T.D., Rilling, J.K., Smith, E.E., Sokolik, A., Casey, K.L., Davidson,

R.J., Kosslyn, S.M., Rose, R.M., Cohen, J.D. (2004). Placebo-induced changes in FMRI in the anticipation and experience of pain. *Science, 303*, 1162-7.

Van Overwalle, F. (2009). Social cognition and the brain: A meta-analysis. *Human Brain Mapping, 30*, 829–858.

van Roekel, E., Verhagen, M., Scholte, R. H., Kleinjan, M., Goossens, L., & Engels, R. C. (2013). The oxytocin receptor gene (OXTR) in relation to state levels of loneliness in adolescence: Evidence for micro-level gene–environment interactions. *PLOS ONE, 8*(11), e77689.

Voss, L. J., Federmeier, K. D., & Paller, K. A. (2011). The potato chip really does look like Elvis! Neural hallmarks of conceptual processing associated with finding novel shapes subjectively meaningful. *Cerebral Cortex.* doi: 10.1093/cercor/bhr315

Waters, E., Hamilton, C., & Weinfield, N. S. (2000). The stability of attachment security from infancy to adolescence and early adulthood: General introduction. *Child Development, 71*, 678–683.

Wilson, E. O. (2012). *The social conquest of earth.* New York, NY: Liveright.

Wiseman, O., Zagoory-Sharon, O., & Feldman, R. (2012). Oxytocin administration to parent enhances infant physiological and behavioral readiness for social engagement. *Biological Psychiatry, 72*(12), 982–989.

Wisner, K. L., Parry, B. L., & Piontek, C. M. (2002). Postpartum depression. *New England Journal of Medicine, 347*, 194–199.

Index

___

In this index, *b* denotes box and *f* denotes figure.